Through "Poverty's Vale"

# Through "Poverty's Vale"

*A Hardscrabble Boyhood in Upstate New York,*
*1832-1862*

A YORK STATE BOOK

# THROUGH "POVERTY'S VALE"

*A Hardscrabble Boyhood in Upstate New York,*

*1832-1862*

## HENRY CONKLIN

*Edited with an introduction by* WENDELL TRIPP

SYRACUSE UNIVERSITY PRESS · 1974

FIRST EDITION

Library of Congress Cataloging in Publication Data

Conklin, Henry, 1832–1915.
    Through "Poverty's Vale": a hardscrabble
boyhood in upstate New York, 1832–1862.

    (A York State book)
    SUMMARY: An autobiographical account of a
frontier family's struggles in a backwoods environ-
ment a century ago.
    1. Conklin, Henry, 1832–1915—Juvenile litera-
ture. 2. Frontier and pioneer life—New York
(State)—Juvenile literature. 3. United States—
History—Civil War—Personal narratives—Juvenile
literature. [1. Conklin, Henry, 1832–1915. 2. Fron-
tier and pioneer life—New York (State). 3. United
States—History—Civil War—Personal narratives]
I. Title.
F123.C6917    1974    917.47′03′40924[B]    [92]
ISBN 0-8156-0098-4    73-19980

*Manufactured in the United States of America*

# Contents

# Acknowledgments

THE editing of Henry Conklin's manuscript, and the vast amount of typing and retyping that this entailed, was the work of "stolen moments" extending over a period of several years. It could not have been accomplished without the help of three publications secretaries at the New York State Historical Association: Mrs. Mary Bliss, now of Ash, North Carolina; Mrs. Deborah Nichols, now of Fort Lauderdale, Florida; and Mrs. Amy Barnum of Cooperstown, New York. From time to time they generously assisted with research, typing, and the search for illustrations.

Mr. Roy Conklin, now living in Livingston Manor, New York, with his daughter, Mrs. Clifford MacArthur, was the first to recognize the historical significance of his grandfather's reminiscence. Inheriting the manuscript from his father, Burton James Conklin, Roy believed that publication would, in itself, fulfill Henry Conklin's original intention and would also make available to modern readers a firsthand account of a bygone way of life. He provided background information on the people and the places featured in Henry's story, and he has shown extraordinary patience throughout the lengthy and sporadic process of preparing the manuscript for publication.

Allusive illustrations reproduced in this book originally appeared in the following publications: William Cullen Bryant, ed., *Picturesque America,* 2 vols. (New York: D. Appleton & Co., 1872, 1874); *The Century Magazine,* May 1885; *Frank Leslie's Illustrated Newspaper,* November 7, 1863; *Harper's New Monthly Magazine,* November 1855, August 1859, July 1880, August 1880; *Scribner's Monthly,* February 1877, December 1877, April 1878, November 1878; and G. W. Sheldon, *American Painters* (New York: D. Appleton & Co., 1879).

# Editor's Introduction

AN Adirondack winter is a long, quiet affair. The deep drifts and icy winds bring ordinary activities to a halt. It is a time for contemplation, and, if one is so directed, a fine time for rumination and for writing. In the winter of 1891–92 Henry Conklin, a sixty-year-old Herkimer County farmer and trapper, was the caretaker and sole occupant of a hunting camp on Hannedaga Lake. A yarn-spinner without an audience, he decided to put down on paper a reminiscence of his life. In five months he produced a remarkable document—a detailed memoir of his boyhood and young manhood on the New York frontier in the years 1832–62.

It is an unusual document. Many men and women, on all educational levels, have kept diaries, and the nation's libraries house thousands of them. But a full-length reminiscence is another matter—a literary form more usual with statesmen than with farmers. When the latter do produce reminiscences, they tend to be brief accounts of great adventures like wars and gold rushes. But Henry, drawing upon a sound memory and a few family letters, chose to tell of the everyday activities of the people he knew in his youth and young manhood. His purpose was to preserve a record of his and his family's struggles in the backwoods environment of over a century ago. In doing so he has given form and personality to a few of the faceless men and women who settled this nation, most of whom, in Lyman Butterfield's words, exist below the level of historical scrutiny.

Henry's story begins in Schenectady County and describes family moves to the Blenheim region of Schoharie County, then to Herkimer County. It is a story of hardscrabble farming on marginal lands in the foothills of the northern Catskills and southern Adirondacks. It presents, in a series of graphic scenes, a man's memory of the joys and sorrows of boyhood and young manhood in a pinched rural milieu—log-house-building, barn-raising, sugar-making, spinning and weaving, fireplace cookery, militia musters, folk medicine, backwoods schools and schooling, children's games, courtship, agricultural apprenticeship, illness, death. Some of Henry's word-pictures—for example, detailed descriptions of log houses, of preparing a log cabin for the onslaught of winter, and of an 1840 Schoharie County schoolhouse—provide rare firsthand accounts of a traditional technology. Especially striking are his memories of the manner in which his family packed their possessions and moved from one part of the state to another. Other memories offer equally valuable glimpses of frontier family life and relationships, the role of individuals in the family, and the facts of economic life in areas where agriculture alone could not support the population.

Despite the lateness of its setting, the narrative can truly be called a pioneer's story. Though the extreme frontier of settlement had moved beyond New York State before Henry was born, that frontier was never an unbroken line that moved westward at a uniform pace. When settlement in western states like Minnesota and Wisconsin was well advanced, large areas of New York State were still sparsely settled, and some parts were still a wilderness. Thus, Henry Conklin, born in Schenectady County in 1832, began life in a log cabin. In Schoharie County in the late 1830s, his family had to clear the land on which they settled, and they continued to live in log houses. When they moved to Herkimer County in 1845, they were among the first settlers in an untouched wilderness. The family spun and wove its own clothing and produced much of its own food. Henry never saw a barrel of commercial flour or a bolt of "factory" cloth until he was ten years old. He received his first pair of "personal" shoes when he was twelve. He was nine years old when he first saw a stove; and when the family got a stove of its own (in 1845), his mother, after a lifetime of fireplace cookery, was not certain how to use it. This, then, was a family living a frontier life when the actual frontier of settlement lay a thousand miles or more to the west.

The central theme of Henry Conklin's reminiscence is poverty. It is sometimes forgotten that the greatest threat to pioneer life was not the Indian or the beasts of the forest or other colorful forces, but simple malnutrition and the disease and debility that accompanied it. The early American colonists had their starving times; later pioneers, throughout the history of the American westward movement, suffered deprivation when they moved to new territories. What is interesting about Conklin's experience is that it took place in the midst of plenty, for New York State in the 1830s and 1840s was settled and prosperous. It held the nation's largest city and several lesser metropolises; farms in the Hudson, Mohawk, and Genesee valleys created a prosperous agricultural civilization; the Erie Canal was a thriving commercial artery; railroads crossed the state; schools, resorts, factories dotted the land. But rural families like the Conklins, living in semi-settled pockets, away from the main routes of commerce, were still facing the pioneer problems of clearing land, scrabbling for a cash crop, and struggling each day for clothing to cover their nakedness and food to sustain their lives.

When Henry Conklin was a boy in Schoharie County, he and his brothers dressed in clothing made of tow—a rough fiber by-product of linen-making—and they went barefoot even in winter. While his mother washed his clothes, Henry stayed in bed, for he had but one set of garments. His diet included little meat, usually pork, and a great deal of breadstuff. With unintentional humor, he says, "We might have gone to the poor house, but there was none to go to."

In 1837, an Ithaca gentleman, traveling by stagecoach, went through the section of Schoharie in which the Conklins were then living, and probably passed within ten miles of their home. Of that region, he said:

> There is a large and grass-growing region or country between Norwich, Franklin, and like towns and the Catskill Mountains, that in 1837 was in a very doleful state. If anyone wanted to travel through woods with openings cut and half cultivated, see ten to hundreds of acres of stumps and blackberry fields and the plainest log huts, with a husband farmer in tow-cloth clothes, a wife in homespun, and several children barefooted, ragged in half clothes, torn straw hats, and in the fall weeds and a sense of defeated farming attempted on a larger scale than the inhabitants could possibly carry out—he had but to ride in these coaches, through this then doleful tract of land.*

Nevertheless, Henry states that these lean years were the happiest of his life. The Conklin family was a unified group, self-sufficient, loving. Henry is occasionally petulant because one

---

* Morris Bishop, ed., "The Journeys of Samuel J. Parker," *New York History* XLV (April 1964), 145.

brother who worked as a farmer laborer did not contribute to the family's support, and he is critical of his father's weakness for "grog"—a factor in the family's economic misfortune—but he emphasizes the love and self-sacrifice of everyone, especially his mother, his brother John, and his sister Ruth. He shows that every member of the family, almost as soon as babyhood was over, contributed his or her labor to the family's support. Each did so, evidently, in a generous spirit, in the presence of the common enemy—privation—and no member of the family was isolated or withdrawn. As a result, though the Conklins had no more material possessions than those unfortunates who inhabit pockets of poverty in present-day America, the family remained industrious, amiable, and hopeful. This further illustrates the nebulous quality of the condition that we label "poverty," and suggests that the privation of the Conklin family deserves a different label.

One of the major themes of American history is the movement of peoples—east to west, country to city, north to south, and back again—and this is also an important theme in Henry Conklin's story. Scores of thousands of American farmers felt that the pot of gold lay somewhere afar—where the soil was richer, the rocks fewer, the climate better. Henry describes an extended visit to an uncle who had removed to Wisconsin, and he himself later lived for a time in Indiana. Two of his sisters settled in Nebraska, another in Minnesota. One brother moved to western New York and later to Illinois. One brother died en route to California. Numbers of his Herkimer County neighbors in the 1850s departed for Ohio, Indiana, and the far west. But in addition to these dramatic journeys in the traditional westward direction, Henry's immediate family and relatives made scores of moves within New York State. Some were journeys of a hundred miles and more; many were just over the next hill. The Conklin family and their kin reveal in microcosm the ceaseless movement that has characterized the American scene from colonial times to the present.

What drove them so? Simple wanderlust could be a factor, but Henry's comments suggest that each journey was stimulated by the prospect of economic improvement, as if, in a sense, socio-economic mobility and geographic mobility were interrelated. In this respect, the Conklin experience was in the American mode.

Their experience further suggests that the most persistent wanderers were marginal farmers of a lower economic group. Prosperous farmers who occupied more productive lands naturally tended to stay where they were. Henry's statement about Joe Curtis's plan to leave Schoharie County gives a personal insight into the phenomenon: ". . . Uncle Joe was talking of moving to Herkimer in the spring. He said he was sick and tired of working among the rocks and stones. He said that he knew of a big farm in Herkimer County that did not have a stone on it big enough to kill a chipping bird, and he was going there if he could sell out. He said that oats there grew as tall as his head." Scores of thousands of American farmers had their own "Herkimer Counties," which drew them from New England and New York and other coastal states across the Appalachians, into the midwest, the plains, and eventually to the Pacific.

Henry's father followed Uncle Joe to Herkimer County. This was inevitable, for Samuel Conklin was the quintessential wanderer. He spent most of his adult life moving from farm to farm, all within New York State, and did not settle down finally until advancing years slowed his pace. His case suggests simple restlessness, yet each move was initiated in hope that his lot in life would be improved, and he was willing to risk his own and his family's security in the endeavor. Clearly he was an optimist, a fact of some importance when we consider that economic matters are often influenced by psychological factors, that the desire for economic betterment and the methods employed to achieve it are influenced by such factors as one's emotional state and outlook on life in general. The American pioneer, after all, was not simply running away from something; he was running toward something.

There are, in this rich document, a number of sub-themes. As one example, students of agricultural history will note that the Conklins, though they cultivated the soil and considered themselves farmers, derived much of their income from nonagricultural activities. At one time, Henry's mother earned half the family's income (or so Henry remembered) by spinning and weaving. Sam Conklin and his sons were frequently engaged in shingle-making, which provided a cash income wherever they lived and could be pursued year-round, as time permitted. In addition, father and sons at times worked as teamsters and as carpenters. Other characters in Henry's tale supplemented agricultural income by keeping bees, making maple sugar, and, in the case of a Schoharie County neighbor, by raising guinea pigs for the Albany pet market.

And, though the family was drawn to Herkimer County, in the southern reaches of the Adirondacks, in expectation of a more productive agriculture, they did less farming there than in Schoharie. Henry became a part-time lumberman; a brother devoted most of his time to gathering hemlock bark, which was used in the tanning industry; a sister became a cook in a lumber camp. By 1860 Henry was working in the woods all summer and coming home only to harvest crops. The part-time lumberman had become a part-time farmer. In fact, the early exploitation of the Adirondacks, not only for lumber but also as a recreational resource, is suggested here and would have been a dominant subject in Henry's story if he had continued it past the Civil War. In the post-war years members of the Conklin family, including Henry, were numbered among the guides and trappers who are so important in the history of the Adirondacks.

Henry concludes his narrative with an account of his service in the Civil War. This too is of special value. Though Civil War diaries and reminiscences are common enough, rarely do we see a wartime journal that includes a detailed reminiscence of the soldier's pre-war life, and it is difficult to understand the Civil War soldier without knowing something of his life before he went to war. Henry presents in detail the circumstances of his enlistment; he tells how the martial music and the recruiting officer's appeal to patriotism compelled several of Henry's neighbors to enlist and swept up Henry too, though he had a wife and three small boys at home. He frankly admits that in a calmer moment he considered deserting and running away to Canada, but the thought of his family's disgrace stayed his flight. He therefore joined his regiment, the 81st New York, and in his concluding chapters describes his training, the move south, and his regiment's role in the Peninsular Campaign of 1862. He was wounded at the Battle of Seven Pines and as a result was discharged a few months later.

Though all of life was an adventure to Henry Conklin, his army service was particularly exciting to him. One wonders, in fact, if his enlisting was not strongly influenced by a desire to take part in the greatest legal adventure afforded by modern civilization. He kept a precise record of his wartime service in a series of letters, which he numbered consecutively and to which he gave the general title, "Soldier's Letters." These documents, no longer in existence, enabled him to be particularly precise in describing his military career. The result is a military memoir that deals with matters familiar to students of the Civil War yet has special meaning because we know Conklin so well by 1861, and because his frankness and literary style combine to present a fresh view of an old subject.

All of these things—the portrait of frontier life, the description of marginal farming, Civil War scenes—are important contributions to our historical knowledge, but Henry Conklin's reminiscence is not only history, it is also literature. He wanted his reminiscences to be read, at least by his family. His style is occasionally self-conscious; but he seems to be carried along by the story he is writing, and he writes as he would have talked—simply and directly, with sufficient use of colloquialisms and colorful phraseology to add a distinctive flavor to his style.

Equally important, he had the storyteller's gift of dramatic organization and the ability to present the growth of individuals, communities, and relationships in a natural and logical manner. He does not, therefore, merely present a series of unrelated scenes; he constructs a living panorama, the central events of which are a family's movement and growth. This is all the more impressive because he did it in a single draft, written that winter of 1891–92, in a blank tax assessor's ledger. By the time he was finished, he had filled every page of the ledger and had completed his story on three additional sheets of foolscap, which he attached to the last page of the ledger. He later read through the manuscript, probably several times if the varicolored ink is an indication, and he inserted missing words and occasionally corrected misspellings. But he did no rewriting.

Henry Conklin was a romantic who could see adventure in the ordinary events of life and who viewed the past in nostalgic terms. His depiction of childhood is poignant, and his love for certain individuals—especially his mother, his brother John, and a childhood sweetheart—is so intensely drawn that only the clear sincerity of his presentation saves him from unintentional hyperbole.

His story also has its minor villains—a cruel brother-in-law, a misanthropic father-in-law, and brother John's slattern of a wife. Henry was too good a chronicler to leave them out and too human to say anything good about them. And, like all sound dramatists, he includes some comic figures, such as the fat and fussy Aunt Amy; the loveable buffoon, Jay Tompkins of Schoharie County; and Jay's mother, who raised guinea pigs and ate woodchucks. But Henry is at his best (though he probably would not have thought so) when dealing with his father, Samuel Conklin, the amiable wanderer. Henry is honest in describing his father's weakness for strong drink, and forthright in condemning it. His characterization of his father contrasts sharply with that of his mother, Mary Conklin. The latter is one-dimensional—all good; the former is more complex—loving, hardworking, but unable to toil for long in one place, too willing to gamble security for uncertain dreams. He could be harsh, as when his stubbornness forced brother John to leave home, but he was also kindhearted and even-tempered. Henry notes that in all his youthful years his father whipped him only once—when Henry ran away and his family thought he had drowned. His attitude toward his father is slightly ambivalent, and this creates an interesting tension in his story.

There is one other literary tension of note. Every man who pens a memoir is conscious of the past. This was especially so in Henry Conklin's case. He was deeply concerned with the rapid passing of time and with the fact of his own mortality. In telling his story, he is trying to save the events and experiences of his life, as well as the men and women he knew, from oblivion. As he writes, he is reliving the past, and he frequently intrudes to mourn his lost youth, to ponder on the hereafter, to comment on the amazing speed of time's passage. But these intrusions are not distracting; on the contrary, they provide us with a fascinating double exposure, for as we see the boy Henry Conklin in a Schoharie County schoolhouse, or the young man Henry Conklin courting his prospective bride, or the young soldier in the midst of battle, we also see the aged Henry Conklin, writing his story in a lonely Adirondack cabin. The double image is an attractive one, and we can rejoice in the writer's victory. The old Henry Conklin has saved the young Henry Conklin from oblivion. And in doing so, he has given us an invaluable portrait of a segment of the American past.

In editing Henry Conklin's manuscript I have been influenced by the fact that this is a literary document as well as a historical document. He wanted it to be read, as his use of "dear reader" and his own insertions and corrections of spelling indicate. I have therefore, with the one exception mentioned below, left his message exactly as he wrote it insofar as the language is concerned, but have used a free hand in correcting spelling and inserting punctuation.

His spelling was quite good, in general, but erratic. He sometimes spelled a particular word correctly (pretty, moccasin, village, oak, ticket, Illinois) at one point and incorrectly (prety, mocason, vilage, oke, tickett, ilinois) at another. Occasionally he spelled a word in two different ways in a single sentence. He corrected the misspelling of a word in some places and let it stand in others. And in making the past tense, he invariably used only one consonant, writing, for example, shiped for shipped, robed for robbed, stoped for stopped, triped for tripped, in a most confusing manner. A *sic* inserted after each misspelling would be a ubiquitous distraction. I have therefore corrected misspelled words throughout, except when the spelling clearly indicates a particular pronunciation, as scairt for scared and handiron for andiron. I have not, of course, tampered with his spelling of family names, even when it looked suspicious.

I have also provided capitals at the beginning of sentences, where he very occasionally neglected them, and have also capitalized the names of villages and states when he failed to do so. He used little punctuation except for periods at the end of sentences, and I have freely inserted commas when a sentence is unclear without them. For example, he frequently used the word "for" as a conjunction ("We didn't do it for mother would have objected."), and in such cases I have placed commas before the "for." I have also placed quotation marks at the beginning and end of all statements that are obviously quoted. Henry frequently did this, but was not consistent, and he occasionally uses italics in place of quotation marks. I have provided paragraph indentation. Henry sometimes indented at the beginning of a chapter, but never within a chapter. Finally, I have supplied all footnotes.

In one case I have interfered with his presentation to the extent of deleting material from the text and presenting it in an appendix. This occurs in Chapter 2, where, in listing his mother's brothers and sisters, he inserts information (including a letter written in 1894 by his cousin Ruth) that is much more meaningful at the end than at the beginning of his story. In fact, since the material alludes to or describes events that occurred after his narrative was written, it is a distraction and not typical of Henry's logical organization. This material is cited in full in Appendix 1.

I have also deleted Henry's poems from the narrative, and have placed them in Appendix 2. Poem 1, on the death of a brother and sister, and poem 3, on the death of a military comrade, were written by Henry himself, on separate sheets inserted in the ledger. Poem 2, on the death of a fellow-soldier, and written in the margin of the original manuscript, may be of his own composition.

I have included in Appendix 3 the complete text of the letter of January 11, 1892, from his sister Julia. In the manuscript he inserted the statement, "See sister Julia's letter," and pinned to the page a copy, in his own hand, of the first half of her letter. He copied the remainder of the letter into the margins of the manuscript. The color of the ink suggests that he did this at a later date. He undoubtedly received the letter after he had begun his reminiscence. It is an interesting document in itself and is an example of the family materials he utilized in his research.

Finally, I have occasionally ignored Henry's own editing of his manuscript. For example, the color of his ink indicates that in later readings he frequently inserted an "and" between sentences and thus made one tedious sentence in place of two felicitous sentences. In such cases, I have ignored his insertions and left his statements as he first wrote them.

Wendell Tripp

Cooperstown, New York
Fall 1973

# *Author's Introduction*

**DEAR READER,**

Today I take my pen in hand to write a narrative of my life from my earliest recollection to the present time, a story I have had in view for years and now the opportunity has presented itself to begin, I being the sole occupant of and in charge of O. L. Snyder's camp on the flat rock near the head of Jock's or Hannedaga Lake as it is now called. A fitting place to write in the silence and quiet, miles from the din and strife of all the rest of humanity.

This is one of the most clear and beautiful lakes in the whole Adirondacks. As I sit here alone today thinking over the past and looking out over the beautiful waters to the eastern sombre November landscape with the outside faded and brown excepting the mingling of the evergreens whose fringe touches the water's edge forming a beautiful picture of autumn's old age reminds me of the many years that are past of childhood, youth and middle age through which I have wandered down almost to old age, still leaving in the frontispiece of life a bright green and beautiful landscape where sweet memory clings with a tenacity of purpose that can never be obliterated while life lasts and memory holds her throne.

Especially are these lines written and dedicated to my father's and mother's families and my own family also. My heros are many, for all the families are large and my humble narrative, dedicated to the memory of so many loved ones, shall be entitled, "Through Poverty's Vale or Fifty Years in the Wilderness." It is befitting for me to say here, they have shared alike with me the joys and sorrows of almost a lifetime. If I live until the seventh of next May I will be sixty years old. Sixty long years through Poverty's Vale, traveling through the Wilderness of Want.

My memory goes back almost fifty eight years of that time, over half a century calling up and resurrecting and revivifying every little event and minute transaction of a life of what might be termed poverty in this day and age of the world. All along through this wearysome, struggling, self denying murmuring Poverty's Vale, the kind loving faces of father, mother, brothers, sisters, relatives, friends and comrades rise up to greet me in every turn of my recollections of my fifty years in the wilderness, along the zig zag path of life's uneven journey.

There shall be no untruth or falsehood intentionally mingled in these pages. It shall be the truth and nothing but the truth, yet there may be a high coloring to some of the joyous or sad pictures but only on the side of good and the nobler instincts of humanity, believing that thereby your thoughts may be lifted to higher and better things.

The events of my life are far as memory goes and what I felt and saw at the time of each event shall be faithfully recorded as well as the events and actions of those around me. Also some of the events happening before I could remember will be as I heard and understood them from my parents, older brothers and sisters and family records. I withhold no names or places connected with this narrative. Yet I may err in spelling some names correctly or fail to locate every place exactly as it should be. It is so very long ago that some of the dates and early transactions may be in the mist and things get a little mixed but all the same you shall have my story from the pen and memory of your humble narrator

Henry Conklin

Hannedaga
November 22, 1891

1     MY grandfather John Conklin was an English-
man. Born in England, he was reared and brought up
there until a young man grown. After becoming of age
he emigrated to America, landing at New York. Here he
made his home for quite a long time or until he married.
He married a French lady by the name of Ruth Barto.
After their marriage they moved to North Hempstead on
the east end of Long Island, where they purchased a small
place on the strand and lived happily together for quite a
number of years.

Grandfather's occupation was that of a fisherman and
he followed the perilous calling for several years or until
he died.

They had four children born to them to care for and
look after. John Jr. the oldest, then Mary, Amy and Samuel who is my father. My father was born on Long Island
June 8, 1791.

I remember of hearing my father tell of when he was a
little lad how he used to go out with my grandfather on
his fishing excursions riding on the dashing waves of the
briny coast and what monstrous great fish they caught
and what narrow escapes they had many times from being
overturned by the angry waves. They were accompanied
sometimes by my father's older brother John.

The boys seemed to take to the sea, for while my father
was only eight years old Uncle John shipped as a sailor
and went and came on several voyages when finally he got
tired of the ocean and bade goodbye to the raging waves,

his home and friends and took his departure somewhere to the far west and was never heard of after by his family or relatives. Aunt Mary Ann married and had one child but died many years ago.

My father continued to live at home, going to school and helping his father in his perilous vocation until he became old enough to ship as a cabin boy when he also went to sea leaving home to try his luck on the perilous deep. He made several voyages with good success, but on his return from his second voyage he learned that his father had perished at sea. Going out as usual one bright morning with his boat and fishing tackle to try his luck. During the day a severe storm came up capsizing his boat and throwing him out. He sank beneath the waves to rise no more.

My father went to sea again on several voyages leaving his mother and sisters at home alone. He used to tell us many stories of his adventures as a sailor. I will write out two of the most vivid ones as I remember them from his own lips.

One time while out at sea there came up a great storm. Waves were dashing over the ship and everyone thought they were going to perish. The passengers, crew and some of the sailors left off work and began to pray thinking their last hour had come when father told them if they wanted to be saved they had better get up and go to work or they would all go to the bottom and that wasting their precious time on their knees would not put the ship to rights or furl the sails or work the pumps and they surely would go down. So they all got up and went to work with a will and soon the ship was in trim again riding the waves in safety. So the ship, crew and passengers were all saved. And here is a little sermon. You may get down and pray all your life for something but if you don't put forth any effort or work with your prayer and faith you will never accomplish anything. God in some way furnishes the means and materials but the work is in your hands to accomplish.

The last time my father ventured to sea he came very near never coming back again and as he used to tell the story to us children while gathered by the old fashioned fireplace, it makes me shudder to think of it now. Returning homeward from his last voyage the sea became very rough and he was sent up the mast to help furl in the sails. His foot was caught in a rope and some way he fell overboard unnoticed by the others. The ship ran over him and while passing over him he tried to clutch at the barnacles growing on the bottom of the ship. He said whenever he thought of it he could almost feel the rough bunches tearing across his back as the ship passed over him. On went the ship and crew heedless of his cries for help until he was missed on board. Then the captain hove to and lowered a boat and sent some of the crew back after him. It was nearly an hour before they picked him up and the longest hour he had ever seen and he thought it would be his last one. When on deck he vowed it would be his last voyage on the ocean and he kept his promise. On returning home he lived with his mother and sisters and worked at the carpenters trade for several years.

In the war of 1812 he volunteered to go as a substitute for another man by the name of Allen and served until the war closed but never drew a pension. He made several efforts to get it and employed attorneys to work for him but he never got his pension on account of a defect in the records of the disbanding of the regiment someway that debarred him from it.* Because he had no written agree-

* There was no conscription in New York in the War of 1812, but Samuel Conklin would have been liable to service in the militia. Reference to disbanding of a regiment, however, confuses the matter.

ment from the man Allen [for] whom he substituted. He went down to his grave in old age just as deserving of a pension as many others that did draw pensions. Technicalities deprived him of his just due from the government.

When Aunt Amy [Henry's father's sister] was twelve years old she went to Duanesburgh and stayed there until she was eighteen when she went back to Long Island and here Uncle Joseph Curtis [Henry's mother's uncle] went and married her and further on I will speak of them more fully.

After the war of 1812 my Father drifted North Westward to the great wilderness of which we will speak further on.

But in justice to us all connected with this narrative in regard to my Father I will say not that I want to mention any faults of his. His habits were formed in his youthful days as a roving sailor used to his grog as such on ship board and no persuasion could induce him to leave it off. He was not ugly or cross . . . when under the influence of drink, but too good natured and funny, and in this way sharpers would get at him and traffic and trade with him getting the best end of the bargain to the dismay of himself and to the sorrow and discomfort of his whole family in their voyage down through Poverty's Vale and our fifty years in the Wilderness of Want.

I have heard my father tell of his three maiden aunts, Harriet, Pattie and Anna Barto. They were sisters of my grandmother Conklin and lived and died on Long Island. Years after father was married he used to go to visit them. They were all in good circumstances and what became of their property my father nor my aunt Amy Curtis never knew.

My grandfather on my mother's side was Abiah Curtis, born September 5, 1777, whose ancestors at some time came from the old country, of what nationality I know not. But I think they were from Connecticut and were always spoken of as American born and were styled by some as Yankees.

My grandmother Curtis was a Holland lady and had emigrated to this country from Holland. Her maiden name was Ruth Cheesman, born in Holland February 20, 1777. She with her father's family was one of the first settlers of that name who came and began what is now called the Cheesman settlement near Theresa in Jefferson County. They came to this country from Holland near the close of the seventeenth [sic] century. That part of the country was then a howling wilderness infested with wolves and all the wild animals natural to an unbroken primeval forest and where the red man of the forest made it his happy hunting ground. And so these early pioneers had the teacherous Indian to guard against and the wild beasts of the forest to molest them.*

My grandfather and grandmother Curtis were married at Theresa in Jefferson County, December 2, 1799. Soon after their marriage grandfather Curtis bought a farm about one mile below Theresa Falls on the west side of the Indian River. Their farm was partly on the river flats and part upland with ledges of stone and pine bluffs. Here they went in the wilderness alike with those early hardy pioneers to clear up their land and build homes for their wives and children.

* The correct spelling is "Cheeseman." In this paragraph Henry may be confused about dates of settlement and perhaps about his grandmother's birthplace. Indians were certainly no problem in Jefferson County in the 1790s. See William H. Horton, ed., *Geographical Gazetteer of Jefferson County, N.Y., 1684–1890* (Syracuse, N.Y., 1890), p. 693.

To them were born seven children, four boys and three girls as follows: Polly or Mary B., born August 20, 1801. (This is my mother, of whom I will speak more fully hereafter.) Next was Betsy, born July 5, 1804. Aunt Betsy never married, but lived at home assisting her parents in clearing up the farm and caring for the younger children. She died in the bloom of youth and early womanhood August 2, 1825. Next was Lydia, who was born November 2, 1806. Aunt Lydia never married, for in her early youth her eye sight failed her, and for many years she was almost totally blind. . . . Sebra Ann was the next, born February 18, 1808, of whom I will write more fully further on. Next was Cheesman, born November 26, 1810. Uncle Cheesman married Mary Chatman of Theresa. They lived on a farm a few miles east of Redwood for many years. . . . Philander was the next one, born November 2, 1818. Of him I will speak further on. Henry, the last, was born February 14, 1820. Uncle Henry grew to manhood living at the homestead and assisting in clearing up the farm. He married Harriet Rider of Antwerp. He was more of a roving disposition than the other two boys and wanted to move about from place to place and at one time went to Wisconsin, where I visited him in the year 1855 of which I will speak further on in my own recollections. . . .

2  I COME down now to my father's family. As I said
before, after leaving the sea and its Long Island strand he
wended his way northwest, sailorlike in a zigzag course,
and in due time he anchored for a while at Theresa in
Jefferson County where he met my mother, Mary B. Curtis, whom he married at Stamphord, March 7, 1818.*

Soon after the marriage my father selected a place to
settle on the Indian River about a mile below Theresa.
Here he bought a forty-acre lot joining my grandfather's
place on the north and lower down the river. It was
partly upland or pine bluff and partly on the river flats.
Here he went to work without anything much to begin
with but his hands, putting up a log house with an old
fashion stone fireplace in it. The people in those days
knew nothing about stoves. They were poor like all the
pioneers in those days. Beginners had to labor and struggle hard for bread and raiment but he managed by mother's help to get quite a start and the next spring, the 15th
day of February, 1819 their first son was born. They
christened him with that good old Bible name John.
Good old brother John was to be the standby of the
whole family for many years down through poverty's vale.

They were doing quite well. Father was clearing up
and fencing his farm summers, and winters he worked

* There was no community named Stamphord in that region. This
may be a confusion of Sanford or Sanford's Corners, a hamlet near
Watertown. See C. K. Stone, *New Topographical Atlas of Jefferson
County, New York* (Philadelphia, 1864), p. 19.

out. In the spring of 1821 another son was born but lived only six weeks, a short-lived bright little boy. Many a time in after years since I was a man grown have I heard my good old mother speak of him as her sweet little cherub gone with the angels, a treasure in Heaven. Yes, a treasure in Heaven and one less to struggle through poverty's vale. One less to stem the tide of a cold indifferent world of sin and temptation.

I have heard my father tell many stories of the then great wilderness along the Indian River and what a wild country it was and what hardships they went through to get a living, carrying their grist many miles on their backs to the grist mill. It was all a wilderness then all the way down the Indian River from Theresa to Rossie Falls. One winter my father was down there to work helping build a dam at that place and coming home every Saturday night. One Saturday evening he lingered too long with his companions over his sailor grog forgetting he had several miles to walk to get home but at last he started going up on the ice as the river was now frozen hard enough to drive on with teams. He got along over half way all right at his leisure and now the moon was slowly rising. He could see the way more plain and began to quicken his pace. But hark! He halted to listen and there was no mistaking that howl away back below him in the distance. It was a pack of wolves, faint at first, but it was wolves. They had come on his track away down the river and were evidently after him. He had nearly two miles yet to go and he put his little bundle of groceries more tightly under his arm and started on a run for dear life while the howl in the distance grew plainer. On and on he went and on the hungry wolves came. Minutes seemed ages to him as nearer and nearer they came. One mile is past and one half mile further up is a bend in the stream, a bluff and forest bank extending out into the river and

if he could only reach that point, for just around its bend he could see the light of his own home and perhaps he could hello to someone, and the dogs or some of the folks might hear and he would be saved. On he sped, thinking of the wolves behind him, his own life and the dear ones in the cabin. He now could see the light of his own cabin as he turned the bend and glancing over his shoulder he could see in the bright moon light the wolves in close pursuit and hear them gnash their teeth. On, on he sped and raising his own voice to its highest pitch he shrieked for help, but the dogs, whose ears had already heard the racket, were coming to his rescue. They were just in time to keep the most foremost wolf biting his heels. Saved at last and before he reached his cabin the inmates had come out to meet him while the dogs drove the wolves away.

One would have thought that this would have been enough to have kept him from his foolish and useless sailor habit for ever but the habit was formed in youth and when with others who drank he soon forgot about the wolves except when he was telling us children the story of his race for life.*

I have heard my mother say they were doing well on their place and at the end of the summer of 1821 he had got over ten acres cleared and fenced with black ash rails, and they had things quite comfortable. The next spring on April 6, 1822 their first daughter was born and they named her Ruth after both of her grandmothers.

My grandmother Curtis had always been a spinner and weaver and my mother learned the trade in her

---

* Samuel Conklin undoubtedly heard the howl of wolves on that lonely walk home, but it is possible that the escape became more and more dramatic with the passage of time. Later in his narrative, Henry tells of his own experiences with wolves in Herkimer County. These animals were fascinating to pioneer settlers and have been the victims of myth and misconception.

youthful days and was now a great help to father, for her earnings were half of their living and if father had let liquor alone he might have been a rich man instead of groveling forever through poverty's vale. My mother had her loom and her two spinning wheels, one for flax and one for wool. Then there were the warping bars, the quill wheel, the swifts, the reel and shuttles. Enough to fill up quite a large room.

In the spring after Ruth was born my father got uneasy and dissatisfied and wanted to sell out although my mother protested against it, and sell out he would and sell out he did. The old wandering sailor habit of moving from port to port got hold of him and he could not resist. So my uncle Philander Curtis bought him out and kept the farm till the day of his death. After my father sold this place he became a wandering planet as my mother used to term it, working from place to place, a little poorer at every move, making a slave of himself and my mother who never gave him a cross word or ill treatment.

They moved from there to Theresa and stayed there one year, and then they moved to the town of Philadelphia and while living there on December 13, 1823 another son was born and they named him Abiah after grandfather Curtis. They lived in the town of Philadelphia until the spring of 1825 but moved three or four times in and about the town. In the spring of 1825 they moved to the Quaker Settlement * and it was no small job to move although they only went a little ways at a time. Instead of buying a piece of land and settling down he was renting land of someone else. While living here at the Quaker Settlement on November 21, 1825, a pair of twins were born—a girl and a boy and they named

* This was the local name for the village of Philadelphia, settled in 1804 by Quakers from New Jersey and Pennsylvania.

them Julius and Julia Ann. So now they had five children to move about with the other traps. From the Quaker Settlement they moved back to Theresa and stayed one year and then they moved to Evans Mills and stayed a while and then they moved to Watertown. Here my father bought 80 acres of land which is now at this date of writing (Christmas day 1891) partly covered by that city.

During his wanderings the past few years he had lived from hand to mouth always a little poorer everytime he moved. His children poorly clad and often hungry, scarcely having the necessarys of life and very humble at that.

At Watertown he told my mother he would stay and settle down for life so he went to work with a will, and a promise that he would leave off drinking, and with my mother's help spinning and weaving, for she had moved her loom and kindred traps. Here my mother said they began to gain some property and in a year or two almost paid for their place (which only cost them two dollars per acre) and were in a fair way to get out of poverty's vale.

My mother's parents had always been very strict in their religion and my mother was brought up under its hallowed influences and in her early youth she experienced religion, and no circumstances, trials, sickness, death or poverty could ever move her one jot from the even tenor of her way. While living at Watertown they had a revival of religion and father experienced religion, was baptized and joined the Methodist church and for a while he was a faithful member until they moved away and then he gave up the church-going as far as being a constant member. He believed there was a good God and a place of happiness and that if people were good though they did not belong to any church they would not be thrust out from the kingdom of God's mercies. He respected all good Christian people and scarcely ever uttered a word of profanity of any kind or an untruthful sentence.

The year after they moved to Watertown on the fourth day of April 1828 another son was born and they named him after his father calling him Samuel Jr. and this was the fourth son living and they now had a family of six children to look after and none to help mother but little sister Ruth and she was only six years old; but young as she was, mother said she done lots of work and would do most all the quilling for mother to weave besides the care of the younger children. Father's work was chopping and clearing land, for it was yet most all wilderness there and Watertown was then only a little hamlet. Everything was fair and prosperous with them. They were doing well and had a good many friends who took an interest in their welfare, and nearly two years more rolled around when another son was born, on the fourth day of March 1830, making seven children. This one they called James, an old Bible name.

The next fall one of my mother's uncles by the name of Silas Curtis who lived at Duanesburg was out visiting grandfather Curtis at Theresa and he came to Watertown to visit father and mother. He was praising up the country where he lived and he got my father on nettles to sell out and move down there. The old roving spirit was again upon him so mother said there was no peace until she gave her consent, and as far as that was concerned when he had them spells of wandering no one could stop him. Sell out he would and sell out he did, going away from a good situation, going from a home almost paid for, dragging his wife and seven children over the country nearly one hundred and fifty miles in the dead of winter from Watertown to Duanesburg.

There was nine in the family now to move and it was

no small job to rig all the children up for the journey, but they got started at last by the help of the neighbors, so they were comparatively comfortable on the road. Father had sold out cheap and sacrificed and lost on his farm and stuff that he had to sell yet he had quite a little money to start with besides his team, harness and sleigh. He hired another man and team to go and take a load, and mother said they were one week on the road traveling through drifts and snow up hill and down dale in the storm and cold. They had nothing to ride in but the old fashioned high sleigh boxes and these two sleighs were piled full. See sister Julia's letter. [Henry pinned a copy of the letter, in his handwriting, to the manuscript page. It is in Appendix 3.]

The old loom, the spinning wheels and kindred parts of course had to go with them, but mother said they sold some of their furniture, some they gave away and some they left so when they got to Duanesburg they had to begin anew to get things to use in the house. When they got to the end of their journey they sent the other team back and by the time they got settled and keeping house they were poorer than ever and their money all gone and no provisions, but the children were quite comfortably clad and all were thankful for a mother who could spin and weave. While living in Jefferson County they were almost continually living in the wilderness where deer and other game was plenty. Although my father was never much of a hunter there were others living in the settlements that could hunt and were successful in the chase and as I used to hear my mother tell it they had many and many a hunk of venison given to help in their poverty.

While living at Duanesburg my father worked out some and hired land to work and worked some on shares and he moved about the place from house to house every year, as mother said he moved every six months.

At Duanesburg the writer of this narrative was born on May 7, 1832 in an old dingy tumbled down log house with a stone fire place in it. They gave me the name of Henry after my Uncle Henry Curtis, my mother's youngest brother. After my birth they still continued to live here, hacking about from place to place, and on the fourth day of January another daughter was born not quite two years younger than I was. They gave her the name of Mary Elizabeth. The first name was after my mother and I don't know where they got the Elizabeth from.

Well, along in the summer of 1834 my uncle Joseph Curtis (or great uncle properly, for he was one of grandfather Curtis's brothers but he had married my Aunt Amy Conklin, my father's sister, so that he was my uncle and great uncle also. Uncle Joe we always called him) had been down to Duanesburg visiting his brother Silas and his grandfather and grandmother Curtis who were still living. Uncle Joe had lived in Duanesburg a few years before but had moved to the Town of Blenheim, Schoharie County, where he was doing well farming and keeping bees. While Uncle Joe and Aunt Amy was visiting us at Duanesburg they persuaded father and mother to move to Blenheim. Well mother said this time she did not care much about it as my father was bound to move about every six months anyway and they might just as well move to Blenheim as anywhere else. So it was decided in the fall that they were to move and Uncle Joe was to look them up a house to move into before winter and my father was happy again as there was another move in progress and he was going to live by his sister Amy, his only sister that was now living.

This time it was not quite so far to move but there were two more kids (myself and sister Mary) to add to the other traps. They moved by wagon late in the fall over the hubs and ruts up hill and down jolty jolt in the old fashioned high box wagon without springs. Now they had nine children to move and eleven in the family in all. Mother said while living at Duanesburg they had bought some new furniture and had had some given to them and when they moved they had three loads to haul over the rough road up to Blenheim and the oldest boys had to walk the most of the way. I don't know how we looked then traveling about through the country with all our accoutrements but I can judge something how it was by my own experience later on after I could remember. I don't remember moving this time but I can remember the old house we moved into after we got there. In her letter of January 11, 1892, sister Julia says:

After moving to Blenheim we lived the first year on one of Joe Curtis's places in an old dingy smoked up log house with a fireplace in it. It was near a great hill and here we rode down hill in the snow and running in by the fire to warm our bare feet. From here we moved over on the north road as they called it and near by a man named Delong who had a brother hung while we lived there. And the winter we lived there my father went to New York to see his sister Aunt Polly as we always called her and while father was gone the boys had a high old time having fun riding down hill and this winter I and the boys went to school. I wore rags and cloth moccasins on my feet. From here we moved to Darling Hollow and then up on John Perry's house on the hill and here we lived until father bought that place over in Tompkins Hollow.

3   I HAVE now got along down to my own recollections, and memory goes back to the long long ago, yes nearly fifty-eight years, over half a century. . . . Memory goes back to loving, trusting childhood. Oh how happy and sweet those days way back in the mist when no sin or thought of sin or evil or knowledge of grief or care or pain loving and being loved, trusting and confiding in the goodness of those who had the care of me. The dim recollection of being trotted to sleep on a father's knee or clasped in the embrace of a mother's arms before a great blazing crackling fire, and as that blessed sweet sleep of childhood came creeping over me, I can yet see other loving forms near me mingling with great shadows cast upon the walls and the great open chimney by the blazing logs and then all would be oblivion. Oblivion, sweet slumber snuggled down warm and cozy on someone's lap. Oh happy sweet days of childhood. How soon they were to pass and never, never to return.

    The first of my distinct recollections is of our folks living in an old big log house on Blenheim Hill. It was all in one room below and a low chamber above. Stoves had not been invented then or if they had the people were too poor to buy them. Everybody had fireplaces, those great old fashioned fireplaces without jambs. The hearths were laid in with great flat stones, three or four feet out in front and six or eight feet long and they were put in all shapes with the smoothest side up. The back of the chimney was built of stones, the logs being left out where the back of the chimney was and the great stones protruded outside the house. They were built up in this way as high as the chamber floor and from there up two or three feet above the house were built square of boards or sticks and laths and plastered with lime or mud and clay, and it was generally more mud and clay than lime.

In these fireplaces they could burn wood six or seven feet long using a great log behind and smaller wood in front resting on stones or handirons. But few were able to have handirons.*

While living here in this old log house, the first one we lived in, in Blenheim, I remember one day of running around in the house playing with the other children. I was in my bare feet and wore dresses yet and as I went to jump along by the fireplace I stubbed my toe on one of the stones used for handirons and I fell over in the fire on my back with the back of my head in the live coals and one arm in the blazing fire. I was quickly snatched out by mother, who was near enough to snatch me from the burning embers but I was in there long enough to burn my scalp so that a piece of the skin came off with the hair and one sleeve of my dress was burned out and my arm burned quite badly. My arm got well and left no scar but I carry the mark today on my head for I have a spot there that hair never grows on. Here my trouble began, for it was a long time before my head got well, for every little bump given it while playing with my brothers and sisters would hurt it afresh. This was the winter and I wouldn't be three years old until the seventh of May, so you see how distinctly my memory comes back to me.

I remember too that winter how my older brothers and my father used to haul in the great back logs on the hand sled and when they opened the great wide door to get in wood for the night we had to stand away back in the

* He undoubtedly means andirons.

corner, for the coals would fly when they put on the back log and the hot embers would sputter and siss. I was so young my mind was not yet in a state to comprehend or understand the true circumstances of our living or of how many the family consisted. Neither could I scarcely distinguish one from the other of my brothers and sisters yet I knew my father and my mother. My mother, yes my own dear mother, who had given me birth and nourished and cared for me until I knew her from the rest. Oh, that sweet childhood memory of my dearest one I ever knew on earth. My mother, first to know, first to love above all others and from that time to this all along down through poverty's vale she has been my guiding star even after it had gone down to rest under the great shadows of this earthly night.

The spring I was three years old I had my first pair of pants and oh how proud I felt. How I strutted about with my hands in my pockets with all the others laughing and applauding to see the young actor, and I more distinctly remember this because there was to be a circus and caravan up at Jefferson that day and I had the promise to go and my mother had rigged me up with a new pair of pants. My sister Julia Ann was then quite a girl and she was to go with me. I could hardly wait for the time to come to start. At last we started, I with my new pants on and a sort of an apron made of flannel and a straw hat made by mother out of rye straw. We had to go from Blenheim Hill down northeastward all the way down hill and through a long deep ravine and around several dugways thus winding down and down until we came to another road running east and west that leads from Patchin Hollow up to Jefferson. Here at the forks of the road lived a family by the name of Darling and here we stopped to wait for a caravan to come along and then we were to ride up to Jefferson with some of the neighbors.

There were a good many here waiting as well as me and my sister was having a good time with the young folks. I also was having a good time playing with those of my own age and some older. Well I was running around the house after some of them and fell down and got my new pants all daubed in manure, mud and dirt, and my sister declared she would not take me to the show looking like that and I must go back home. About this time the cry was set up, "The caravan is coming, the caravan is coming," and sure enough we could look back way down the road and sure enough led by his keeper there came the great old elephant with his majestic tread and great ears flopping and long round tail switching from side to side and then the long train of wagons with the other animals inside went by which we could only get a glimpse of through the grates, and while they passed how we children trembled and kept back out of the road and after they got by we went and looked at the great tracks the elephant had made. How I did want to go, but no my sister was resolute and cross at me for my carelessness and home she would go, not daring to send me home alone. She said she would never take me anywhere again but she did all the same. My sister was sadly provoked, for she had anticipated a good time. I thought at the time she was quite rough with me and I did not blame her much. All the way back up the hills and the winding dugways she carried a whip in her hand full of little twigs and she drove me ahead of her whipping my bare feet as we went home. Well we got home at last, but did mother scold me? No, oh no, but instead she took off my pants and washed them out. But she scolded my sister for whipping my feet. From that day on my sister was always good to me and was always a kind and loving sister. No matter what my faults they were always overlooked by her excepting once which I will tell you later on.

4   I<small>N</small> the fall when I was three years old our folks moved from Blenheim Hill down to Darling Hollow.* It was only a few miles to go but all the same it was pick up and pack up and string along the road with a big family of children. My father never could anchor at any place a great while at a time. We had a smaller house this time and newer and made of logs and chimney some like the other only not so large. We lived in sight of where we was when we saw the elephant tracks, only a little farther east.

After we moved here another daughter was born on the 29th day of December 1835, another little one to love and caress and she was a little twit of a thing, rosy fat and good natured and they at first called her titmouse but finally named her Casandana, I believe after some great fairy in a fairy story book. So we had a fairy to go with us through the vale of poverty and another one to feed and clothe and move about from place to place with our other traps.

While living here in Darling Hollow the spring before I was four years old our folks made sugar, my father and older brothers, John, Julius, Abiah and Samuel doing the work. It was about a half mile from the house up to the hill and they used to carry me up to the boiling place and let me stay by the fire while they gathered sap and cut wood to boil it down. The snow was on yet and I had nothing to wear on my feet so they carried me up. I can now look back over the long past and see just how they

* Now known as Cole Hollow.

looked and see the fire blazing up around the great kettle vibrating with heat and boiling sap. My brother James, two years older than me, used to come up to the bush barefoot to play with me around the boiling place where the snow was melted off and when we got hungry and tired of this we would scud to the house and when we got there our feet were red as geeses feet and oh horrors how they would ache and smart while holding them up to the fireplace. How glad we used to be when the snow was gone.

Oh happy times then running in the woods gathering wild flowers, six or seven of us almost of a size one a little taller than the other like a pair of stairs. We not only gathered flowers but used to go after leeks for greens. Oh what a treat thus to ramble in the woods and get something to eat besides rye bread and johnny cake. Here is my first recollection of how mother used to bake in an old fashion flat bottom iron kettle with cover on and legs on the bottom. It was as large as a half bushel. She used to set it over some coals on the hearth, then put the great loaf in, made of rye or corn meal and then put the cover on and coals on top of that. Oh what delicious bread, so moist and sweet. Many a time she used to bake johnny cake on a flat stone set up towards the fire and potatoes baked in the hot ashes then were as good as cake is to us now. The trammel pole was fixed in many different ways. It generally was fastened up over the fire and held in place by a notch in the jambs or if there were no jambs it was fastened with a chain or hook. From the trammel pole hung other long hooks of wood or iron that came down low enough to hang the kettles on. I can see mother now and just how she looked when reaching over the fire to hang on the great dinner pot. In my imagination it would hold a bushel. Well there were a good many to eat and oh so hungry.

While living here I began to learn, remember and distinguish my brothers apart. John was the oldest and biggest and I loved him the best. He was in the prime of youth, almost a man grown then and was always at home with father or working out with him. There was nothing done but what he was called on to help, toiling from morn till night for the whole family, self-sacrificing, kind-hearted, true and loving, good natured brother John. If anyone was to be scrimped for clothing or food, it was John not thinking of himself but giving away to all the others unmurmuring and uncomplaining. Oh how I loved him. In the evening before a great blazing fire when I got to be quite a lad I used to sit on his lap while he sung me to sleep. Not only me did he watch over and caress but the younger ones too got their share of kisses and caresses from brother John. In fact, John was all in all the old standby of the whole family, my dear oldest loving brother John. Some time in this spring I remember the first money I ever had, my brother John gave me one of those old fashioned pennies with a hole in it and he put a string in it for me. How rich I was in my imagination. I could have bought clothes with it enough to last a year. I kept it for a long time and one day I was playing with it out with my brother James and was twirling it around my head by the string when the string broke and away it went. We looked hours for it but never found it and every time I was near the spot I was looking for my penny but it was gone. Thus away went all my riches and all my imaginary happiness.

While living here I saw the first dead person I had ever seen. It was Mrs. Darling our nearest neighbor just west of us. Mother was with her the night she died and helped lay her out, and in the morning after mother got home she let us children go up and see her and I never shall forget how pale and quiet she looked lying there with her hands folded on her breast. It was sad indeed to us. How soft and still we walked in our bare feet afraid we would wake her up thinking she was only asleep.

The next winter I remember of riding down hill with my older brothers. Back of the house towards the sap bush was a great long hill and when going up with their sleds they would draw me up all bundled up hands and feet

with some old blanket or garment to keep me from freezing, then the downward run sitting on their laps in front covered and almost strangled with snow. What fun! If it was cold we did not care, and what tricks they used to play with each other. One day one of the boys chopped a great hole in our path and filled it with loose snow and what a ducking I got then as we went in the hole, tipping over, and the sled and John on top of me and they had to dig me out. I did not want to ride anymore that day. The boys had trapped John and me, and how they roared and laughed to see us crawl out of the snow. Brother Julius was the ring leader in such mischief.

While living in Darling Hollow I remember of my mother and oldest sister Ruth spinning and weaving. In fact the spinning wheels and loom was the means of over half of our living. Mother and Ruth were at work early and late spinning and weaving for someone and they used to take work of this kind to do for some of the neighbors. They had three wheels. The small low one was to spin flax on and they could sit down when they worked with this wheel for it went with treadles. The big tall one they spun wool on and they had to walk back and forth when they used this and it was no play to stand at this wheel all day and walk and work. And then there was the quill wheel I will introduce later on. I never heard of a carding mill in those days and I used to sit for hours and see my mother sitting before the great fireplace in the winter evenings carding wool into great flat rolls for spinning. About the first work I ever remember doing was picking wool for mother or sister Ruth to card. All these wheels, the loom, warping bans, shuttles, reeds, reels and swifts had to be trucked about the country whenever we moved, for they were the indispensable article of furniture helping us out of the wilderness of want many times and smoothing the way more pleasantly through poverty's vale. And the loom, what a great big piece of furniture it was with its harnesses, treadles, swinging beam, warping beam, reeds and shuttles, and to look back upon it now I think that if cut up into four foot wood there would be a cord of it. It also had to have its place in the house in winter and was generally erected in some warm corner by the fireplace and many a time have I crawled under the old loom and gone to sleep in the warmth of the great blazing fire and someone would drag me out and put me to bed. In summer the loom was either upstairs or out in some shed by the house. [See Julia's letter, Appendix 3.]

5    ANOTHER move in progress. My father was always taking farms to work on shares or hiring some place of somebody so he was constantly clearing or working some-one else's land, never having any of his own. If he bought a piece of land he never was contented to stay long enough on it to pay for it, consequently he never had a home of his own. No wonder we were poor. No wonder we were half naked and sometimes hungry and cold and no place to lay our heads that we could call our own, free from all encumbrances. And what a happy time if we only did have such a place. No, but it was a continual struggle to keep soul and body together. We were down deep in the vale of poverty wandering in the wilderness like a sailor seeking a port to anchor and finding none. Mother's protests were of no avail and reason and argu-ment amounted to nothing.

My father had hired a place or rented it, I don't know which, of John Perry up southwest from Darling Hollow towards Blenheim Hill perhaps a mile or a mile and a half, and sometime the fore part of April we moved (I would be five in May). The snow had not gone off yet and I never shall forget that move. It was only a little ways to go but what a time. All that were able to go on foot walked and everyone carrying something. Mother and my two younger sisters, Mary and the baby—Cass was the baby then, still our little fairy as we called her. Well they rode in an old wood sled with pieces of wood pinned on for shoe runners. I can see how it looked as it wriggled and creaked as the horses pulled it along over the bare spots in the road. Some of us were bare foot and some had a sort of moccasin that was leather or old coarse cloth sewed on the bottom of old stockings. Father and the oldest boys wore great coarse shoes laced up with leather strings and leggings tied on over them coming most up to their knees. Oh how we looked straggling up the hills to our new home. I called it home; well it was, if we only stayed one night. My sister Julia Ann carried the looking glass and all the way along up the hills and around those old dugways she would let some of us at a time look into it and ask us if we wanted to see an April fool and then again she would hold it so that by looking in corner ways we could see a group of movers and call it her circus and caravan, and circus it was. I laugh to myself yet sometimes thinking of it. I know I carried the broom, an old fashion splint broom, for we had no other kind in them days unless it was a bunch of hemlock brush tied onto a stick. One of the older boys, I think it was Julius, got plaguing me because my pants were torn behind and said I had a letter in the post office. I got my dander up a little and went for them with the broom and came very near breaking the looking glass, and then they let me alone in peace the rest of our journey. I don't remember as yet that we ever had a cow to move but I presume we did.

It seems that John Perry owned two places or farms, for the one we moved onto had a house and a barn a little ways west of where he lived. It was a double house. That is, there had been an addition of a frame part built on the west side of the log part. And this was the first frame house we had ever lived in and that was only half of a house. On the east end was a log woodshed where mother had her loom in the summer. There was a double fireplace, one in each room, and the chimney was modeled over to suit the new part. This new part was fitted up by the girls for a parlor and us children had to look out how we ran through it with dirt. Parlor did I say? Oh yes they called it their parlor where all the visitors used to sit and chat and take snuff and where the table was spread when they had company.

But in winter the loom and its relative parts occupied this room, for here I learned to quill for mother and Ruth to weave. The older ones had done the quilling before this but now my turn had come. The quill wheel was constructed something like the big wheel for spinning wool, only not so large. It ran with a string band from the wheel to the spindle where the empty spools were put on to be filled for the shuttle. The spindle was made tapering so that you could crowd the spool on so it would not turn only as the spindle turned. The great skeins of yarn were put on swifts as they were called and then the end of the thread was wet a little and carefully rolled on the spool by turning the rim of the wheel and then with one hand steadying the thread, while you turned the wheel with the other and so on until the spool was full enough to fill the shuttle. And here I used to sit day after day and month after month when they had any weaving to do and tired, oh so tired I thought then, but not so tired as the dear old mother plying the shuttle and bumping up the threads with the swinging beams, changing hands to catch the shuttle as it came through and then using the treadles with her feet first up and then down all day long, clash clash year in and year out to keep us clothed and to keep the hungry wolf from the door and never a word of complaint. Blessed good old mother, good to every one. Where oh where shall her reward be but in Heaven among those who have come through poverty and tribulations.

When it was not quilling it was handing thrums, putting in a new piece to weave.* At times I used to get out in the lots where father, brother John and Abiah were at work and here I remember of their sowing wheat and buckwheat. The rye was most always sown in the fall. All kinds of grain was ground in the mills nearest home and there was no flour in the markets then put up in sacks or barrels as it is now and everything was used for bread or pancakes even to wheat bran. It was a world of new experience for me then to learn how they raised the grain and how it made our bread.

Here was the first place I ever went to school. I went with my oldest sister Ruth, she leading me by the hand. Oh my good sister Ruth. I wish my pen could describe her to you as she seemed to me then, one of the good angels that I had heard my mother tell about. She was not very tall but slender and trim and always looked so neat and loving, with dark brown eyes, rosy cheeks and black hair and a sweet and loving disposition. And it seems but yesterday when I received from her lips those loving kisses and fond caresses and she loved them all alike. I don't know how far off the school house was but I should say over a mile. We went through a piece of woods and then clearings and again more woods and here was a small clearing and a farm house on the north side of the road and a little frame schoolhouse on the south side of the road on a knoll by a swamp. It was a small building with

* Thrums were the fringes of warp threads left on the loom after the web had been cut off.

30

a fireplace in one end of it. All the way along my sister kept telling me I must go up and read and not be afraid of the teacher. I was a little afraid at first but we soon got acquainted and I was alright and could read and play with the rest of the scholars and at recess and noons we used to go in the swamp and gather flowers and wintergreens, the first I had ever remembered eating. One day all of us scholars, sister Ruth and the teacher got evergreens and trimmed the schoolhouse.

I went there to school all summer only when I had quilling to do but Ruth did not go to school much when they had spinning and weaving to do or work at the neighbors. That year in the fall my sister Ruth went away to work and when I went to school the next summer Julia Ann or some of my brothers went with me but as soon as any of the children got old enough to work out, school was neglected. Consequently the most of the children had a very scanty education. In fact we were so poor we could not pay our rate bill many times as the teachers were paid by a rate bill, every day's schooling costing the ratio according to the teacher's wages. My father always seemed to be behind with his bills and constantly in debt and it was always work and scrub and dig with the whole family to pay up and live.

The older boys and girls were all good to work but oh how discouraged sometimes they got in trying to get along and live and be clothed decent, and a great deal of our poverty was caused by my father's foolish habit of drinking, for sailorlike he still wanted his grog and especially when he went to mill or away on business with his team. He would get among some other fellows that loved whiskey and to have a good time over their glass and then it was all trade and traffic in old horses and other useless traps that did not amount to anything and yet they all had to be paid for and no wonder the boys were all discouraged. As they used to term it, working hard to pay for old dead horses.

Yet I would not have the reader here to understand that I mean to wrongfully cast any bad reflections on my father's character or actions in regard to the family. When not in drink he was always at work, always trying and striving to keep us above want, always kind and loving and scarcely ever spoke a cross or angry word to any of us or to mother, but when he came home full of rye whiskey he was far too loving for mother's own good and in fact he was so mellow, soft and funny (if I must use the expression) that we could not lay up anything very serious against him. When in liquor he was rich, oh so rich that we never should want for anything and he would clothe us like kings and princesses and feed us on the fat of the land, but when he began to get over these spells he became sad and dejected and discouraged and poor. In fact, again groping his way down down through poverty's vale and the wilderness of work, toil and care.

I remember the second spring we lived here father and brother John took a job of John Perry to chop a fallow of quite a number of acres.* It was west of the house away down on a steep side hill. Father and my older brothers were out there to work one day and James and I went also. James had an axe and sometimes helped cut the small trees. But this time we went after some basswood bark for strings to play horse with. James was chopping into a small sapling to loosen the bark at the bottom so we could strip it off. Well I thought I would take hold and help strip it off too so I grabbed after some and at the same time James was chopping, when whack down came the axe on the back of my right hand (I am looking

* Conklin here uses the term *fallow* to mean uncleared land, though it usually refers simply to uncultivated land.

33

at the scar now), cutting a gash almost across it letting the blood fly in all directions. Well I tell you there was trouble in the camp now and what to do we did not know and James was awfully scairt and called for help when brother John came running to us. Brother John, the ever present helper, was near. We had no cloth or rag to do it up so John unbuttoned his pants and tore off his shirt tail and quickly bound it up and started for the house with me, the blood trickling as we went. I got pretty faint before we got to the house for there was two of the veins cut off. At the house the remedy was at hand. Someone ran upstairs and brought down some puff balls and mother split a large one in two and bound it on and in a few minutes the blood was all stopped. I had a very sore hand and it was a long time before it got well and I had quite a rest and my brother James or some other one of the family done the quilling.

After I cut my hand I went to school until huckleberries got ripe and then mother used to take me with her to help pick berries and always wanted me to carry a great long stick for there was lots of rattlesnakes on the huckleberry hills. While watching for snakes I would help mother pick berries and I could just pick berries in them days, for I was quicker than chain lightning (as the other boys said). I have helped my brothers kill many an old rattler and drag them up home by a string around their neck and then cut off the head and burn it up, for the poison was in their teeth. After destroying the head we would drag the carcas about until it began to come to pieces and then we would burn that also.

There was lots of sweet fern growing here and we used to gather it for tea when we had no other and sage was cultivated as regular as any other garden stuff. Our folks were too poor to buy much tea, and sweet fern and sage was a very good substitute. The summer I had my hand cut I remember of going up that fall on Blenheim Hill to my Uncle Joseph Curtis's when they were taking up bees and straining honey for market and boiling out beeswax. I went with my mother and we stayed over night while mother helped them with their work. Uncle Joseph and Aunt Amy were always good to us. Uncle's folks had a large family also and when part of both families got together it was fun in the camp and Uncle Joe as we always called him was first and foremost in the fun and play with the rest. Oh what fun, and Aunt Amy scolding us all the while, for she was a great scold, but we did not mind her much. Uncle said she was like a barking good natured dog that would never bite anyone. Oh how I delighted in going there to eat honey. Uncle used to make methiglin (as they called it).* It was made from the rinsing of bee comb and when it began to work it was a very good drink and sometimes it would make us dizzy for a while and then Uncle would get us to walk a crack and how he would roar and laugh to see our crooked walk. They kept a good many bees and every fall they took honey and beeswax to the Albany market. Their bees were as profitable as the farm. And how much different were the hives then than now. Then they were made of rye straw made in great rolls and wound around from top to bottom and sewed together with elm bark strings. A hole was left in the top and filled with a straw plug. What bees they took up; all had to be killed and what a wholesale slaughter of the little workers.

Uncle Joseph had quite a large farm but oh so stony. It was almost impossible to plow it unless the rocks and stones were first removed. Most of all his fences were great stone walls.

* Metheglin, or mead, is a fermented beverage made of honey and water.

There were so many of us at home now and we were so poor that father found a place for Julius and Samuel to work out. So they were bound out until they were twenty one years old. Julius went to Nelson Hagers and Samuel to Shavers. These men both of them were Dutch, and they were sometimes called low Dutch or Mohawk Dutch. They lived down on the Schoharie flats below what was called Patchin Hollow and they owned and worked large farms. They were hard working old farmers, working early and late and were in those days termed rich, but oh how stingy. They would sell all they could sell and what they could not sell would feed to the hogs and what the hogs would not eat they lived on themselves. The boys were to have three months schooling each year and their clothes (but they went in rags or dressed in cast off clothing far too large for them). They were to have a little spending money on general training day to buy gingerbread with and when they became twenty one years old they were to have one hundred dollars apiece.

The boys were worked and starved almost to death, deprived of a minute's play even on Sunday as long as the chores would last. While living here I went down and stayed with Julius over night and we slept away up in the great old garret in an old dingy room large enough for a soldier's barrack and no fire to warm the room and the bed was not as warm as the one I slept in at home although we were poor.

While down there one time my brother took me over the creek in an old scow boat. It was the first time I ever rode in a boat and I was awful afraid of being tipped over and drowned so when we got near the shore on a long sand bar my brother tried to rock the boat over to show me there was no danger. Their cow pasture was along the creek and my brother had to go over after the cows most every night, as they used to swim over. I was down there one time with mother on foot and in the afternoon when we started to come home one of the women that lived to Hagers, a great tall one, and she came about a mile with us for a walk and to visit with mother and she had her knitting work in her hands and knit as she went—walking and knitting. Methinks I can yet hear her needles click, click as she strode along. I thought mother and Ruth could knit fast but this woman beat anything I ever saw.

In the fall I went down to see Julius again and father went with me this time with a team. I and Julius went and gathered some butternuts on the flats for me to take home and when going back home we stopped and got a lot of apples and put them in the wagon with the butternuts. They got badly mixed up before we got home. The apples were well stained with the butternuts shucks.

My brother Samuel lived up the creek three or four miles above Hagers and I did not go to Shavers until the next year. So now that two of my brothers were away from home there was less work for mother and two less for her to care for.

At this time childhood was fleeting and I was gradually stepping over the land of youth. Yes, early youth with more brightening eyes, more red and more rounded cheeks and curly brown hair. Oh glorious awakening to youth and sweet childhood.

6   THE land of youth. We still lived in John Perry's house. The fall before I was six years old was spent at home scarcely going to school any as I had no shoes to wear and my time was spent mostly helping mother and sister Ruth at spinning and weaving, for the fall was a busy time with them, while Julia Ann did the housework. James was now old enough to help father and John about the work on the farm. Julius and Samuel were away from home at their adopted places, and Abiah worked out, for in fact he was a money grabber, always working out and always had good luck in getting his pay. He carefully saved all of his wages and in the fall brought home his earnings to share them with mother, his brothers and sisters.

He went to school winters, paying for his own schooling. On days when there was no school, he used to help father and John get up wood in great big logs that a team could hardly draw, and he and John used to race chopping to see who could beat one another—that is, to see who could cut off the butt log first. It was about an even race but John generally came out ahead. Wood was all chopped in those days, for they knew nothing about sawing off a hardwood log with a cross-cut saw. Cross-cut saws were not yet invented for sawing hardwood.

That winter wore away as usual with our fun of riding down hill and brother John is now on hand again, making us boys hand sleighs. Evenings when he had nothing else to do he would tinker away by the great blazing fire for hours making or repairing a sled. And such hand sleds, we thought they were splendid. No wonder we all loved John.

Early in the spring sister Ruth went away to work at Uncle Tom Peaslee's, a farmer living a few miles west of us. His farm was next joining where Uncle Joe Curtis lived. Ruth never came home again to stay but frequently was home on a visit and brought us lots of presents. Dear sister Ruth, how much she loved my mother. How sweet she looked in her womanly Christian beauty for she had long before experienced religion and was now a respected and faithful member of the Methodist church. How we used to cling to her whenever she was home. But now she had found a good place to work, plenty to wear, plenty to eat and was now fairly on the road that finally led her out of poverty's vale.

After Ruth went away to work sister Julia had to take her place at the wheel and loom and I was old enough to help them to do chores about the house. My work was sweeping, washing dishes and helping mother to wash and do most all kinds of indoor work as my sisters older than I were occupied elsewhere and sister Mary was not old enough to do much. In fact I was my mother's boy girl and I believed it for mother said so. If she went away anywhere I had to go with her to help about something, to keep the snakes away while picking huckleberries and when visiting to either carry the bundle or the baby. I could carry Cassie, as we always called her, for she was so little. I was then nimble and stout with curly brown hair, blue eyes and rosy cheeks and in my own eyes quite a lad, just blooming into youth. Although we were poor I was blithesome and gay, caring not for poverty or care or trouble, happy go lucky in the morning of the sweet time of youth. Oh how glorious and bright and happy seemed the hours and days and the sweet slumber at night. No brain racking or planning, restless, uneasy, sleepless nights but calm and sweet were my slumbers as a summer evening.

Well I remember this season. Father, John and James worked hard but did not seem to get along well. Crops were poor and everything went wrong while hiring places. So father said they would look around to buy a place somewhere. They went over into what was called Tompkins Hollow in the Town of Fulton, ten or twelve miles north of Blenheim Hill and here they found and bought a small place of fifty or sixty acres with no buildings on it and most all woods. Now we were to move again as soon as they could fix a place to move into. So whenever father and John could get away for two or three days at a time, they used to drive over and work, taking some lumber each time, for we were to live in grand style in a framehouse. Father was quite a carpenter, for he had worked at the trade when a young man while living on Long Island. Father hewed the timber and John drew some logs up to a saw mill in the hollow about a mile above our new place towards Rosman Hill. In this way they gathered lumber to start the building. Mother was well pleased with the undertaking and did all she could to help them along by cooking up a basket of provisions each time they went over to work at the house. They had what they called their dinner basket. It was made of wide splints, round like a cheese box and a high cover on it made of splints also. The cover was fastened on with splint hinges. In my imagination it would hold a bushel.

Oh what Eldorado stories they told of our new home. Such nice spring water near the house and what a lovely brook full of trout running right past the door. It was nothing but talk of the new home and moving over to it, all in the latter part of the summer or late in the fall and to hurry matters along one day it was finally decided that father and John should go over and get their new neighbors together and make a bee to put up the house. So over they went and let the people know what they wanted and they soon got enough together, some bringing nails, some shingles, and some lumber and some of this and some of that, anything that was needed to carry it along and they set at it old fashion bee style, with a basket of dinner and a jug of old rye whiskey and before night they had the house so far constructed that father thought it would do to move into.

The next thing was to pack up and move. They had taken over a part of their old useless truck and traps, what they could, every time they went over, so there was not so much to move when the family went over. It was late in the fall and it was getting cold weather and it was hurry up, hurry up. Finally there was a day set to go. Father and mother made all preparations and the day before we were to start they packed up everything except what we needed that night. I was old enough now to assist and entered into the business of moving most heartily for I longed to get over in the new frame house and see the brook where the trout were. At last the morning came for us to start and it was all hurly burly. John, father, mother, Julia Ann and James were all at work. There were not so many this time to go as usual for Ruth, Julius, Samuel and Abiah were away at work but there were six besides father and mother, making eight in all to go. My father had a team and one of our neighbors had volunteered to come over and take a load. The loom and all its relative traps had gone on the advance a few days before, for I remember it stood in a pile in the new house when we got there.

At last we got started, two loads of us in the clumsy old fashion high box wagons without springs and the road was rough and stony and it was jolty, jolty, jolt as we went. We had to go down through Darling Hollow past where we had once lived on the same road where I saw the elephant then down through those crooked dugway hills that I had traveled many times, then from Darling Hollow northeast down and down great long hills until we came to Patchin Hollow. Here was a little hamlet, a post office, store, hotel, gristmill and a few other dwellings. From here our road turned toward the northwest up the hills again through small clearings and pieces of woods for three or four miles and then we came to a big piece of woods three or four miles long. While going up the last hills John, James and I had been walking for the wagons were heavy loaded.

Brother James had on his feet a pair of father's old worn out shoes that were too large for his feet but he had managed to get on stockings and old rags enough to fill them up and they were tied on with tow strings and so he went skuff, skuff with these great shoes swabbing over the frozen hubs. I had on my feet a pair of old stockings with two or three thicknesses of cloth of some kind sewed on the bottom which mother had fixed for me to wear while moving. My feet were good and warm at first, but after leaving Patchin Hollow the boys had to walk most of the way, and before we got up the hills my moccassins were worn to tatters on the bottom and my bare toes were on the frozen hubs. But what did I care then for any such a thing! I had been used to it all through childhood.

Happy, oh I was happy now for we were on our way to the new home over in the promised land. Well, when we came to the woods how dark and dismal they looked. They were second growth pine and great towering dark hemlocks. In the center of these woods was a great swamp and it was called Wolf Swamp because in the early days of settlement it was a rendezvous and hiding place for wolves. While going through the swamp my brother John and father were telling some awful wolf stories and I got so scairt I clumb on the wagon until I got past it. On we went and out of the woods to a clearing where lived a man by the name of Boyd and from his house it was only half a mile across down a great steep hill through a piece of woods and then over the brook to our new house. This was a foot path and I traveled it hundreds of times after. John, James and I went across to build a fire while the teams had to go by the road which led towards the west for about half a mile and then turned and wound around down the hill on the flats then east by another new house and our nearest neighbor, Jay Tompkins. One half mile east was our new house.

After we left the teams we boys skipped pretty lively down the hill through the woods to an old clearing of two or three acres. Here was the brook and when we crossed it John says, "Here boys is where the trout are." I looked in the deep holes as we crossed over on a log but did not see any. We soon got to the new house and John went to work with a flint, a piece of steel and some punk and there he sat over a pile of dry sticks and slivers. Whackety whack, click, click, click, and at last he struck fire and soon had a good blaze. For good old brother John had prepared for this beforehand by getting a lot of pitch pine slivers. We soon had a roaring fire but had to watch the chimney and boards above the fireplace for they had only time enough to build up the back of the chimney with stone as far as the chamber floor, and above there and out of the roof were tacked on temporarily a few boards for the smoke to go up out until they had more time to complete it. The door was not hung yet and there was only one window in and only a part of the chamber floor was laid yet. We got the castle good and warm and along about dark on come the rest of them, and then it was unload and carry in the truck.

The lower part of the house was all in one room and before the teams had got along we carried the old loom, wheels and warping bars to the farthest corner from the fire so as to give room for the family by the fireplace. After we had all gotten in and settled and warm the next thing was supper. Mother had prepared for this by baking some great loaves of rye and Indian bread baked in the big iron baking kettle. We also had tea, cold meat and potatoes—baked in the ashes, for they had not gotten the trammel pole up yet and so could not boil them in the dinner pot. What a good supper it was to us hungry movers as we had not stopped to get dinner on the way except to eat a lunch while the teams were being fed.

That night Jay Tompkins came down to see us and I never shall forget him. What a rollicsome fun-loving fellow he was and what hours of fun and laughter he made for us for years after. He would heat the fire shovel red hot, then lick it with his tongue and not get burned and then he said he could swallow us if he had some grease to grease our heads with. Many and many a time he used to come over to have fun with us, chasing us around the house to swallow us. That night he and my brother John got to singing songs. Oh happy, happy John. He was happy that night, and why should he not be? He had hacked and jogged and toted about as the main stay of the family through Jefferson, Schenectady and Schoharie counties all his life and now they had got and were going to have a home of their own where mother should have a little rest.

That night we all slept on the floor, not having time to put up the bedsteads. The trundle bedsteads were left outdoors that night. We had old fashion cord bedsteads made of four by four hardwood scantling big enough for barn timber and great ropes for bed cords. I remember how we looked that night in beds scattered over the floor with the great shadows of the fire flickering over our heads on the beams and rafters and roof inside.

Time went on and father and John finished the chimney by lathing the inside of the boards and plastering them with mud and clay mixed together. Then they finished the chamber floor and put in two more windows and hung the door on great wooden hinges that John had manufactured. Then they made a pair of stairs for the chamber in one corner by the chimney, and in the other corner they made a cupboard, and by banking the house on the outside up to the windows we were quite comfortable for the winter.

After they got the house fixed they put up a sort of barn or shed of logs for the team and a place for hay, and during the winter father and John used to go over on Blenheim Hill and draw their hay over on a slight for the teams.

Abiah came home as usual this winter, and he and Julia Ann went to school part of the time. They had to go over two miles away over towards West Gilboa or Rosman Hill. It was so far I could not go.

Towards spring Abiah bought a cow out of his last summer earnings and gave it to mother. I do not remember that we had ever owned a cow before but I presume we had.* How proud mother felt with her cow. She was a great big nice one spotted red, white and cream color and what a pet we all made of her. That spring when she gave milk I used to go with mother and watch her milk.

I was then seven years old and I thought that if I could only milk I would soon be a man and sometimes after

---

* Cows were usually beyond the financial reach of a family as poor as the Conklins. See Philip L. White, ed., "An Irish Immigrant Housewife on the New York Frontier," *New York History* XLVIII (April 1967), 185.

mother would get her milked she would let me strip
her out.* In this way I soon learned to milk and then I
used to milk her all the time. I was so small I could not
carry in the pail of milk alone and when I got her milked
I would call for mother or someone to carry in the milk.
The milk pail was made of wooden staves with three or
four large wooden hoops on it and a wooden bail, and
in good feed the cow would fill this pail.

We called our house a frame house. Well it was a
frame house of hewn timber just put together with pins
enough to keep the wind from blowing it over. It was

* Stripping is a final milking to drain the udder.

double boarded up and down, and for the time being they had made the roof of boards, but in the spring father and John made some pine shingles and shingled it.

The farm was in a narrow valley running east and west perhaps thirty or forty rods wide. This was good rich tillable land and partly cleared. Through this valley ran a nice gravelly brook where the trout lived and they were quite plentiful when we first came there. The brook ran within twenty feet of the door and just over the brook in a little bank was a clear cold crystal spring. We had a little bridge over the brook to get to it. On the south side of the valley was a very steep hill covered with forest growth running the whole length of the farm. This too was good land but a terrible place to get crops off of. On the north side of the valley was a sloping side hill just steep enough to ride down hill on, and here was our coasting ground in winter with our hand sleds. But this side hill was very poor land. The soil was a sort of clay and it was mostly barren with the exceptions of a few second growth pine, oak bushes, sweet ferns and huckleberry bushes, and up in here were the rattlesnakes. Our land on the west joined Jay Tompkins and they had cleared down to our line perhaps fifty rods from our house, and we could see up to their house. Across here we had a foot path to their house but the wagon road ran along the south side of the valley and that was further around.

Father and John went to work in the spring that year clearing land, and with what help James, mother and I were to them, they cleared most of the flats west of the house and got it into spring wheat, corn, potatoes and flax. Our folks most always raised flax and while living here I first learned how to help take care of it from the time it was pulled, dried and thrashed, then rotted in water and dried again and stored away in the barn or shed. Then in winter or stormy weather it went through the process of breaking and hatcheling until it was ready for the wheel and then mother would spin it for towels and clothing. The tow was made into coarse cloth for bags, towels and our summer pants. The fine flax was spun and wove into fine linen for sheets, shirts, table-cloths, dresses and Sunday pants. In this way my mother supplied the household with linen until she got so old, worn out and feeble with hard work that she had to give it up, and then we also stopped raising flax.

Down along the brook east of the house on the flats we had a good sugar bush, and father and John made quite a lot of sugar that spring. Down on these flats we gathered leeks, cowslips, and adder tongues for greens. That summer we got along quite well for we could live on most anything in the summer. And trout, we had never had such nice trout to eat as we got from the brook, and we used to fish down a mile or two to where there were some great deep holes in the gorge.

When the berries came it was nothing but pick berries with mother and the children that were old enough to go. The berries were picked and dried for winter use and to sell. The huckleberries were most always sold for they brought the most in the market. I went many and many a day with mother taking our dinner and picking berries to dry.

We used to go northwest of us to a place called huckle-berry plains. There were hundreds of acres with nothing but scrub oak, pine, white birch, elders, sweet fern and berry bushes, and in berrying time there were a good many people there picking berries. And the snakes, I killed many a rattler for I carried an oak stick five or six feet long, and when one made his appearance I went for him with a vengeance. I was spry then and could get around quite lively. One or two walloping blows would lay them out. When we came to a nice patch of berries I ran around it poking my stick in under and around to see if there were any snakes under the bushes and ferns before mother would go picking. Brother James used to go with us when he could be spared at home, and mother would send him after water in some ravine, for he knew where the good springs were. Thus it went year after year while we lived in Tompkins Hollow. How we enjoyed the dried fruit in the cold winters when other luxuries were scarce.

I think sister Julia worked out the first summer we lived here. But when at home she used to go with us to pick berries or took care of the house and our two younger sisters, Mary and Cassie, still our little fairy, as we called her. I remember how she looked, so fat and chubby trying to walk and talk. She was the pet of all the household. I don't know but I must have felt a little jealous, for most of the kisses were lavished on the younger ones and I thought I was slighted. The kisses now for me were few and far between but I knew where my kisses came from and a good rousing kiss and a hug from mother made it all up, and I was old enough now to appreciate them too. Oh those sweet kisses, love tokens of the dearest one on earth I knew at that time.

That summer we raised quite a lot of wheat, some corn and potatoes and buckwheat, and we also had quite a garden. Mother did most of the garden work with James and my help weeding the beds. Before this I did not know much about garden work. Our garden was just over across the brook by the spring. After this year I always was my mother's helper in the garden and became quite an expert in the business.

That fall father and John built an addition to the barn. It was a threshing floor to thresh grain on. I remember also of raking buckwheat up in bunches for sister Julia to set up. After the corn was husked it was set in pans around the fire to dry so we could get an early grist.* One evening we had a shelling bee to shell corn. We all sat in a ring before the fire. I remember of John sitting on a barn shovel using the blade to tear off the corn. This was glorious fun for us as we talked of what nice johnny cake we were going to have and we would live now on the fat of the land. Only think, wheat and corn of our raising and just going to the mill.

That night we got the grist ready, put up in bags and set in the corner by the door, and next morning father and John started off to the mill. I think the name of the place was Cobleskill, and they went northwest over the hills by Rosman Hill school house and then down through Sapbush Hollow and so on to Cobleskill. It was late when they got home and I was in bed and to sleep. Next morning mother had a rousing big sweetened johnny cake, sweetened with maple sugar. And the wheat flour, what nice sweet bread it made, but rather dark. And the wheat kernel, what lovely pancakes baked on mother's great big round griddle with a bail on and a swivel in the top so she could turn it around to turn the cakes as it hung over the fireplace. Then we had good sweet milk. Johnny cake, milk and pancakes of our own raising. What jolly treats they were to us then. Yet perhaps no better than we had had at other times, but we had all been more or less interested in the first crops on our new farm.

On the twenty ninth day of September 1838 another little sister was born. They named her Amy Catherine after our aunt Amy Curtis. She was not so tiny and small as Cassie but large and fleshy with large bright blue

* Grain ready for grinding. The term can also apply to the meal or flour after grinding.

eyes and light hair. Now we had another one to love and caress. Another one to provide for and go with us along down through the vale of poverty. Another one to share our joys and sorrows through life's uneven way.

None of us went to school this winter, for the school house was too far off. Abiah was away from home this winter working for his board and going to school. My brother James and I were setting snares for rabbits. Down below our house along the road that leads to the Schoharie Flats or Creek was a large piece of second growth timber of birches, oak and pine, and here the rabbits had their runways. Early in the winter there came quite a deep snow, almost knee deep. We started out one day to look for the rabbits with our snares made of linen thread good and stout. We had no shoes nor boots to wear on our feet so we contrived a plan to go and not freeze our feet. We took a great big sheep skin that father had tanned with the wool on and started running as far as we could without freezing our feet, then we would lay it down wool side up, get onto it and pull it up around our feet until they got warm. Then we went on again and so on until we set a few snares with spring poles. On going back to the house we did not stop so often.

The next morning bright and early we went to the snares taking the sheepskin for a foot warmer. Sure enough we had one in a snare. He was caught around the middle and was alive, jumping about like a horse, but we had him all the same and quickly dispatched him with a club. How proud we felt carrying him home. Our feet were not cold now running through the snow. One had the rabbit and the other the sheepskin, whirling them around our heads in the air. Oh what a feast we would have now. We decided before we got home it should be a potpie, and potpie it was, made by mother's own hands,

51

cooked in the big dinner pot. And such dumplings—none but a mother knew how to make such dumplings. So we thought then, and many and many a rabbit did we get after that in winters while we lived there. It helped us along quite well through poverty's vale. But the sheepskin we never used after that winter. We managed to get some old cast off shoes given us by some of the neighbors and if we did not get old shoes we sewed rags on our feet to tramp in the snow.

The next spring and summer went along as usual only I had gotten more acquainted with most all our new neighbors. Mr. Tompkin's family were the nearest and we went there the most. There was old Mr. and Mrs. Tompkins or Aunt Peggy as we called her. She was a great big fat good natured old lady most always out to work in the lots. She had two great big dogs and she would take them and go up in the lots on the side hill and dig out woodchucks. The dogs would hole one and then the fun would begin. The dogs both digging and she with a hoe or shovel. I tell you, the dirt would fly. When she got after a woodchuck everyone in the neighborhood knew it by the noise she made yelling, "Sic 'em Tige, sic 'em Tige." Brother James and I used to skin up across lots to help her and see the fun, and fun it was. The fat old woman would work and dig until the sweat ran off her face to get a woodchuck for a roast, for they used to eat them.

The old lady kept guinea pigs. They were a little chunk of an animal about half as large as a rabbit with short legs, shore ears and short tails and a nose like a little pig. They were fed on grass and clover winter and summer. They were spotted, black and white. In summer she kept them in a large tight yard outdoors, and in winter she kept them in boxes or cages in the house under her bed. She raised them for the Albany market, taking them there every fall, all but two or three pairs to breed from the next year. The rich people in Albany bought them and kept them in great cages for pets just the same as people now keep canary birds. She used to get as high as five dollars a pair and that would depend on their beauty as to the spots. She made more clean money out of her guinea pigs than they did off the farm. I have stayed over there many an hour to look at the guinea pigs and help her pick clover to feed them on.

The old gentleman was a very quiet sort of an easy going worker, always busy and always quiet. But there was their son Jay. As I told you before he was full of fun and frolic. He used to come down to our house to torment us children. He would open his great wide mouth and chase us around the house to swallow us, and he said many a time he could do it if our heads were greased.

His wife Elizabeth was as full of fun as Jay only not quite so noisy. They had two children Joshua and Hannah. Hannah was the baby, and when she was little Jay come over one day and flattered me up to go and work for him until I was twenty one years old. He was to give me Hannah for a wife, a pair of guinea pigs and an old frozen footed hen that he said went thump, thump across the barn floor. So I went over with him and stayed all night but I did not sleep much. Next morning he set me to rocking the cradle that Hannah laid in. He said if she was to be my wife I must begin to take care of her now, and after breakfast he would show me the old hen.

When breakfast was ready he said I could go to the brook and wash. So I went out and the minute his back was turned I scud for home. I got some ways before he saw me and he hooted but I did not stop until I got home. I left my hat behind and sent James over after it. But how he did plague me after that. I never heard the last of it.

The Tompkins people were always good to us and ever ready to help in time of need.

Directly south of us up a great steep hill one half mile through the woods lived the Boyds. Their farm and ours joined. They were good neighbors also and quite well off. Mr. Boyd was a carpenter by trade, and they had a nice frame house and barn. There were four in the family. Mr. and Mrs. Boyd, a girl named Ann Eliza and a boy named Henry.

I took a great notion to both of these children, and boy style, I fell in love with Ann at first sight and Henry was my best chum. After this I went to Mr. Boyd's more than anywhere else. I thought at first that Ann was dreadful homely with her big brown eyes and long nose, but when I got more acquainted with her I did not notice her nose and her eyes became more beautiful. Her beauty was her kind ways, gentle manners and good behavior. I was always happy in her presence and will tell you more further on. It is enough to say now that I loved her and she was my angel.

The second summer we lived there father and John went to making pine shingles to take to market. A little east of the house, they built a shingle camp of old pine logs and made a fireplace in it. The timber for the shingles was taken from old pine tops that had lain there for years. The butts of the trees had been taken away for lumber, leaving the tops to rot and waste. The heart of these were good yet although the moss was growing over some of them. They dug these out and between the rows of knots they would get two or three good shingle cuts.

James and I were busy now helping them, as we were as much interested in the shingle business as the older ones, for the shingles were to go to the Albany market to be traded for some things for winter. All through the summer and rainy weather and odd spells we worked at

54

the shingles, and in the fall they had enough made for two loads. They got Jay Tompkins to go with one load and our own team took the other. They were gone four days and when coming home my father's old team tuckered out and had to be left several miles back at one of our neighbors, and Jay brought my father's stuff as far as his house. It was late at night when they got home but not so late but that us children heard what they had to say about the trip.

Among the articles they had gotten was a barrel of wheat flour raised out west somewhere and ground in the new style.* We had never seen at any one time a whole barrel of flour and packed in a barrel too. How they did talk about that barrel of flour that night, and they decided to go over early in the morning and carry it home across lots so some of it could be baked for breakfast. Early in the morning they started. All of us children that could walk had to go along to see the curiosity. There was father and John, Julia Ann, James, Mary and Cassie, the little fairy, and myself, and how we looked stringing along cross lots, and when we got over there, father and John tied some ropes around the barrel of flour and put in two long sticks so they could carry it.

Among the things they got that time was a new tin baker constructed like an open camp with a cover to turn back.† This they let Julia Ann carry and she carried it

* Conklin may be referring to new methods of milling, which produced a finer flour, developed by Oliver Evans in the 1790s but not popular for another four decades. The date of this statement, about 1840, accords with a period of increasing imports of western flour into New York by way of Buffalo. See John Storck and Walter D. Teague, *Flour for Man's Bread: A History of Milling* (Minneapolis: University of Minnesota Press, 1952), pp. 178–80.

† Conklin frequently uses the term *camp* to designate a forest shelter, probably four-sided with a peaked roof—the apparent construction of the tin baker. See Mary Earle Gould, *Antique Tin and Tole Ware: Its History and Romance* (Rutland, Vt., 1958), chap. 2.

on her shoulder. When all was ready we started, father ahead and John behind carrying the flour. I shall never forget how we looked running along beside them gabbing and talking all the way, and then when we came to the fences (there were three) they would stop to rest while James and I would lay off the top rails so they could step over, and in this way they lugged the flour home.

We were rich then for we had a whole barrel of flour and a new tin baker to bake biscuit in. What a wonder the new tin baker was and who could be smart enough to invent such a thing. The barrel was soon opened and the tin baker in position before the fire, and for breakfast (though rather late) we had some splendid white biscuit almost as white as snow. How we did live then and how the neighbors came to visit us and have a taste, as I thought of the biscuits made of boughten flour put up in barrels and brought from Albany. Mother prized the tin baker very highly as it was so nice to bake pie in. Pie was another luxury mother learned to make and bake in the new tin baker, but the pies were not so big and thick as those baked in the iron bake kettle.

7   THE summer I was eight years old, in the fall, we did not go to school any, for the school house was away up on Rosman Hill most three miles off. That fall the neighbors got together and formed a new school district, but it was so late they could not get the new school house done for a winter's school. But they built it during the winter and put it away up on Fulington Hill a mile from where we lived directly west. We had to go by Tompkins and turn a little south up around a hill and dugway in the woods, and then out in the clearing past the Fulington's and up up another long hill to the top.

Here was the new school house by the road side in the edge of a large grove of second growth oaks, pines, beeches and birches of eight or ten acres. The school house was built of great oak logs nearly two feet through and four logs on a side brought it up to the eaves. It was, I should say, eighteen feet by twenty-four. The door was in the middle under the eaves on the east side. The other three sides had one window each with double sash of six lights each and when opened slid by each other. There was a writing desk on three sides against the wall so when we were writing our backs were to the teacher. A long bench went away around on three sides and then there were two or three low short benches without backs for the small scholars. The door had great wooden hinges and when opened or shut it would creak, creak so you could hear it a long ways. It had no chamber floor, but there were two big beams acrost overhead for the chimney to rest on. The chimney was made of stone and mortar. They had a stove in it, yes a great big box stove and the first one I had ever seen in use. It would take in wood about three feet long. The boys had their side and the girls theirs. One half way around to the middle of the back window was the girls and the other the boys. I describe this more particular so you will see what takes place afterwards.

They got it done towards spring and in May our school began. I was then nine years old. We had seen the new school house, for they had dedicated it by holding Methodist meetings in it. We could hardly wait for the first day of school in the new schoolhouse and when the day came, Julia Ann, James, Mary and I started for school. On the way there I had fell in with Ann Boyd, and we were the first ones there of the scholars and had the choice of seats. The teacher was there ahead of us. I think her name was Catherine Buit.

The teacher gave Ann and me the choice of seats, so I chose the one by the back middle window and so did Ann and so our seats were side by side. I was the lucky boy and she was the lucky girl and so for three years in summer we sat side by side in school hours. I have said before I loved her as my best girl and her brother Henry as my best chum. And Ann and I studied together out of the same book, and read from the same book, and when we wrote, used the same kind of pens. Our pens were made by the teacher of goose quills, for steel pens were unknown then. To make a good goose quill pen was one of the essential qualifications of a teacher. Well, as I said we sat side by side. We simply lived in each other's presence.

Of course you may smile at this but all the same it was my boy love. I could not help it and excepting my mother she was the dearest, sweetest one I knew then and many a kiss did we snatch and take, and talked of the years to come when we should be grown up, and instead of a little bush play house in the grove, we would have a great big real house of our own, and instead of acorns and acorn shells for cups and saucers we would have real earthen dishes. And so the time passed with us happy in each other's presence. Oh golden happy hours. Many a time we divided dinners with each other in our noon time rambles through the grove.

We had quite a large school that summer and winter. Let me see if I can call the roll of the winter's school which is most vivid. It is so long ago and some of the names are in the mist. Let me think. Yes memory has it. Of our family were—John, Abiah, Julia Ann, James, Mary and myself. And Ann and Henry Boyd. Joshua Tompkins. Of the Fulingtons were Ephraim, Josephine, George, James and William. Almanzy and Marganzy Baker. Susan and Henry Weaver. Of the Tripps there were Sally and Emma and Myron. Of the Gibsons there were Harriet, Mary, Debora and Helen. Of the Joslins, Meranda, William and Joseph.* Twenty-nine in all that came the first winter, and the school was full.

What fun we had riding down hill, boys and girls together, and the teacher among us. We could ride on our sleds almost half way home in winter for there were two big hills to go down. I had nothing but cloth moccasins to wear on my feet winters while going to school, and many a time my bare toes would be on the snow before I got home, and in the evenings my mother would fix

* Stone and Stewart's 1866 atlas of Schoharie County centers these family names in southern Fulton Township. Henry's spelling is not always precise (the name was Jocelyn, not Joslin; Fullington, not Fulington), but the atlas corroborates his memory. It locates the schoolhouse some six miles west of Breakabeen. Stone and Stewart, *New Topographical Atlas of Schoharie County* (Philadelphia, 1866), p. 33.

them up again for the next day. In this way through snow and cold I got the most of my education. Not half the time did we have books sufficient. But I got along very well for I had one good friend and that was Ann who let me study in her books, and in summers what a chit chat we always had for our road home came over half the way together and then hers turned off by the dugway in the woods, and here was our trysting place, our parting place at night and meeting place in the morning. Oh long long ago in youthful time and where is Ann now? How sweet memory dwells on the place at the dugway where the road separates.

The next summer father and John built a new frame barn. They had two carpenters to help them a few days. One was Mr. Gifford and the other a man by the name of Hillsinger. He was a great big tall heavy man, with high cheek bones, a great big mouth and a voice like a lion, and you could hear him talk and laugh a mile away. Swear, oh how he could swear. I thought then the reason they called him Hellsinger was because he was always swearing about hell.*

This fall on the first day of November 1840 another little brother was born. He was light in complexion, light hair, rosy cheeks and blue eyes, a good natured loving little boy. They named him Leonard Kinney and I shall style him my youngest brother. I loved him for his good qualities and his beauty. If Cassie was a little fairy, he was fairy's brother.

During this summer father and the older boys had chopped and cleared quite a piece on the south side hill so we could see up through to Boyd's. It was good land

* The name was probably Hilsinger. Stone and Stewart's *New Topographical Atlas* locates a family of that name in the section of Fulton Township where the Conklins lived.

but steep and stony. That summer had passed away very quickly, with me helping mother in the garden, going to school, picking berries, and fishing, for we had learned to catch trout, but now winter was coming and it was hurry up for the winter school.

There were six now to go from our house, John, Abiah, Julia Ann, James, Mary and myself. We used to take our dinner and not infrequently it was nothing but a sweetened johnny cake. One time that winter we got out of flour and meal and father had gone to mill but was delayed and could not get home that night so mother had nothing to bake for our dinner. So she kept Julia Ann home and if father came with the grist in time enough she would bake something and send it up by her to the school house for us. Noon came but no dinner came. We were hungry and looked with anxious eyes down the hill toward home but no Julia Ann. The other scholars and teacher ate their dinners and then we all went out to play, riding down hill. We had a man teacher, and he was "the master so cruel and grim." All the same he had his fun with us. I forgot about the dinner until school was called at one o'clock. I looked in vain down the hill for sister to come but had to go in with the rest. After we had got nicely engaged with our lessons and it was most recess time in came Julia Ann with a big sweetened johnnycake steaming hot. Father was late home but mother had done as she agreed to. The big boys, John and Abiah, colored up in the face and were so ashamed they would not touch it, but at recess, James and Mary and I had a good dinner, no matter about the older ones, but I noticed there was none to take home. John and Abiah and Julia Ann finished it on the way home.

Ruth used to come once or twice a year to visit us, and what happy times it was for us then when she was with us and the nice presents she brought for mother and us children. She still worked for Uncle Tom Peaslee as we always called him. He had two sons, Sheldon and Nathan Smith.* Sheldon the eldest had married my cousin Mehala Curtis and lived on a farm north and joining Uncle Joe Curtis's place on Blenheim Hill. Smith lived at home with his father and mother. Sister Ruth had worked there quite a while through the summer seasons and going to school winters and in the spring of 1842 on the thirteenth day of March she and Smith were married.

As I said before, when sister Ruth went there to work she was on the path that would lead her out of poverty's vale, and now she had got a good home and plenty to eat and wear, and everything to do with, and a kind, loving husband. No more poverty for her. A good home, a kind husband and an abundance of this world's goods. What is more she had gotten out of the wilderness of want. Yet they had their hard and honest toil from day to day, from year to year. It was work, work for all hands on the farm. They had a large farm well stocked and well worked. Ruth never forgot us, for many a token of liberality was bestowed on us years after.

I was ten years old the spring Ruth was married, and that spring and that summer father and John chopped the remainder of the side hill on the south and up towards Jay Tompkins'. Early in the fall they burnt it and logged it and got in a crop of rye. Father worked so hard this summer he lost the sight of one eye. Father used to change work with the neighbors, and there was a man by the name of John Hanely living about a mile north of us on the edge of the huckleberry Plains. He used to change with us.

He and my father were well matched for having poor

* Smith was Nathan's middle name.

old worn out horses or plug teams as the boys termed it, and each one generally lost an old horse or two each year. Father and he were poor and could not get enough together to buy a young team, and so it went year after year. It was a common saying with the boys that the crows had a mortgage on their horses, and when I saw the crows gathering up in the fall I thought they were after my father's and John Hanely's teams.

Sister Julia went away this spring to work down in Patchin Hollow near Hagers where Julius lived, and mother. They did not get much sleep that night and Julius started to come home one day—Julius on a visit and Julia to stay all winter to help mother and go to school. They got belated and before they got half way past the Wolf Swamp (I spoke of before) it began to get dark. But on they came following the road all right in the dark, when the first thing they knew they ran against an old tree fallen across the road, and they thought they were out of the road. They began to wander about until they got completely lost and hooted and hellowed to the top of their voices but no answer from anyone. Thus they wandered about two or three hours and finally gave up getting out until daylight and made up their minds to camp somewhere. There was no matches then, and as they were not prepared with steel flint and tinder or punk they had to go without fire. So they curled down beside an old log, and all they had for a covering was a piece of new factory cloth they were bringing home to mother. They did not get much sleep that night and toward morning they heard Mr. Boyd's rooster crow, and they got up and started out of the woods. They were not over forty rods from the clearing. They got home before we got up.*

* Julia describes this incident in her letter of January 11, 1892, and Henry has related it nearly verbatim. See Appendix 3.

I remember how they looked coming in that cold morning with the bundle of factory cloth. And what was factory cloth? We had never seen any before. Julia said they got it for sheets and to make dresses of for the girls. Before this we had always had homemade woolen sheets, and mother and the children's clothes were either made of flannel or worsted that mother had spun and wove.

The next day mother sent us to the woods to get some soft maple bark to color with. (We knew where it was for we had got it to make ink.) So mother colored some of it for the girls' dresses. It made a sort of purple color. The dresses were made plain from head to foot without gathers, something like the Mother Hubbard dresses with a band around the middle. And how they did look in these long straight purple robes and proud. Yes how proud they felt and acted, and they pounded us boys when we called them Catholic priests. But the girls found out they were not half as warm as the woolen dresses. And the sheets were cold things to sleep in with a harsh coarse seam in the middle. James and I slept together, and if one or the other got over the seam there was some tall kicking. We slept in the trundle bed, and through the day it was pushed under a large bed. Mother used to tell us if we did not stop kicking and behave ourselves she would put a long stick of wood between us.

Julius stayed a few days with us and went to paring bees and parties and got acquainted with the young folks and did not want to go back, for they—the Hagers folks—had not given him any schooling much. Instead of three months each year it had not been three weeks and his clothing was so poor and shabby he was ashamed of it. Father and mother persuaded him to go back but he declared he would run away the first chance.

Father and mother used to go over on Blenheim Hill now and then to visit, so after Julia got home they went over to visit Ruth and Smith and see how they got along after they were married. They took baby Leonard with them and left the rest of us for John and Julia to look after. The second evening after they were gone John went away somewhere and stayed over night. So now Julia was the boss, and us children got playing and tearing around for we had our fun when mother was gone. Julia had the churn near the fire to warm so she could churn, and in our play I ran against it and tipped it over on the floor and hearth, and away went the cream and milk, and what a mess it made, and how sister did scold and jaw but she did not whip me. She said she would tell father and he would give me a peeling. She did not say mother for she knew mother had never struck one of us a blow in her life.

Tripping over the churn ended our fun that night. Sister was cross and sent us to bed flying, and she went to work mopping and cleaning up the floor, and if I looked towards her from the trundle bed she would mutter something about a peeling when father got home. Next morning we had no butter for breakfast and all the forenoon sister was cross and says, "You will catch it when father gets home tonight."

There was a little snow on the ground in some places, so after dinner I got hold of an old pair of worn out men's shoes and put them on. Then I found an old summer hat and a roamabout coat torn at the sleeves, and my pants were thin tow summer pants. Thus fixed up I sauntered down the brook through the sap bush. My intention was to hide somewhere and let them look me up. But I got so cold I had to keep moving to keep warm, so on down past the sap bush I went looking at all the good fishing holes where we had been in the summer. I soon came to the gorge where there was some deep holes, and here I crossed over the brook on a log that lay over the

deepest hole. I had made tracks in the snow all the way till here, and after I got over to the other side on the side hill there was no snow. Now I thought I would go up to the road and go home, and so I came up the road but stopped to consider whether to go home and take a whipping or run away, for I thought of what Julius said about running away. So I said to myself I will run away.

I had been down this road a number of times to see my brother Sammy who lived at Shaver's. And I knew the way. It was quite warm along this road and the snow was melted off. So I took off my old scuffs and tucked one under each arm and started. I had several farm houses to go by and wondered what they would think of me in such a plight. I consoled myself with the thought that there were lots of just such poor boys about the country. The grass did not grow under my feet, and I skipped along quite lively, and just before I got there I tucked the old shoes under the fence. I had been there before with mother and knew just where they lived. It was most dark when I got there and my brother was doing the chores. He wanted to know what was the matter and was bound I should go back home that night. At last I told him and they let me stay over night.

Next morning Mr. Shaver and my brother went down on the Schoharie Flats (for the farm lay along the creek) to draw in cornstalks. Mr. Shaver let me drive while he loaded and my brother pitched them up to him. We had nearly got the first load on and who should I see but sister Julia coming, and I knew she was after me. Now I thought if I could only get down and run I would hide away forever. Yes, I would go to the ends of the earth before going home and be whipped for one churn of cream.

I declared I would not go home with her, but she said mother was sick and had slept none all night, and none of them had slept any, and I must go home and see mother anyway. So for her sake and a promise from sister that I should not be whipped I consented to go.

The day before, towards night, when father and mother got home and found out I was gone down the brook, for the other children had tracked me part way, and I not coming back there must be something the matter. I was lost or drowned. So they began to search. It was now dark and with lanterns and pitch pine torches they traced me out to where I crossed the log over the deep hole but could not trace me any further, and then they went to poking in the water with a long pole but did not find me, and finally give up the search for the night and got back home about midnight. No sleep at home that night for mother. At daylight father, John and Julia came down the road to where I came to it. They saw my barefoot tracks in the mud and then they knew where I had gone. So Julia came after me.

When I consented to go back home Julia hurried me from the cornfield to the house and one of the women gave me an old pair of men's pants worn and patched, to wear home over mine. We were soon ready, but she hurried me along so fast I forgot the old shoes, and I suppose they are by the fence yet.

When we got within half a mile of home (I knew the spot, for here is where the rabbits were) we met father. He had a gad in his hand four or five feet long cut from the top of a little beech. I knew what was coming. My sister protested and said I did not mean to tip over the churn. But he said it was not for that he would whip me but it was because I had run away and he would learn me better tricks. Then he grabbed me by the collar and gave me an awful thrashing with those long limber beech twigs cutting my legs and feet and as I danced around him how I wished for the old shoes to shelter my cold bare feet. But thanks to the woman for the old pants, they saved my legs from some of the blows and at the same time got the dust whipped out of them. Well I danced the pigeon ring for about five minutes or until he got tired, and then he drove me ahead of him towards home. When he got in sight of the house he threw away the cat of nine beech tails. I thought he acted ashamed of what he had done and did not want mother to see the whip. (I saw the whip next spring and counted the twigs, and there were nine.)

When the whipping began Julia scud for home. That was the first and last whipping my father ever gave me. I can say that of him, whatever other faults he had, he never pounded or whipped any of the children but me and that only once.

Well, as Julius said, when he went back to Hagers he would run away, and sure enough he did. He came home the fore part of the winter, but father scolded him some for leaving his place, so he went up on Rosman Hill and went to school, working for his board at Jerry Gilson's. Mr. Gilson and his wife were good people and they belonged to the Methodist church, and they were the life of the prayer meetings. They were always kind good neighbors. They had no boys but six girls so Julius made it his home here working for Mr. Gilson three or four years.

Julius was a good looking young man when he dressed up and a good boy to work. He soon slicked himself up and went in the best of company, but dress and schooling took about all he could earn, so we did not receive much of his wages. We loved him all the same as he frequently came to see us and have fun romping with us boys.

That winter they had revival meetings in the log school house on the hill, and sometimes mother let me go along to carry the baby or lantern (she always had a baby to carry). The lantern was made of tin with slits cut in it for the light to shine out. There was a place inside to set the candle. It did not give much light all the same. Mother loved the meetings so we went even if it was dark.

Mother had always from a girl belonged to the Methodist church and she was a true and devoted Christian if there was one on earth. At all times and places she exemplified the Christian character, always reading and studying the Bible, so she took an active part in these meetings. She did not have much of a voice to sing but her prayers and exhortations were the sweetest and best I ever heard, and oh I too loved these meetings and longed to take part in them but thought I was too young. Yet I loved the Saviour and all good Christian people, and those glorious old hymns that were sung in that old log schoolhouse on the hill are sweetly and lovingly ringing in my ears today as my pen traces these words I am writing down.

Thus the winter wore away with our revival and prayer meetings and going to school and spelling schools. In our school we used the old elementary speller, the English reader, and Daboll's arithmetic. I knew almost every word in the speller by heart and frequently used to spell the whole school down.

The next winter I went one time with the other scholars up to the Rosman Hill schoolhouse to a spelling school. Two schools together, over forty in all, and lots of them young men and women grown, and when we stood alone and no word in the speller could bring me down, so the teacher got the geography and then I had to come down. I felt proud that night and my brothers and sisters were not ashamed of me after that although I was poorly clad and wore old rags on my feet. I was then eleven years old.

The spring I was eleven, father and John had some

difficulty one day when I was at school. When I came home I found my mother in tears, for John had gone off in a passion and declared he would never come home again. Father was blustering about and did not know what to do, for his best helper was gone and all through his fault of scolding. A desire to go out and work for himself, and a few sharp words from father had driven John away. And come to think it over now I did not blame him. All that summer none of the family knew where John had gone. Sad were the days and nights during the summer and fall, for John, our good old brother John, our ever present helper, was gone. How we missed him, and who would make our handsleds now? After all I did not blame him much for going. Abiah and Julius could dress up, putting the most of their earnings on their backs, giving up what little they had left to the rest of us, but John scarcely ever was nicely dressed. All he had earned had went for the support of the house and family.

That summer Sammy came home from Shaver's and would not go back. His clothes was in tatters and rags worse than mine and his education poor. I or my sister Mary, two years younger than I, could read and spell better than he could. But little schooling had he got. He would have to stay four years more before he could get the one hundred dollars. He would not go back, so father let him stay at home and that summer we had lots of fun fishing for trout with our older brother and picking berries.

James and I were old enough to help a considerable on the farm, and sometimes James would work for Jay Tompkins, and one day about the last of haying they were up in the meadow north of the house on the side hill. The dogs got something in a hole and began to bark. Pretty soon we could see the old fat woman, old Mrs. Tompkins, hurry up there with the hoe and shovel on her back. We could hear her holler, "Sic em Tige, sic em Tige," and she went to digging. This was too much fun for me to stay at home so I scud up there, and James and Jay quit work and went to digging. When we got down there near the bottom of the hole my brother says this don't smell like a woodchuck. The old lady looked at him and says, "How can you tell? Don't you suppose Tige knows what he is after?" I was looking at Jay and could see him wink at James and me, and knew something was up. By this time the dogs had got most to it and began to dig and bark faster, and the old lady says, "Take em Tige. Take em Tige." And the dirt began to heave up and down in the hole. Then Jay says, "There it is mother, kill him, kill him," and with all the vim she had she jammed the hoe down in. And oh whew, whew, a skunk skunk. The old lady got out just in time to save herself but poor Tige and his companion tore and jerked the poor skunk out of the hole and around on the grass until he was dead while Jay and us boys lay on the hay roaring and laughing. The old woman started for the house declaring she would never dig out another woodchuck. They might starve for something to roast and the blamed woodchucks might eat all the clover up and she would not care. Jay plagued her so after that, she dug no more woodchucks while we lived there.

We did not live so well this summer and fall as usual, and if it had not been for some neighbors we would have went hungry many times. We might have went to the poor house but there was none to go to. We never heard of a poor master or a county house.

The fore part of that winter, the first of sleighing, father started off to mill with a grist over to Patchin Hollow leaving us to home without flour or meal except a little wheat kernel, and that was gone the first day, and we expected him home that night. But no father or flour that night, and all next day he did not come, and the second day he did not come, and that night there come a heavy snow storm, and mother thought he was froze to death somewhere, and there was no one to send out, for John was gone. For the past two days we had lived on potatoes, milk and dried berries. We looked in vain up the road before dark for father but he did not come, and mother got no sleep that night, and as soon as it was light (this was the third morning) we began to look up the road towards Tompkins' where the road turns to come to our house. At last we heard him hollowing at his horses way up on the side hill towards Boyd's. Among the stumps we looked, and sure enough it was him, and the cry went up, "Father is coming, father is coming." The loose snow was about three feet deep and he had cut crosslots. Down he came, the team and sleigh swimming in the snow, making a great deep furrow all the way down the hill and across the brook to the house.

Father felt quite jolly and had been trading horses as he generally did when under the influence of liquor. He had had a good time over his sailor grog and that was what kept him so long. It was all talk about his new horse. At last mother told him we did not care about his new horse but to get the grist in so she could bake something, for we had had nothing to eat the last two days but potatoes and salt. Abiah and Sammy had gone off to some of the neighbors that morning and got back to dinner, and they scolded father for trading horses, for he had made a poor trade.

Thus time went on and Christmas morning came, and we had heard nothing from John, and that evening as we all sat around the fireplace someone knocked on the door. Father said, "Come in," and who should walk in but John and Jay Tompkins? Yes it was John, our lost John. He couldn't stay away from home and mother any longer, and such a greeting. We were all happy that night and so was John. Oh happy happy John. He had stopped to Jay's and eat his supper, and Jay had come over with him to share in the greeting.

John had a bundle under his arm which he gave to mother, and it proved to be a calico dress, and what was calico? We had never seen any before. What a wonderment. And how did they put so many flowers on it? Now we said mother could dress up in calico, and how good she would look in it, for it was given her by brother John. Us children were remembered also, for he had a packet full of good things for us and some jews harps for James and me. He had been down below Duanesburg all summer to work and did not let us know where he was.

After the greeting was over he and Jay went to singing songs. They sung Caroline of Edingburg Town and lots of others. How we clustered around John that night. Sitting in the corner by the fire, he had his lap full of children. And I, as big as I was had to hang around his neck. What happy times we had that winter with John, for he was all boy yet. What did we care now for poverty and rags? John was with us once more.

That winter after John got home, father, mother and I started to go over on Blenheim Hill. John went with us around as far as Boyd's to help us over the drifts. I was fixed up good and warm, for mother had worked over some old clothes to fit me that some of the neighbors had given her. I had on a pair of Julia's old shoes and her hood. So I was fixed up alright I thought.

We got most around to Boyd's and the horses got off the road and broke the harness, and John would have to go back and get something to fix it or toggle it up there. While they were fussing up the old harness mother and I got off and went to Boyd's, mother carrying Leonard in her arms through the deep snow. Stopping to Boyd's

74

suited me for I had a chit chat with Ann and Henry, as I had not seen them for most two weeks. When they got the harness fixed, on they came.

From here the roads were better, for it was woods for about four miles and John went back home. The roads were quite passable all the rest of the way and we got to sister Ruth's that night. Here we visited a day or two, and also over to Sheldon Peaslee's. He had married my cousin Mehala. They were very religious people and used to fast every Friday. It must have been Thursday night when we stayed there, for in the morning neither one, Sheldon nor Mehala, would eat a morsel of breakfast. Neither did they eat any dinner. They got victuals for the rest and sat by the table and waited on the others. I remember how down cast they looked and how sad all day long with great long woebegone looking faces and hunger gnawing at their vitals. Now and then their lips would move as in silent prayer. All day long they worked until supper without eating a morsel. I thought if this was religion or pleasing God I never wanted religion, and as for God I thought as long as they had such a plenty of good things stored away in the house that God had already given them, it would be a pleasure to the same good God to see them eat it and not work and toil in hunger.

From Sheldon's we went over to Uncle Joe Curtis's, and here it was all fun and bustle. It was winter and not much farm work was going on, and so they were gathered around the old fireplace, cracking butternuts, eating pop corn and drinking cider. They had a large family, and all went to school that were old enough except John. Yes, they too had a brother John. He was the oldest of the family but Patience and Mehala. John was lame. His knees crooked in, so he could hardly walk, so he had learned the shoemaker's trade, and while we were there he was at work on his bench in one corner by the great blazing fire earning something for himself and the others, for he was like our John in that respect. He was the ever present helper in his way, for none of the family went barefoot as long as John could lift a hammer or drive a shoe peg. He was kindhearted, full of fun and a living disposition, good old cousin John.

We had a splendid visit here but Uncle Joe talked of moving to Herkimer County in the spring. He said he was sick and tired of working among the rocks and stones, and said he knew of a big farm in Herkimer County that did not have a stone on it big enough to kill a chipping bird, and he was going there if he could sell out. He said the oats there grew as tall as his head.

From Uncle Joe's we went over to my mother's Uncle Benjamin Curtis's. They lived toward Summit or Jefferson. We had a good visit there. They were quite well off, had a good farm and lots of stock. They were nice pleasant people but not so full of fun as Uncle Joe's folks. They had only four children. We were welcome here with Uncle Ben but Aunt Eunice could not scold like my Aunt Amy. When we came away she gave my mother a great bundle of second hand clothing to work over for the children. Father and mother visited with some of their old neighbors but I would rather have stayed with sister Ruth. We were gone over a week and made lots of visits, and mother had a good many presents given her. Everybody liked my mother and always called her Aunt Polly, and my father was Uncle Sam.

8   We come now down to the spring of 1843. I would be eleven in May and almost six years of youth is gone. Oh my earliest joys and my earliest griefs, my childhood's sweetest dreams. Try how I will, those days will always form an epoch in my life, and side by side with the recollections of the privations that darkened my early youth will remain the recollections of its joys. Joys that will remain forever the sweetest flowers of memory.

The fall before, father had bought some sheep of John Hanely and this spring they wandered back. One of them had two little lambs over in the woods. The snow was not all gone yet but James and I had to go in our bare feet. We found the lambs. Each of us took a lamb and started for home with the old ewe following us. It was after dark before we got home and John came to meet us with a lantern and wasn't we glad to see John that night in our bare cold feet lugging the little lambs along. After this they kept them shut up till grass came.

This spring Abiah and Samuel went away to work and they did not come home until winter. That spring James and I went up to the mill pond to see them wash sheep. All who owned sheep near there would get together to wash them and have a good spree drinking rye whiskey and washing sheep at the same time, and James and I went to see the fun. There was a man there by the name of Winny, a great tall, gaunt man, consumptive looking with an impediment in his throat that made his cough sound like the bark of a dog a little way off, and they

called him barking Winny. He got a little too much rye
and fell in over his head and when he came up he called
for help and went down again, and when he came up
again, Julius grabbed him by his hair and others helped
to drag him out, then they rolled him on the grass quite
a while before he came to, and when he did they passed
the jug to him but he said he had got enough and went
home.

That summer was my last term [of school] in that place
but I did not go as much as usual. Work in the garden,
helping mother, and picking berries, and spreading and
raking hay took most all the time. Yet I went part of the
summer with Mary and Cassie, and what happy times we
had to school. Our playground was the grove and a little
green spot under the hill where we played fox and geese
and sung green grows the rushes oh, kiss her quick and

let her go, the needle's eye, and lots of other plays, and the teacher was among us, and in my lonely retreat here tonight I can almost imagine I am back there once more at play in the rosy tint of youth.

In them days they used to have county and general training. This fall James and I had the promise of going if we were good boys to work. So we worked like good fellows picking berries and all other work on the farm that we could do. Our last work before training day was setting up buckwheat, and this Julia helped us finish. The day came at last and off we started, father going with his old team and John with his old big bass drum, the only music I ever knew him to play.

The training was up at Jefferson, a little village ten miles southwest of where we lived. We started before daylight and got there about nine o'clock, and found a big crowd already collected. Pretty soon the roll was called, and they stepped into the ranks and the officers formed them into companies, and then they went to marching and drilling. The old men and boys had to stand out of the way now as the militia marched about the town. I thought they made an awful racket with six or seven bass drums and as many snare drums and fifes. I tell you it almost raised us off our feet when they were all playing together, and how proud I felt marching under the flag along outside of the ranks close by brother John. How he did pound the old drum, and how proud and noble he looked and what a stately tread as he kept time with the music. Little did I think then that he and I, the oldest and youngest brothers, would ever be soldiers marching to real battle under the old flag. Soldiers in earnest. Soldiers in uniforms with our lives in our hands going out in the scene of a dreadful war to defend the old flag with our heart's blood. But such was the fact. And little did I think then that the same good old brother I was trying to imitate in keeping step was to fill a soldier's grave.

We had a good time that day. Father and John got our dinner and gave us ten cents apiece to buy a cake of ginger bread, for that was about all the go them days and was about all the luxury that was peddled that day. It was baked in a square tin eight by ten and two inches thick, and I thought then it was the best cake I ever ate. Father and John got a few loaves to take home and what a treat. Father was too old to train but he always went for the fun of it. This time as usual he went home quite tipsy, mellow and funny. It was in the night when we got home.

That fall father and mother went over on Blenheim Hill for a visit, but they did not find Uncle Joe Curtis there, for he had sold out to his son-in-law, Sheldon Peaslee, and moved to Herkimer County in the Town of Brunswick or Ohio as they called it afterwards. They did not make a very long visit this time for father had caught the roving spirit again because Uncle Joe was gone.

After they got home he went off down to Herkimer County and was gone about two weeks. When he got back he was all taken up with Herkimer County. He was full of great prospects and thought he had found a country where he could get rich and he was bound to go there if he could sell out. He would go where land was cheap and easy to till.

Mother and John tried to persuade him to stay where he was another year. But no, he was going that winter so he could get in a crop in the spring. Mother saw he was bound to go and knew it was no use to try and reason with him and, uncomplaining, she tried to make the best of it.

It was now getting late in the fall and mother had lots of work to do to get us all ready. It was finally decided we should move to Herkimer County sometime before spring. The thought of moving so far filled us with dread especially in the winter through the cold storms. So the

80

grain was thrashed and taken to mill and everything sold that we could sell that we could not take along. Some things were traded off with the neighbors to pay for teams to help move us to Herkimer County. The sheep were sold, all but one, and that one had got in the notion of running with the cow, and mother said the cow and this sheep should be moved to Herkimer and that some of the boys could walk and drive them. John then and there said that he would drive them if he had to do it alone. But little Sammy volunteered to go with him. So far that was settled to mother's satisfaction.

Along in January father went to mill up to Jefferson where the general training was. On his way home he got caught in a great snowstorm on the hills. It snowed and drifted so the team could not get along, and father had to leave them and go on foot for help. It was over half a mile to the nearest house and that was Mr. Baker's (his two boys came to our school). He was now two and one half miles from home. The road was so full of snow he had to wallow up to his arms, but he soon got tired of that and tried to crawl along on the fences, but they were stone walls and he made poor headway. He had now got to where he could see the glimmer of a light through the blinding snow, and from there to the house he crawled on his hands and knees.

He was very near dead with cold and exhaustion, and his clothes were frozen with snow and ice. Mr. Baker's folks gave him some warm supper and got him thawed out and warm, and in a little while the storm abated, and they turned out with lanterns and shovels. They went back and got his team so they would not freeze, leaving the load in the snow banks. It was three days before he got home. Mother began to worry so about him that John and Abiah started out with shovels and met him coming home and helped him through.

We had school that winter as usual, also our fun riding down hill, and the young folks had their parties and pastimes. We had lived here now six years and we were all acquainted with each other, and all had our favorites and chums, and the thought of now going away to some other place was not very pleasant. But it seems it was to be so. And we must leave the school and the scholars, friends and neighbors behind and go away among strangers, to meet with other struggles and cares and duties, and all we could say for ourselves was, the best of friends must part.

9 IT was all excitement that winter making preparations to move, and visiting back and forth with the neighbors, for we had been there six years. While living here we had been so poor that we had only one suit of clothes to our backs, and when mother wanted to wash them she had to do it while we were abed at night or undressed and go to bed in the day time while she washed and dried our clothes. Many a time I have lain in the trundle bed and looked at her while she washed and dried my clothes by the open fireplace. Minutes would seem hours while I was waiting.

We always had to use a steel and flint to kindle a fire if the fire got out in the fireplace, and lots of times the older boys were sent to the neighbors on a cold frosty morning to borrow a brand of fire if the tinder, flint and steel did not do the work. The first one up would peek out and if any of the neighbors were fortunate enough to have a smoke [showing from their chimney] someone would scud after fire.

It had been a hard struggle, the last six years, to live and pay for books and schooling and we had not gained much property. Well they got everything most ready to go. It was now the first of February, and it was decided to start some time the next week, so that week we was told to bring our books from school. This meant that we were to bid our playmates and teacher goodby forever. When the last day came they all seemed more dearer than ever.

From childhood I had grown up with them to my middle youth, the happiest time of our lives, and I shall never forget the sweet goodbyes given and taken, tokens of sweet remembrance. And Ann and Henry, how we lingered along the road to where the road separated by the dugway in the woods where for years we had bid each other goodnight and good morning. And now it was to be farewell and that forever. But our youthful hearts did not realize it thus. A hand shake and a sweet loving kiss given and taken. Then we parted. Ann, I never saw her again but shall always remember the love light of those sparkling eyes as I saw them for the last time forever.

What ever became of Ann and Henry or their father and mother I never heard. Goodbye to my boyhood love, goodbye to the old log schoolhouse on the hill and its playgrounds. Goodbye to playmates and all those scenes that for six years had been dear to my heart. Alas and alas they will never return.

On getting home I found the day was set for us to start. This was Friday and the next Tuesday we were to go. On

Sunday some of the neighbors come in to see us for the last time, and it was goodbye goodbye to many more. I for one was feeling quite proud that day, for a week before I had had my feet measured for a new pair of shoes. As John measured my foot he made me stand on one foot and my heel against the door post, and then he stuck the knife down close to my toe in the floor. Oh that cold sharp jack knife, I trembled lest he would cut my toe. When done with this operation he said step away. Then he cut a stick just as long as my foot, allowing for the stockings. Then they sent it to the shoemakers, and sure enough Sunday morning I was presented with a new pair of shoes—the first I had ever had in my life and I was most twelve years old. I was happy not withstanding my sad goodbyes the day before.

All day Monday was spent in packing up for the next morning. We were sure to start. For a year to two back mother had not spun and wove as much as usual. But the loom and all its accoutrements had to go. Monday afternoon the other two teams came down and partly loaded up all except what we needed that night.

Julius worked at Jerry Gilson's yet but was going with us to drive Jay Tompkins' team to Herkimer County and take it back. So was William Fulington with his team. And then my father's team made three teams.

There was not much sleep that night, for Julius and William stayed with us and Jay Tompkins and his wife stayed quite late. What a roaring fire and jolly time that night. It was a goodbye also to the humble shelter we had so long called home. The best we had ever had up to then.

Morning came at last and the three long sleds with the old fashioned high boxes were at the door. Father drove his own team and the back seat was for mother and Leonard, my younger brother, and me, while mother had the baby. Oh yes I have not told you I had another little brown-eyed, rosy-cheeked sister who was born the March before and she was now not quite eleven months old. They had named her Lydia after my aunt Lydia out in Jefferson County. Our seat was full. In front of us was a barrel partly full of pork with the brine turned off and the barrel headed up and a soap tub of soft soap, perhaps half of a barrel.* The remainder of the sleigh was piled full of boxes and bags way up above the sleigh box with some chains tucked in to keep the stuff on. Father sat on the side of the box to drive with his feet hanging out. That was our load. William Fulington had Julia Ann, Amy and Cassie, a part of the loom, some chairs and part of the bedsteads. The four girls sat in the hind seat and had a good place to ride. Julius had James with him and his sleigh was piled so full they had to hang on anywhere they could to ride. John and Samuel drove the cow and the sheep and had to walk, and they started on ahead quite a while.

Well when all was ready, off we went, bidding adieu to the dearest spot I had then ever known on earth. I never shall see the old place again. It was a very pleasant day but we found lots of drifts and bad places in the road. . . . As we went by Mr. Tompkins' the old folks came out to shake hands with us, and Jay stood there by the others and tried to grab me off the sleigh in fun and said I was going away and he should have to give Hannah to someone else, and that the old frozen footed hen was dead.

Well on we went going northwest up past the Joslins and Jerry Gilsons, past the Rosman Hill schoolhouse. Then we turned northward down and down a winding road toward Sapbush Hollow. Here the road was drifted

* "Brine turned off . . . headed up." He probably means that the saline solution in which the pork was preserved had been poured off and a new cover, or "head," secured on the barrel.

and was very sidling, and father kept stepping from side to side to keep from tipping over. The other teams were in sight below us winding round the hills and we could see them now and then. We had just overtaken John and Sam with the cow and sheep. As we went to turn a bend in the road over we went, pork barrel and soap and chairs and boxes with mother and myself and the children all in a pile in the deep snow. Father cleared himself by jumping but the rest of us went under. John and Sam ran to our assistance and dragged mother and the baby out but where was Leonard? Well they heard him squall and it sounded half a mile away but they soon found him under the pork barrel crushed down in the loose snow. He was soon dug out, without any bruises, but the soap was spilt all over the snow, and how mother took on to see her nice soap go to waste. There was a farm house close by, and they came and helped mother and the children. There we soon got warm by the great roaring fire. When the men got loaded up again they came after us. While we were there the woman gave Leonard and the baby each a cloak, and mother told the woman she could have the soap and tub in welcome as father said it was all on the snow.

Well on we went but mother fretted and pined for her soap all the way to Herkimer County, and afterwards whenever the circumstances were mentioned she always remembered the soap and how they dug Leonard from under the pork barrel.

I had been once before to Sapbush Hollow but from there on it was all new to me. But on we went and when it came noon we all stopped at a great big tavern for dinner. In the bar room was a great big fireplace and a rousing hot fire. In riding I had gotten chilly and cold and got so near the fire I almost burned my clothes. What fun the boys had telling how we tipped over. Just as we were about to start again on came John and Sam with the cow and sheep, but father told them they must not try to keep up with us for the cow could not stand it. So I did not see them again until two days after we got through.

Before they started, father and the teamsters had to take a horn of whiskey. They made me drink some and said it would keep me warm. Well I took a horn too, and not being used to it I began to get dizzy and began to talk funny, so Julius got me to get off and run behind his sleigh. I said I was not cold, the whiskey was keeping me warm. But they dragged me out and made me walk or try to walk and so I could, by hanging on the sleigh. Then Julius drove like everything and I fell down and then he would stop and let me get hold again, and the second time I fell I knew nothing more until middle afternoon, and when I came to they had me by a big fire trying to turn salt or something else down me. I got over it soon but would not touch any more of the accursed stuff the rest of the way.

Well that night we got to Oppenheim where one of the Peaslees lived by the name of Tom Peaslee as they called him. I think he is a cousin to Sheldon and Smith. His house was always a stopping place for the friends going and coming from Schoharie to Herkimer County, and we were always welcome although it was late in the evening. Mr. Peaslee was a middle aged man full of fun and had seven children of his own and with our big family he had a house full.

After we had our supper we all gathered around the fireplace in a great big room. What a visit and what a time eating apples, drinking cider, cracking butternuts and eating popcorn. Tom Peaslee then got me and James wrestling with his boys, and we had it there for nearly an hour, a regular rough and tumble. When it was bed time they took in some of our bedding and made a great long bed clear across the room where the fire would shine on us all night. So the boys all slept on the floor in a row. I thought it was kind of nice to move after all this fun and had almost got over my adieus and goodbyes of the two days before.

Well, the next morning we were again on the road and found good roads until we began to come up out of the Mohawk Valley, and it was fearful up through Salisbury where we took dinner. After dinner we again started coming through Norway, and over half the way from there the roads criss crossed through lanes and fields, over drifts and fences and stonewalls, until we got to what is now called Sam Hemstreet's sawmill.

When we got up in Fairfield father said, "This is Herkimer County." Mother said to him, coming along through Norway, "I thought you said there was no stone in Herkimer County and that it was all smooth sandy land." "Well," he says, "I will show you some nice smooth land before we get there," and when we came up the hill from the sawmill father says, "Here is the nice rich flats I have told you of."

Well it was almost dark now. We were all cold and tired, and the baby and Leonard were crying half the time. The old team was about played out, and we were behind, for the other teams had gone on. But all the same we got there at last. When we got so we could see the light father says, "There is where Uncle Joe lives." And sure enough we found him and Aunt Amy, the same old hospitable people they were over in Blenheim. The same old kind and generous welcome and the same old fun and good humor pervaded all. And wasn't we glad to get in the old log house, good and warm with a fireplace in one end and a great cook stove in the other. No need of complaining of being cold between two fires. And this was the first cook stove I ever saw.

Well, we had all arrived that night except John and Sam. We were well fed and well cared for and well housed thanks to good old Uncle Joe and Aunt Amy. There was a house full that night, and it will not be out of place to name them from the oldest to the youngest. To begin, there was father and mother, Abiah, Julius, Julia Ann, James, myself, Mary, Cassandana, Amy, Leonard, Lydia and the teamster William Fulington. Ruth was left at Blenheim and John and little Sammy had not come yet. Well now for Uncle Joe's family. I think they were all at home but Mehala. She was at Blenheim living, neighbor to Ruth. I will call the roll, Uncle Joe and Aunt Amy, Patience, John, Ruth, Silas, Mary Ann, Nicholas, Benjamin, Amy, Lorena, and Jammy, twenty five in all. Every crack and corner of the old log house was full that night. When the beds were made, spread out on the floor, for there were not enough bedsteads, you could not step without stepping on someone.

Well, I had heard father tell so much about Herkimer County and the Town of Brunswick or Ohio. Some called it one and some the other, and after a while no one called it Brunswick.* In the morning it looked dreary enough, with four feet of snow and more coming.

Uncle Joe lived on the place where Henry Hiney lives now.† Most all of the land on the south side of the road where Uncle Joe lived was cleared and mostly new for the stumps were visible just sticking out of the snow. On the north side of the road it was most all woods with the exceptions of an acre or two around the barn and a piece

* The township was formed in 1823 and named West Brunswick. In 1836 the name was changed to Ohio.

† The Curtis and Hiney homes are located about one and a half miles northwest of Ohio City in B. Nichols, et al., *Atlas of Herkimer County, New York* (New York, 1868), p. 26.

of new ground on the sloping little knoll northeast of the barn. Over here they had a turnip patch the summer before and they had not pulled them all, leaving some on purpose to have nice fresh turnips in the spring, for the ground scarcely ever froze. Uncle Joe told us we could have all we could dig up, and so James and I went at it. Uncle Joe told us where they were the thickest. We took shovels and went to work, and in about an hour we got down to them. Such great flat Dutch turnips, they were as big as a large plate, nice and crispy. What a feast we had at the house. All that spring we did not lack for turnips. They just came in play to help us spring out as Uncle Joe said.

They had a great big barn besides a large straw barn as they called it where they put straw, leaving it open around the bottom and with sticks standing up and down like stanchions so the cattle could stick their heads in and eat at any time. Their barn was full from top to bottom of hay and grain. The land was new and produced good grain and hay.

Off northwest of the barn was their great maple sugar bush of several thousand great big giant maple trees. Here every spring they made tons of sugar. They made most of it in little brown cakes like the bung of a barrel weighing two or three ounces apiece. These they took to the Utica market and sold them for a good price.

The next day after we got there Julius and William started back for Blenheim. John and Sam were four days coming. The cow and sheep were all right and mother felt pleased enough to think they had got through safe. Everything had come alright but the soap.

The next day father began to look about him for a place to move into. There was no empty house except [about a mile away] a little frame house, ten feet by twelve, with a low chamber. It was small but there seemed no other alternative, for we could not all stay at Uncle Joe's. So we moved over there, all but the old loom and its kindred parts. There was no room for that so it was stowed away for the time being in Uncle Joe's barn. I was glad for once that it was left, for it was my dread, and it had haunted me from my babyhood, especially the old rickety quill wheel and warping bars.

There was no fireplace there, but father got a little cook stove somewhere with only two griddle holes and a little small oven big enough for one little loaf of bread at a time. It took wood only a foot long and the house was cold and we came near freezing many times. And what a time mother had cooking and baking for so many. She had never used a stove before and her old iron baking kettle had to be set to one side for there was no place for that, and all it could be used for now was to take up ashes in. The old tin open camp baker too was of no account anymore, but was used up for a plaything to drag about in the snow by the children.

We had only a little ways to move this time, and by the time John and Sam were along we were nearly settled again or squatted down in the little ten by twelve pigeon hole. All the same it was a shelter. There were thirteen of us to stay in this little house and when the beds were set up there was scarcely standing room left.

Here we stayed until the snow went off. John and Abiah went to work making shingles on shares for Uncle Joe. They had their shingle shanty a little west of the barn in the lot and here the boys worked until spring. Little Sammy, for I shall call him thus after this, went to work for Uncle Joe and helped them through sugaring that spring. James and I passed the time away digging turnips, cutting wood and gadding around to see the new neighbors, now and then getting around to the sugar bush in time to eat warm sugar.

Uncle Joe had brought some of his bees with him from Blenheim and they always had a plenty of honey which suited my taste very well. Aunt Amy was always good to me when I came there, and that spring I used to gather up eggs for her for I could get around where she could not, she was so large and fleshy. But it was the same old scold scold all day long about something, or simply nothing I might say. She had got in the habit of it and could not leave it off.

There was a little old log barn where we lived where we kept the cow and sheep, and some of the boys bought a few hens. When we had new milk again we got along very well. But the house was too small so they looked about to see where they could find another one that was larger. So they went over and hired the old log school house where Wm. R. Ash's place is.* It was built so low that there was not standing room in the chamber except in the peak. But there was more room below than where we were living before.

* Ash lived one mile west of Joe Curtis. Nichols, *Atlas of Herkimer County*, p. 26.

I think it was about the first of May when we packed up again and moved down in the old school house. We did not have far to move and all that could walk went on foot, and all carrying a bundle of something. It put me in mind of the time we moved from Darling Hollow up to Thom Perry's house on the hill, only we had no hills to climb or snow drifts to get through with our bare feet, for we all had shoes now. Still we were yet a poor band traveling through poverty's vale and had not got out of the wilderness of a woeful want. We enjoyed one good blessing for which we were all thankful and that was good health.

The old loom and wheels except the large spinning wheel was left stowed away in Uncle Joe's barn. The old tin baker was used up for the children's plaything, but mother clung to the old iron kettle and the great old big dinner pot and the pancake griddle. She said they might come in play yet.

The baby, that is Lydia, was now over a year old and began to walk and talk a little. She was the beauty of the whole household, such lovely brown sparkling eyes and dark hair, and so good and sweet we all loved her, and that spring if she could get hold of any wild flowers she was perfectly happy with her posies as she called them, and she would carry them about all day or until they would wilt and fade. My younger brother Leonard was her guard and helped her gather the spring flowers.

The old schoolhouse done very well for summer but it was all open between the logs, for the plastering was mostly out, but we could never live in it in the winter. So father, John and Abiah began to look up a place to buy or hire to move to before winter. They soon heard of a place over by the West Canada Creek where there was lots of wild woodland, a plenty of shingle timber, and lots of fish and deer. They went over one day and looked at a place on the flats where John Flansburg lives now and concluded to buy it. Shortly after that father went over to Utica and bought a hundred acres of J. Watson Williams, taking a contract.* They were to pay five dollars per acre. So it was settled—we were to move again before winter, and when father, John and Abiah could get away a day or so they used to go over and work, getting ready to build a log house and barn and clear some land so we could move the first of sleighing. They either had to go around by the McIntosh bridge or up around through Wilmurt, for there was no highway, only a road zigzagging through by the Flansburg Bridge, but when the creek was low they used to go that way and wade it. It was most all a wilderness from Ohio over to the creek.

While living here in the old schoolhouse we did not go to school much, any of us, that summer except Mary and Cassie. They went part of the summer to the Ohio school. The boys worked out most of the time, and Julia Ann went away to work also during the summer. Father and John worked some land on shares, and cleared a little over the creek and put up a log house and log barn. James and I worked around a little among the neighbors but it did not amount to much.

The little village of Ohio was more lively then, and more business going on there than there is now. Albert Abeel kept store and hotel and a law office. R. H. Wood was then young and in his prime. He ran a large and then quite productive farm, making butter and cheese.

* James Watson Williams was a lawyer, editor of the *Weekly Observer,* and sometime mayor of Utica. See M. M. Bogg, ed., *Memorial History of Utica, N. Y.* (Syracuse, N.Y., 1892), pt. 2, pp. 91–92. The location of the lands may be determined by reference to 1868 landholders in Nichols, *Atlas of Herkimer County,* p. 26. In sale by contract, ownership is not transferred to the purchaser until all payments are completed.

He was justice of the peace for many years and kept a law office, and there was scarcely a week but what there were several law suits.

Mr. J. M. Gallt was the blacksmith at Ohio about this time and here he toiled at his trade for several years. Mr. Gallt was always an honest, upright Christian man and his timid wife was beloved and respected for her Christian character and quiet and peaceful disposition. They had only one son, Alex, a lad with a quiet, shy, bashful disposition in his early youth at the time we lived in the old school house. His parents doted on him and fairly idolized him and well they might for he was all they had, a noble and self sacrificing boy struggling for an education. But when attending school in his boyhood days he got in the habit of wearing glasses, more to hide his very large and lustrous eyes than anything else for he was very sensitive and anything said about his eyes was taken to heart badly. But I never thought that a disfigurement. His large and noble looking eyes showed he had a large and generous uncomplaining heart.

The farms of Ohio and around in that vicinity were mostly lately-cleared and generally very productive. They were sown to oats just as long as they could get half a crop, and in this way were finally oated to death and run out by one continuous crop.

The most of the people that lived there then are now dead or moved away so there is but few old settlers left. The little grave yard opposite the church contains about two thirds of the old settlers of forty years ago. Here they are quietly sleeping awaiting the final awaking at the last day.

I have not space to enumerate all we got acquainted with while living in the corn crib, as we called the little house, and old schoolhouse. But we found them all kind hearted, generous, and willing to help. I had my chums and play fellows as well here as I did in Blenheim only I did not fall in boyhood love with any of the feminines as yet, for my boy love had passed and gone. But I will mention a few of the boys. There was Nathan and Allen Hemstreet then living on the corner west of Uncle Joe's. Our nearest neighbor was Gilbert Furgason, and he had some rollicking fun-loving boys and with them we were more intimate. There was Charlie, Jo (as they called him then), Lupp or Gilbert, and they called him Lupp to distinguish him from his father. Then there was Benjamin with an impediment in his speech and not over bright, but he was as quick at a joke as the best of them. We were near neighbors only that summer, but we made things rattle generally with our sport and mischief. James and I were at Hemstreet's or Furgasons or they were at our house whenever we could get together, and memory clings to the happy times we spent together.

That spring my brother Sammy and John Furgason went in swimming in R. H. Wood's millpond, and took cold while Sammy had been exposed to the mumps, and when he came down with them he came very near dying, and I think he would if it had not been for another new acquaintance who will hereafter be another heroine in my narrative. She was Margaret Potter, Chauncy Potter's wife. They then lived in a house below R. H. Wood and ran his sawmill. The sawmill and dam have been buried years ago by a freshet. She was always a good woman in sickness and went far and near to help those in distress. Everybody called her Old Mag. She heard Sam was sick and she come over. In ten minutes she was acquainted with us all and found out what was the matter, and she ordered a bean poultice "as quick as God would let you," and she flew around like some great doctor and she saved him. In reality she was better than some doctors.

Then along in the summer father was sick with inflamation in his bowels and the doctors gave him up, and Mag come again and looked at father and says, "Well I can save him," and she turned around to James and me and says, "Here you little devils go and dig me a quart of fish worms." I thought she wanted us to go fishing, and I looked at her and thought I would not want to go off when father was so sick. Then she said she wanted them for a poultice, and we dug them quite lively but she did not wait for a quart but came out with a cloth and picked up a few while we were digging and went and put them on. In a few minutes she came out again with the same cloth but the worms were as black as dirt. Well the fish worms saved him and she stayed until he was out of danger.

That summer I was up to Uncle Joe's frequently while his bees were swarming and helped him some with his bees, and I went with him one time down on the Wedgewood flats to get elm bark for strings to fasten the rolls or straw together for making bee hives. This was the first time I ever crossed the West Canada Creek or the McIntosh bridge.

The fall we lived in the old schoolhouse they had general training at Norway. James and I and John and father went. John had brought his old bass drum with him from Blenheim and he took that along. John did not belong to the company but he took his drum all the same. Uncle Joe and his boys went too and the boys were in the ranks. I thought Norway was more stony than Blenheim, and the hills just as bad and the drums made the same old thundering noise and John was in his element again, pounding the old drum until it quivered as though this was music. Well, it was martial music in case of a battle to deafen the cries of the wounded and dying.

We had a good time that day, if it was noisy. The ginger bread peddlers were plenty and we got all we could eat and some to take home. The genuine old fashion ginger bread. Its manufacture is one of the lost arts. That night coming home William Hemstreet rode with us as far as his place, and he and father were quite happy, and Hemstreet got to telling bear and panther stories all the way along the road. It was so dark through the woods I thought we never would get home. He got me so afraid I got way down under the seat by father and covered up my head, afraid the panthers would jump in the wagon and get me, and wasn't I glad when Hemstreet got out, for I knew then I should hear no more panther stories that night. Years after, I got to thinking that Mr. H. manufactured most of his stories for the sake of talk.

That was the last general training I ever went to, but one summer they tried to get up a training at Ohio, but that was a fizzle. I think that James or Sam Cooperhall was captain. They did not get enough together for an awkward squad and no gingerbread either.

There is another one I will mention here, and that is R. H. Wiggins. He lived by the Vicary Sawmill near Casper Emery's. He tended that sawmill. He was living then with his first wife. Cloe I think her name was. I thought she was the most beautiful woman I ever saw. They had two children, John and Annie. Mr. Wiggins was in his early manhood then and a noble looking man, full of jokes and fun. But the old mill has gone to decay and the rafters have fallen in and it is all quiet now in the place of the noisy old mill.

10   ANOTHER move in progress as it was getting late in the fall and we wanted to get over the creek in our new home before winter set in. Everything again was hurly burly. Mother was not very well that Fall and Julia Ann come home to help her and to help get the children ready. Although we had only a few miles to go there was lots to do in fixing things together in shape to move.

On the twenty ninth day of November my youngest sister was born in the old cold log schoolhouse. We called her Merinda but afterwards it was shortened up to Rinda when she got old enough to write her own name. We had plenty to do to keep warm in the old shell, and along in December we began to have snow enough for sleighing. Father and the boys were busy hauling hay and old stuff we had stored away ever since the February before when we moved from Blenheim. The old loom in particular and all the spinning wheels, swifts and warping bars had to go this time for sure.

Mother never did much weaving after Rinda was born and very little spinning. The old loom and its kindred parts were disposed of. Some of the reeds, shuttles, warping bars and little wheels were sold or traded or given away to others who were more able to use them than mother, but the old loom was finally stowed away in the hog pen chamber and years after was used up piece by piece for kindling wood. The old relic met a sad fate at last after being hauled all over through Jefferson, Schenectady, Schoharie and Herkimer counties. It had been the means of earning hundreds of dollars by mother and my sisters and helped to furnish covering for our bodies and to stop the gnawing hunger of the whole family thus far through Poverty's Vale. The old quill wheel, my dread all through my early youth, also met its fate. James and I and the girls Mary, Cassie and Amy got the rim one day and played roll the hoop with it until it fell to pieces and lost its rim, and then we ran it on the spokes until it was used up and burned for kindling wood at last. No more spinning, no more warping, and no more weaving for my poor old worn out mother.

Mother got well enough to move soon. On the fourth day of January 1845 we moved over the creek coming around by the McIntosh bridge (called so for the reason that Nicholas McIntosh lived only a few rods below it) and then up on the north side of the creek past old Henry S. Conkling's place where he had a small clearing, a log house and a barn and a shingle shanty, and from his place to where our house stood. It was all woods, a great tall dense forest.

We all got to our journey's end this time without any mishaps or accidents. I have often wondered why we didn't have some accident, for there were so many of us. We went stringing along, some on foot and some riding, laughing and joking. Mary and Cassie called it the caravan of wild animals. There were father and mother, John, Abiah, Julia Ann, little Sammy, James, myself, Mary, Cassie, Amy, Leonard, Lydia, and Rinda the baby. There were fourteen all told. The family was all together then but Ruth and Julius. Julius still worked for Jerry Gilson on Rosman Hill in the town of Blenheim. We were all well and healthy, thanks to plain food, plenty of outdoor exercise and a father and mother with iron constitutions and no hereditary disease lurking in their bodies. What a tough lot of children we were. Although poor and at times pinched with hunger we were comparatively happy going to our new home in the wilderness. I had often wondered how they ever kept soul and body together until I had nine of my own to provide for and rack my brains studying how to keep the hungry wolf from the door.

Mother had clung to the old cow and sheep, so we had those two old friends to accompany us to our new home. What friends the cow and sheep were. They were so attached to each other—where you found one you found the other, and they always stood side by side in the barn and ate out of the same manger, and more strange yet, the old ewe never had any lambs. These two friends were always our pets and were always welcome to share our humble lot. The old cow furnished us milk and butter almost the year round and the old sheep's wool made our mittens and stockings as far as it went.

Well we landed all right and John and the other boys soon had the cook stove set up, for they thought it would be cheaper to use a stove than to make a fireplace. That summer father had gotten quite a good cook stove somewhere almost new. It was the first style of the elevated oven and took in wood about two feet long.

Let us glance at our surroundings in our new home. The house was built of logs eighteen by twenty feet inside. The lower story was seven feet from floor to beams and the chamber was just high enough under the eaves to set a low bedstead. The one who slept in the back of the bed had to be careful or he would bump his head on the rafters. The lower part was partitioned off with two small bed rooms in one end, one for father and mother and the other for the girls. Our table was made of rough boards and occupied the room with the stove, wood box, stairway and buttery. Our stairs was a ladder made of round poles. We boys slept upstairs and it got to be a common saying among us or our visitors when it came bed time, "Take your merchandise and travel on or climb the pole." The house was shingled. Father and the boys had bought the shingles and lumber that was on a house that John Ash had built a few years before, a mile and a half back in the woods on the Gulf Stream.* They had got this lumber and shingles and hauled them out to cover our house. We had three small windows below and one upstairs and the stove pipe running up through the roof and about four or five feet above the roof. There was chinking of poles and split sticks between the logs and then calked with moss gathered from trees, and every fall the old moss was dug out and new put in.

The old house stood about four rods southeast of where John Flansburg's house is now. The log barn stood on the knoll north of the house and most to the hill. The road or highway proper ran south of the house on a line from the present bridge up past the row of maples (these were set out by my own hands) south of John's house and coming out in the present highway near Jerry Flansburg's barn.

After we got moved, father and us boys built a log shingle shanty south of the house across the road towards the creek, and here the manufactory of shingles began and was kept up winters for a good many years—our only source of support, the boys making them and father drawing them to Utica and Herkimer and elsewhere.

It was all a dense woods of great long nice spruce along the creek, and back further on the flat it was cherry and maple the width of two or three lots. On this cherry flat a few years before two men by the names of Ambler and Cook had girdled the timber on these lots and cut and

* A narrow stream, a few miles long, that empties into West Canada Creek.

burned the brush and sowed it to buckwheat. The old settlers said they never harvested it for the frost took it. But the trees, most of them, were dead and their old crumbling tops were crashing down in every wind storm.

It was my work that winter to cut the wood for the stove and it kept me busy most of the time. But I did not have far to carry it or draw it on the sled that John had made for me. They had cut the big trees close to the house but the smaller ones stood so near I fell one on the house one day and gave the inmates quite a fright. After that I was more careful how I fell timber.

Packing shingles was my first work in that line of business that winter, and if I had a dollar for every bunch I have packed since, I would be a rich man. The spruce shingles in the market then brought from $2.00 to $2.50 per thousand, and Father used to go away with a load most every week all winter and be gone two or three days every time. I tell you we had to work or starve. We never heard of a poor master to run to if we got cramped for provision or clothes, and I don't think we had ever heard of a county house.

I suppose it will be in place to say something about our neighbors as we had to deal with a good many first and last. Our nearest neighbor was Spencer Wilkins. He too had moved there that fall from Fort Plain and he had taken up the lot joining us on the west and had built a log house and barn that fall and had moved a short time before we did. They had five children— Spencer, Jr., Jane, James, John and George. John was about my age, somewhat taller, and George was two years younger. These two boys were our constant playmates, and one day George was up to our house. I was falling small trees for wood, and as one was coming down I told him to run out of the way, and he ran just wrong and the tree came down on him and crushed him down in the loose snow and held him there until I called for help to get him out. I thought I had killed him, he was under the snow so. But he came out alright with a few bruises. He was on the lookout after that when I was chopping trees. He was a friendly chum and always hanging on to me wherever we went.

Jane, their only daughter, had married David Dunn. He and Spencer Jr. and James were boatmen and followed the canal for a living during the summers for several years after this. The old man and two younger boys were clearing up the farm.

Our nearest neighbor on the east was Peleg Tripp. He lived down by the creek. Here he had a log house and a few acres cleared. But he went away that next fall so we did not get acquainted much with them.

One neighbor on the east was Roswell Wooden. They lived on the lot Mr. Shufelt owns down by the creek. There was only him and his wife, but they were nice people and ever ready to help in time of need.

It was all a dense forest the rest of the way until you got to the Henry Paul place. Here was a small clearing and a log house but empty. The spring before a man by the name of Simons had lived there with a poor cripple for a wife and one little boy. His wife had went on crutches for years, but one day he and his boy went off, and when they came home she was gone. He aroused the people about and they searched all over but could not find her. Finally they looked down the creek. *Simons said maybe she has drowned herself.* But how could she get there without the crutches, for they were at the house? So they went down in the gorge and down along the creek, and sure enough they found her in the water, dead. But she had not filled with water. This happened one day when father and John were over looking up the place, and they chose father as one of the jury. The ver-

104

dict was accidental drowning. They buried her by the road just west of Henry Paul's barn. When they found her she had one slipper on and the other was found by Aunt Mary Stevens years later thrown in among the rocks where the path goes down in the gorge from the house. Reader, you can draw your own conclusions concerning her fate. But I am digressing from my story.

The next clearing on the east is where Ed Wilkerson now lives. Old Uncle John Paul as they called him lived here, and of him and his family I will speak later on. So you see we were in the wilderness in good earnest.

Our nearest neighbor on the west was two miles down the creek. It was Henry S. Conkling's family. They had a large family. At the time we moved over they had nine children. There was Smith, Lemuel, Alvin, Morris, John, Almira, William, Daniel and Mary Ann. They had three more born afterwards—George, Sarah Elizabeth and Amy Catherine. They all lived mostly by making shingles from year to year. They were poor like ourselves and had a hard struggle to get a living. They were no relatives of ours, but spelled their name the same excepting the "g" on the end of their name.

We soon got acquainted with them and visited back and forth during the long winter evenings. Smith and Alvin played the fife and fiddle, Lemuel the snare drum, and our John the bass drum, and both families, that is the boys, got together about once a week for a *wild wood* serenade, generally meeting half way or going half way home to separate, and I tell you we made the wilderness ring.

I was still in my youth and enjoyed these good old times, and as I sit here tonight in my lonely retreat memory goes back to the long ago, and I almost fancy I hear the fifes and drums and the wild warhoops as we danced around a large pile of burning shingle shavings saved for the purpose. But alas the lips that blew the fife are stilled and silent forever and the hands that held the drum sticks are folded in the long sleep of death.

Our nearest neighbor over the creek was Nathaniel Tripp and his wife Mum as they always called her. They lived in an old log house. Here they had lived for several years, and made a clearing, keeping a team and two or three cows. They were kind hearted and accommodating. The old man was a shoemaker, and evenings and stormy days he sat by the fireplace and mended shoes. I used to go there to sit by the great roaring fire and hear the old man tell stories. They were the most loving old couple I ever saw. Later on I worked many a day cutting four foot wood for the old couple.

There was a sort of wagon road down from Ohio past the Madison Bunce farm and zigzagging down through the woods and over the hills past Mr. Tripp's and so on to the creek where there was a fording place near Mr. Wilkins's.

That first winter was a hard one for us. We didn't have hay enough for the cow, sheep and horses, and we were too poor to buy. So every day James and I used to fall birch and maple trees and drag the tops up for the cow and sheep to browse. The horses too were pinched down to browse sometimes.

As soon as spring opened we all went to work chopping and clearing. What a crashing there was in the old dead girdled trees as they came crashing to the ground under the mighty strokes of the axe handled by John, Abiah, Sam, and father, and by fall we had quite a clearing and had raised considerable stuff for winter.

How Leonard and Lydia enjoyed the spring and summer. All day long they would wander together picking the wild flowers that grew in the woods, and making their play houses and flower pots. Lydia would carry

106

them around until they would fade and then go and gather more until tired out and would then fall to sleep with her hands full. These two children were so good and happy it made us all love them.

Mother was pretty well worn out, and no wonder. She had borne fifteen children, and nursed and took care of them, and this time they were all living but one, the second little boy, who died when he was six weeks old and was buried in Jefferson County. But after all her hardships and hard work she was happy here in the wilderness. She declared she never wanted to move again and wanted to stay here until she died, and even picked out a place to be buried just across the road north east of the house. Here with Rinda in her arms she, Leonard and Lydia used to go to gather the wild flowers that grew there. She said she never wanted to move anywhere, only to this sacred spot.

We did not any of us go to school that summer. Our nearest school was the Cummings District, over two miles away and there was no bridge. That summer we had a plenty of trout. The boys used to go fishing after supper and would sometimes get enough for three meals a plenty to last all the next day. Some times they would catch a big pan full in an hour or two, and such great nice beauties. During the summer season for ten or twelve years our table was well supplied with fish, and they helped us along wonderfully. Some times we had venison during the summer and fall. There was no law against killing deer anytime of year. Or if there was it was never put in force. Winters we used to crust them,* and it was no uncommon thing to have a half dozen deer

* Deer cannot travel quickly on crusted snow, for they break through the surface. Dogs, light enough to run on crust, were trained to drive the deer out of their yards into crusted areas where they could be overtaken by the hunter.

hanging up against the old log house. Everybody got
them and supposed they were free as water. There was
never any wasted, for they were not killed expressly for
their saddles to supply the market. No, they were killed
because we were poor and had to have meat and none
was wasted.

I went to school in Cummings District some during

the second winter, crossing the creek on the ice but it was a long and crooked road. I had to start at half past seven in the morning and would not get home at night until six o'clock. After dark many a night I walked over the treacherous ice striving to get a little education. The second summer I and Mary and Cassie and Amy all went over there to school after the creek got low enough so we could wade it. But sometimes we used to cross in a canoe. My brother John had made one out of a great big hemlock tree and we had it on the still water just above the island. It would hold only three or four of us and they pushed it across with a pole and John was our boatman. Dear old brother John, the most trusty of all with the old canoe. But one spring it mastered him. The creek was high and Abiah and Sam had been away somewhere and they came and called for John to bring them over. John went after them and crossed all right alone but when they got three in coming back the current took them and on they went. The old canoe was unmanageable with the pole and they called for help and we all ran to the creek as the cry went up "The boys are going down stream." Sure enough there they went and John had lost the setting pole and they were helpless and they dared not jump for they were in the middle of the creek but they sat down in the old canoe and clung to her sides. On they went over the foaming dashing waves and rocks down by the slip bank. Here was a short stillwater and a bend in the stream and the most of the current running to the north side and here the old thing drifted within ten or twelve feet of the shore and when they came there they all jumped for dear life. John and Abiah got out without getting much wet. But little Sammy went under kersouse and had to be pulled out by the others, dripping wet to the skin, and the old canoe went on down and we never saw it again.

Then they made a boat of boards and that lasted quite a while and one summer we had an old tin sap boiler to cross in. It was about five feet wide and eight feet long and one foot deep and there could not but two cross at a time. It was quite a bother to us to run and ferry people over and it took us many an hour from our work and wasn't we glad when they began to talk of a bridge.

The first and second years we lived there other new neighbors began to move in and by the third year we had quite a settlement. David Dunn, Mr. Wilkins's son-in-law, took up the lot eighteen, east of us. He sold part of it to Jacob Phelps. He had two sons and a daughter, Darmer, Willard and Louise. Ammon Stevens had moved on lot seventeen and built a new log house in the turn just beyond the schoolhouse and the old bottom logs lay there yet. Well, he had three boys James, George and Will and one girl Sarah. Uncle Ammon and Aunt Mary as every body called them were friends to everyone and James and George were our chums in all the mischief and sport we could get into. They were two of our rollicking companions. They were poor like our selves and had always made shingles for a living.

Mr. Dunn did not go on the canal as usual now but stayed at home and cleared up his farm. Old Mr. Marvin Sackett had moved on the Woodin place. He had four sons who moved there with him, Herman, Roswell, James and Byron. Herman lived where Frank Flansburg does now. Roswell lived where Seamen Shufelt does now. The old man lived down by the creek.

**11** THE first summer we lived over the creek our folks had bought another cow and they raised some heifers and the second summer we had three cows and one sheep and some calves, so we were getting along very well.

All the cattle in the neighborhood ran together in the woods, everyone fencing the cleared land, and by the third summer there was quite a drove of cattle. There were ours, Mr. Wilkins's, Mr. Dunn's, Mr. Phelps' and Mr. Stevens's. There were a dozen or fifteen all together and seven or eight bells in the drove and when together there was quite a bell-band. They had over two miles square of woods and notwithstanding all the bells it was quite a job to look them up every night. This was my work for years accompanied by John Wilkins, sometimes my brother James, and James and George Stevens. We would start at five o'clock in the afternoon in the summer and in the fall at four o'clock. We most always had a dog or two and sometimes our guns and sometimes we had neither. We would take the cows tracks and follow them up until we heard the bells and then we would hustle them home.

One afternoon we started without dog or gun and there were four of us—John Wilkins, James Stevens, brother James and myself. Well, we looked until most night and finally found the drove way back on the Ash ridge about one and one-half miles from the creek and just about the time we found them we heard a great howling like some angry dogs and it did not sound like dogs either. So we listened and my brother James says, "It is wolves." We were quite scairt as we had neither dog nor gun. James Stevens says, "My God boys they will have us. What shall we do?" So we took hasty council and decided to each one of us get hold of a cow's tail and hang on and they would take us out. By this time the wolves had got quite near and the cattle began to be scairt and we grabbed on to the cows' tails and away they went over logs and brush, every bell a clanking and the young cattle bellowing and we hanging on for dear life on a dead line for the clearing. In about half of a mile we came to a deep hollow and down it we went a whooping and yelling and we followed this hollow until we came out to the creek. And weren't we wet with sweat and the perspiration rolling off of us and the cattle were panting and puffing.*

This hollow is on my place that I own now and to this day it is known all over this section as Wolf Hollow. It was a frequent occurance for wolves to be prowling around where the cattle fed. The deer sometimes used to be seen feeding with the cattle.

The second fall our folks fatted and killed the old cow we brought from Blenheim and the old ewe took on so, bleating and running about looking for the old cow, her mate and friend and it was so pitiful to hear that mother said we had better kill her too for she was fat and would make good mutton. But father or none of the boys would kill her. So they got one of the neighbors to do it for us. Thus ended the lives of two of our domestic pets and

* If wolves were such a menace, one would think that the cattle could not have survived unguarded in the woods. It would also seem that a wolf could outrun a cow, especially a cow dragging a boy, if the wolf meant business. As is indicated elsewhere in Conklin's narrative, wild creatures stimulated the pioneer imagination.

friends. How well they had contributed to our wants through poverty's vale.

We could summer our stock very well the first years we were there. But we had to cut browse for some of them in winter and we used to go in the woods in the summer and cut fly hay that grew on the heavier meadows.* Our folks and Mr. Wilkins used to cut the Cummings fly and haul it out in the winter. The first time I ever stayed in the woods in an open camp was at the Cummings fly.

---

* The term *fly* is a corruption of *vly*, from the Dutch for meadow.

One time we stayed there, there were seven of us, Spencer Jr., James and John Wilkins, my brothers John, James and Abiah and me. The big boys mowed and us younger ones spread and raked. In the morning it rained. So we came out and the bushes was wet so we took off our pants and rolled them up and carried them on our shoulders and ran through the bushes in our bare legs and it was lucky there was no briers then. I never shall forget how the great long bare legs looked going through the bushes. At the clearing we had dry pants to put on.

We used to cut and skid our shingle timber on our fly road and we had a road also to haul our vension out on. I remember one winter James and I went deer hunting and we drove a pair of steers before an old wood sled up almost to the fly and turned the sled around and un-hitched the steers, tied them to a tree and fed them and then we went for the deer. We had a good crust dog and by one or two o'clock we had killed three deer and dragged two of them to the sleigh, and we went back about half a mile after the other and was dragging it along and our dog began to whine and ran past us. We were upon a little rise of ground and looking away back saw the glimpse of two great gaunt-looking wolves. They had smelt the fresh venison and were following us up. They set up an unearthly yelling and we left the deer and scud and wasn't long getting back and loading the two deer and hitching the steers on the sled. All the while we could hear the wolves howling. But after we got hitched on we went as fast as the steers could go for some time until we got out of their hearing. Well, it was after dark when we got home and the next day we went back to look, leaving the steers at home that day, and the wolves had eaten the deer all up and there was nothing left of it but the hair and a few bones.

Julius came to visit us the second winter. He helped

us make shingles most all winter. But in the spring he went back to Blenheim and made his home at Jerry Gilson's. So we had no more of his earnings.

We used to frequently go over to Uncle Joe's, visiting, and the third winter we lived here on Christmas day Father and Mother and Rinda the baby went over there visiting. I remember it was a very warm, thawy day and the snow was quite packy and that day Leonard and Lydia shoveled out and made a play house in the snow at the east end of the house. They had made steps and seats in the wet snow and had got some evergreen twigs for a posy pot as they called it. Here they played a long time until towards night. We thought nothing of it at the time but on New Years day they both came down with the scarlet fever and they had it terrible bad. They had not been anywhere to catch it, neither was it in the neighborhood. But they taking such a cold [at] Christmas it had resulted in the fever. Well Mother and all of us went to work trying to help them but it done no good and then we got the doctor but all of no avail. They were getting worse all the time and burning up with the fever. They could take their medicine and once in a while drink a little broth. Mother stood over them night and day and the neighbors came in and done all they could. Aunt Mary Stevens was in to see them every day. On the morning of the eighth day Lydia began to rouse up a little and tried to set up in the bed and she looked so bright and her brown eyes fairly sparkled and her cheeks so red with the fever. I thought I had never seen her look so beautiful in all her life and as she looked around the house at us I thought she was better. Soon she began to murmur, "I want to eat. I want to eat." Mother gave her a few spoonsfull of broth but she could scarcely swallow and she began to sink away and tried to raise her little hands to put them around my mother's neck and then mother pulled them up around her neck and oh what a pleasant smile she gave us as she murmured the words, "Kiss me Mama," and then her little hands loosened and dropped down and she was gone. Gone with a mother's kiss upon her brow. Gone from poverty's vale. To that great inheritance where the flowers never fade in our Saviors Kingdom and there kneeling beside the little trundle bed and with trembling hands my mother closed the beautiful brown eyes for ever to earthly things and pressed the now thin pale lips together that had only a few moments before been wreathed in smiles.

It was in the dead of winter and Leonard was so sick they had no preaching. But the neighbors came in and sung a hymn or two and old Mr. Farnicrook made a prayer and then they took her out and buried her where she and mother had picked the spring violets and the drifting snows soon obliterated all signs of the burying place until spring.

Leonard revived up a little and for a time was getting better, but he took another cold and the disease settled in his spine and for weeks and months he suffered terribly. He was cupped and blistered and went through all kinds of torture without a word of complaint. He could eat but little and under the terrible pain he sank away to a skeleton. All through January, February, March and April he lay there and suffered and no one, not even the doctor, could give him any relief and along the last of April he was delirious by spells and at such times he was living over the times when he and Lydia had rambled together after the wild flowers. He sank lower and lower and got so he could not speak. But oh how patient, and with all the pain he was suffering would smile through his tears and when the first day of May came he was still living in the morning. Along in the forenoon he lay very quiet and mother stepped out a few moments and when she returned he was gone. Yes gone so quietly that none of us knew it until we looked at him laying there in the cold embrace of death with a smile still resting on his thin pale face, and how mother wept as she closed his eyes and smoothed his marble forehead. He too had gone from poverty's vale to share the lot of one of the redeemed and dwell forever where no want, sickness, pain or death shall ever enter. United again with sister Lydia on those bright eternal plains where flowers immortal grow, and we buried him by the side of sister Lydia as the violets were budding.

Thus two of the loveliest of all the family had gone from our midst and they are now two of our Savior's brightest jewels. Their graves were frequently visited by my dear old mother whose trembling limbs would scarcely hold her up to get there and back. Lydia was four years old and Leonard six and these two loving ones left quite a sad and vacant spot in our family. And so Rinda the baby now was our pet, ours to love and care for and caress.

When Lydia died it was in the dead of winter, deep snow and no road only around by the McIntosh bridge so they concluded to bury her where mother had picked out a place for herself to be buried in. When the first of May came and Leonard died also and we had no roads then, and there was no other way only to bury him by the side of Lydia and thus they were sleeping side by side. Our folks frequently talked of taking them up and burying them at Ohio in the cemetery, but mother insisted they should lay where they were as she said time and again she wanted to be buried by the side of them. But little do we know where will be our last resting place.

Thus time passed on. Years came and went and their graves were partly neglected and forgotten only by a few friends and the members of the family. But the spot where they are buried was never molested or torn up by the hand of the plowman although the farm has been cultivated by strangers since 1861. In a few years after they were buried a clump of wild thorn sprang up over their graves and the owner of the land, John Flansburg, has never molested them and here year after year since 1847 the wild violets still thrive and blossoms every spring in the virgin soil and mould of a thousand years. Those beautiful flowers that were the favorites with the two loved ones who still sleep beneath the wild thorn. [Henry wrote the preceding paragraph on a separate folded sheet, which also bore the remark "Flowers from Leonard and Lydia's grave picked May 4, 1892," and a poem. The flowers are no longer in the manuscript. See Appendix 2, poem 1.]

The summer I was sixteen was the last summer I went to school, I and my three younger sisters Mary, Cass and Amy. We went over to Cummings District. But we did not go very steady for we had to wade the creek or cross in the boat and sometimes the creek was high and we had to stay at home.

I was still in my youth. And my youth was passing now like the fleeting wind and I was awaking to duty, sorrow, passion and pain. But how I did enjoy this last summer of youthful schooldays and what happy times, although mingled with sorrow. There was a very large school over there then and I will mention the names of those along the way and some of those who will hereafter be some of my intimate acquaintances and figure in the narrative through poverty's vale.

Joseph Hane was the first one who had children to send. There was Arthur, Marthy, William H. and Emeline. But Emeline was then too young to go. Next was Edgar Hane, John Hane's boy and Esther. They lived

118

then down on the high bank of the creek on Henry Ash's place. Next was Alida Farnicrook. They lived on the old place beyond Mr. Ash's. Next was Peter Hane, Elizabeth, Silas and James—they were Peter Hane's children. Next was B. Flansburg. They had a large family. There were Lucinda, Frank, Cornelius, Sarah, Philo, John, Elizabeth, Harriet, Jerry and William. That summer only John and Elizabeth went to school. The rest were to work out or too young to go and by the time we got to Flansburg's there was quite a drove of us coming from this way. From Henry S. Conkling's were Almira, Alvin, William, Morris and Lemuel. Then there was Ellen Cummings, Lavina Hammond, Ellen, Rhoda and Mary Wedgewood. But I will not enumerate them all for there was about forty attending school that summer and if we didn't have play and fun no school ever had. Elizabeth Cummings was our teacher and everyone liked her, she was so motherly to us all and in fact we called her our mother and all must hang on to her somewhere and walk along, hold of hands with her or some of the rest who did touch her. It was like a ring with a galvanic battery attached. And such play and sport and the teacher was in the midst of it too. Hornaway was the favorite game,* for this gave us a good exercise for our studies.

But what bothered us scholars most was Richard Wigins used to happen along quite often and take up our teacher's time at noon or recess. He had been a widower for two or three years and us scholars soon learned that he was sparking her and we could see that she loved him and no wonder for he was a handsome

---

* Hornaway was probably a chasing game in which the chaser represented a horned animal of some kind. See Iona Opie and Peter Opie, *Children's Games in Street and Playground* (Oxford, 1969), pp. 70–71, 94.

man, and always appeared so good to every one. We felt a little jealous but that availed nothing for they were married afterwards. But whenever we met her we called her mother. They are both living yet and their home is in Remsen.

Well, my favorite of all the girls was Almira and I thought I could always love her. She was the best looking of the oldest girls, so I thought then. John Flansburg was my boy chum, and his sister Elizabeth was a shy and timid girl and would hardly say her soul was her own. Us boys were full of our jokes and I said to Elizabeth one day, "What a homely old woman you will be when you get old," and how she took it to heart. She tells me of it now quite often. But I have changed my mind on that and think she gets more beautiful every year of her life. The old saying is that handsome is that handsome does.

Well time sped away that summer and our school was soon over and my youthful school days ended and with what sad regrets, as many and many a time have I looked back over those ten years that were past. Ten years of youth and the reader will say is that not enough? No I was not satisfied. I wished for an eternal youth where the roses on the cheek never fade, where the curly ringlets always hold their auburn hue and the sparkling blue eyes never grow dim and the sprightly frame shall always be nimble and active. Alas and alas, we are born to bud and like the flower blossom, then wither and decay, and when the fire is burning low the blaze of heat is gone and the bright coals shine with warmth for a while and then we dissolve to *ashes and dust* and we are earth to earth. I had passed through my boyhood love and manhood's budding morn was now beaming upon me and I was only sweet sixteen.

That fall was the first I ever went from home to work. I worked for cousin Benjamin Curtis at Russia Corners.

He lived just below the village towards Graves Hollow and that winter or part of the winter I went there to school and worked for my board and that was the last schooling I ever got. I was quite well along in my studies and my education was as good as the average teacher in these times and one term more would have fitted me for teaching but my folks were poor and I had no clothes, only what I earned myself, and my younger sisters went in rags if some of the boys didn't help supply their wants. So I give up going to school and worked out here and there only when I was actually needed to get in the crops in the spring. Our winter's work was making shingles at home or away to some of the neighbors, making them on shares.

Mother was getting more feeble now and could not do much hard work, and Julia Ann my older sister and Mary and Cassie the next two younger had the most of the house work to do. Mother could mend and sew. But her time was mostly occupied in reading the Bible, the old fashion fine print Bible. After a while we sent and got her one with great large plain print and she kept it as long as she lived and she read it so much she got it threadbare as the worn pages now testify. The good old book was her solace and comfort in the many years she was helpless.

**12** IN the summer of 1849 there was a highway laid out from the neighborhood south of the creek and it crossed the creek where the Flansburg Bridge now stands and so up to intersect the highway in Wilmurt near where Jerry Flansburg now lives and that fall the Town of Ohio had completed a new bridge over the West Canada Creek which was a great advantage to us as before this we had to ford the creek or go around by the McIntosh Bridge in Ohio or up across the covered bridge in Wilmurt.

We also had several new neighbors move in and some moved out, but they got together and formed a new school district in the month of November, 1849. The first school meeting was held on November 17, 1849. It was held at the home of Samuel Conklin. The officers chosen were: Chairman Samuel Conklin, Clerk Jacob Phelps, Trustees David Dunn one year, Samuel Conklin two years, R. R. Sacket three years, Collector Spencer Wilkins, Librarian Abiah Conklin. They built a small frame school house on the site where the new one stands only down closer by the road and here my youngest sister Rinda first went to school, not five years old yet and so small that some of the boys had to go and carry her home through the snow.

Abiah now worked out most of the time and was saving up his wages for himself, for he was a money grabber, only buying his clothes and once in a while giving mother and his younger sisters a small present.

John too was now away to work for himself the most of

the time and only helping through the winter. Little
Sammy also worked away from home almost the year
round and made it his home to Uncle Joe's. So during
the summer I was seventeen my brother James, father
and me done the work on the place.

Thc firm of Hinkley and Ballou were now running the
new mill at Gang Mills and they were buying spruce and
hemlock logs and the boys and men in the neighborhood
were engaged working for them or cutting logs and bank-

ing them for the new firm.\* This together with peeling hemlock bark made business quite lively along through our place. The tan bark was hauled to Poland, Middleville, Pardeeville and Grant. The wilderness began to be stripped of the hemlock and spruce and good shingle timber was scarce near the creek.

The winter I was seventeen I made shingles for Ammon Stevens. He lived then on the place where George Potter lives now.

My father did not now go off on the road teaming as he used to but he was just as spry as he ever was for all I could see and did just as much work. James went ahead now with the work on the farm and the teaming on the road. For planning and calculating and going on with the work, he "filled a father's place," and since good old brother John had gone out to work, James was the staff now for the family to lean on.

In the fall of 1849 Mr. Wilkins folks were sadly afflicted with the cholera morbus or diarrhea and old Mrs. Wilkins, James and George all died with it within a week in spite of all the doctors they could get and all the neighbors could do was of no avail. Thus almost half of the family was gone and it was a severe blow to them. George, my youthful chum, was gone. He had been my right hand companion for a few short years and we were always the best of friends and how I missed him, for always if we were walking together he always had one arm around my neck. My fishing days with George was now over and I would never have him for a companion again and it ap-

---

\* Gardener Hinckley of Russia, New York, and T. P. Ballou of Utica, owned individual mills on West Canada Creek and became partners in 1846. They built mills at Gang's Mills (renamed Hinckley in 1891) in 1849. Henry Conklin's dating is quite accurate. See Nelson Greene, ed., *History of the Mohawk Valley*, 4 vols. (Chicago, 1925), III, 705–6.

peared to me then a sad picture to see one in the bloom of youth be taken away in a few days and be buried beneath the clods of the valley.

Mr. Dunn's folks lost a little boy with the same disease that fall and Louise Phelps also died with it that fall so there were five gone out of our little neighborhood in a few short weeks.

While we lived here, I think it was the winter of 1847 and 1848, my grandfather Curtis and Uncle Philander, Uncle Henry and Aunt Sebra Ann come from Jefferson County and made us a visit. They stayed about a week visiting with us and Uncle Joe's folks. I don't remember of their bringing mother any presents and don't think they did although they had abundance at home. This was the first time I ever saw any of my mother's relatives from Jefferson County. Uncle Henry Curtis come once after this and stayed five or six weeks and tried to trap it but did not have much success and so he went back home. None of them ever came from there after that to visit us.

Our little neighborhood was now quite prosperous and we thought we were getting out of the wilderness. We had a new bridge and a new schoolhouse and everyone seemed to take a great interest in each other's welfare. We had no quarrels, disputes, or backbiting selfish ones among us. All was peace, love, fun and quiet.

Alexander Gallt taught our school this winter of 1849 and 1850 and the term was an excellent one. I did not go this winter but my four younger sisters went all winter. In them days the teacher boarded around but I thought he come uncommonly often to our house this winter, but I was not long in doubt why he come so often. I soon discovered he and my sister Mary were on the best of terms and the best of friends and I concluded he loved her and would some day take her away bodily. I don't know as I blamed him for loving her for we all loved our blue eyed, rosy cheeked sister Mary, always so pleasant, good natured and trusting. She was sixteen this winter and it was the last term of school for her.

This year in the winter of 1849–1850 I made shingles for R. O. Paul. I made them to the halves and he boarded me.* I worked in the shop (it was new then) which is all gone now. Mr. Wilkinson used it up for an ice house. I made 150 bunches that winter and I gave most all they come to to the folks at home only keeping enough for my clothes and boots and a little spending money. But I did not spend any money foolishly. I thought more of giving my mother or younger sisters a present than of tobacco, cigars or whiskey. I knew the value of something good to eat and wear by bitter experience and every dollar helped us along through the vale of poverty.

Old Uncle John Paul and his wife were living then and they and Richard lived together. The old gentleman went about with a cane doing chores and light work but the old lady was very smart for her age and done most all the work in the house and she was always knitting or mending. I think she could get up the best boiled dinner I ever eat. In the long winter evenings after I quit work in the shop I used to read stories to the old couple. The old gentleman was a great story teller, lively and full of jokes, which made the evenings pass away very pleasantly. They were church members but of what denomination I did not know.

In the spring of 1850 we had revival meetings in the new schoolhouse. We had been deprived of having meetings or going to church so long that we had almost become like the heathen and needed a good shaking by something.

---

* "To the halves." He and Paul shared the profits equally. For a description of shingle-making, provided by Roy Conklin, Henry's grandson, see Lloyd Blankman, "Burt Conklin, The Greatest Trapper," *New York Folklore Quarterly* XXII (December 1966), 291–92.

Still, we used to go over to Wilmurt Corners to church and to sabbath school when we could get over the creek. They had meetings regular over there every two weeks but only a few went excepting the young folks from our side of the creek. But folks up in the Paul neighborhood and from towards Ohio were regular attendants.

Elder Thurston lived to Wilmurt Corners and was the preacher in charge then on the circuit and he came over and preached in our new school house in the winter of 1849 and 1850 and in the spring of and summer of 1850 he held evening meetings with us. Sometimes he would wade the creek and go back home the same night taking a lantern with him. He done a noble work for us and brought many a hardened old sinner to repent and come forward to the mercy seat. Not only the old but a good many of the young people were brought to a saving knowledge of the truth.

Our little schoolhouse was always crowded, and such glorious meetings. It was getting like it was in the old log schoolhouse when I was a little boy down in Schoharie County and one night I could not stay away any longer and so I went forward with others for prayers in great faith of receiving forgiveness of my sins and while others prayed for me I prayed also for myself and when we rose up I felt a change of heart. Oh the sweet peace of that blessed moment. I loved everyone and if I had ever had any hate for anyone it was all gone and I thought I was away back in the good old days in the long ago when but eleven years old mingling again in the songs of Zion and drinking in the sweet inspiration of the halleluahs and soul reviving music to the loving peace of the soul.

Thus it was I found the savior, he who can speak peace to the troubled soul and is ever ready and willing to receive all who come to him in faith believing. Oh how I loved and revered him that night as I arose as a living witness of his blessed mercies. Would that I could have always lived thus in the loving, forgiving heavenly spirit of those revival meetings. How the sweet and loving prayers and those old revival hymns fill our souls with joy and what a thrill would pass over us as we joined in and mingled in the praise with sweet accord.

Oh how I loved the church people and the meetings, taking active part in the services and tonight (March 2, 1892) while I am penning down these lines I am almost set back to the time of those glorious soul-stirring prayer meetings, and memory brings to mind the worshippers, a few of which I will mention. There was my good old mother with her prayers and exaltations, the first on the list for I loved her most. In our neighborhood were old Mrs. Marvin Sackett, Mrs. Jane Dunn, Mrs. Jacob Phelps, James M. Gallt and wife, David Dunn and Spencer Wilkins Jr. From the neighborhood over in Ohio were Joseph Hane and wife, Mrs. Sally Davenport, Francis Holenbeck and wife, Henry Ash and wife, old Mr. Farnicrook and wife, Uncle Peter Hane and wife, B. Flansburg and wife, John Emery and wife and William R. Ash and wife and then from Ohio village were John V. Furgason on George DeLong's place, Casin Nicholas and Silas Curtis and many others of the younger class that I have not mentioned.

When we all got together we made the schoolhouse ring with the heavenly music and the prayers and the soul reviving exhortations as one after another rose to their feet. Methinks I can hear them tonight as I bring to mind each soldier of the cross that I have mentioned above. But alas and alas how time has flown. How the many years have come and gone since then and the dear old prayer meetings are glorious days of the eventful past, and the forms that gathered in the little old schoolhouse to worship and praise God are laid away in the silent graveyard, their hands folded to rest and eyes closed (the most of them at Ohio). And the lips that uttered the prayers and the soul-stirring exhortations winding up with, "Pray for us that when it is well with you that it may be well with me also." And the hearts that sung and joined in with us in those soul reviving anthems of praise to God are stilled forever to earth and their ransomed souls are tonight singing the song of the redeemed around the great white throne.

That spring of 1850 after the creek warmed there were quite a number of us baptised kneeling in the pure running waters of the old West Canada Creek and having water poured over our heads. I joined the rest in these church rites and was taken in on probation and afterwards into full membership. I did not think the baptising was a saving ordinance but showed our respect to the church and to the commands and teachings of our Savior. I think it was Elder Thurston that baptised us.

Those were the happy years to me spiritually and bodily, I might say too, for I never saw many sick days. I was enjoying the privileges of a sort of Christian experience and sweet hallowed moments and days when grief or the harrowing and cankering care were not mine to share. I had many youthful companions, both boys and girls, and mingled with them in our sports, hunting, fishing and rambles in the forest. Some of the old neighbors had moved away and others had moved in. I still visited Almira and we were on the best of terms and in winters yet the boys from her family and ours frequently got together for a drum and fife serenade, but they were not so frequent as years before, for my brother John was away most of the time and there was none to beat the old bass drum and our bonfires of shingle shavings were getting scarce.

This spring one day I was helping father plow. It was my birthday, the seventh of May 1850. Joseph Hane came over and said old Mr. Tripp was dead and father put out the team and went over and helped lay him out and the next day they buried him up on the hill under an old apple tree which is standing there yet. After this I went over frequently to work for old Mum Tripp as they called her, and many a dollar I earned working for her.

In the spring and summer of 1850 our folks' family were getting pretty well scattered and separated. Julius still lived to Schoharie County in the Town of Fulton and had married one of Jerry Gilson's girls. Her name was Harriet. But the next year or the year after, they (that is Julius and Mr. Gilson) sold out their farms in Schoharie County and moved to Wyoming County in the Town of Vernal near Attica.

Julius had not been to make us a visit but once since we moved from Blenheim. Sister Ruth came a few times to visit us in the winter when she could get away the best. The winters were sad and dreary looking and deep snow and she missed seeing the beauties of the great forest in the summer bloom of flowers and foliage and never got a taste of the delicious trout that swam in the old West Canada Creek. Although Ruth was fading and thin by hard work the same old sparkle was in her brown eyes and the same lovely disposition and pleasant voice and her step as sprightly as it was the morning she led me to school in the long ago. Her husband came with her and one time they brought their little boy Aurey along with them. He was a lovely little boy but he died when he was six years old.

Brother John worked out summers with the farmers over in Norway but made it his home with us winters, making shingles or working in the lumber woods. Little Sammy worked out also and made it his home to Uncle Joe Curtis's and he hardly ever came home. Abiah worked in the lumber woods for Hinkley and Ballou but frequently came home to get mother to knit and mend for him and in fact we all knew what it was to have a good old mother to mend and knit for us. Mother was not able to get around and do the house work, so some one of the girls had to stay at home for that. Sister Rinda was all the little one we had now to love and torment. She was very sensitive and any little joke she took it in earnest and when she was thus vexed the fire would fairly fly out of her black eyes, but after all, we loved her for all that and done all we could for her to help her along in her studies. She was all books and school, and I thought sometimes it was because she was born in a schoolhouse.

In the spring of 1850 the family of James M. Gallt moved from the village of Ohio over to the Town of Wilmurt. They bought the place that Henry Paul now owns west of where Mr. Wilkinson lives by the gorge where the woman was drowned. There was an old log house and barn there then and that summer and the next fall they built a frame house. Alexander Gallt was now a little closer to sister Mary and on the third day of July 1850 they were married, and after they were married she went to Mr. Gallt's to live. This summer and the next Alexander and his father were very busy building and clearing land. I was there frequently to see them and sister Mary. Old Mr. Gallt was a good story teller and many an hour I passed away with him listening to his fish stories and some of them were awful yet very interesting. Alexander's mother was very quiet and still and most always reading the Bible. She was always afraid her husband or Alex would get trees fell on them and when they were out chopping fallow she would listen whenever a tree fell and they had a signal, after the tree came down and they were all right, they would pound on the log with the axe three times so she would know they were safe.

Our old home was now being robbed of its loved ones.

It was sister Mary this time. She too had got a kind and loving husband and a good home but was not entirely out of poverty's vale or above want, for their family like ourselves had to toil and work hard for the necessaries of life. But as far as I could judge, sweet contentment pervaded their home—no cross words, no quarreling, no unkind words or actions. Everything was peace and love and quiet and harmonious.

In the fall of 1850 a man by the name of Truman Simmons moved into the neighborhood. He lived in the log house east of the schoolhouse. He was a carpenter by trade and he and his wife were both very deaf, and if they were talking to each other you could hear them away out in the road. Mr. Simmons was a rough swearing fellow and fond of his whiskey and had it all the time. He bought it by the gallon. He and my father and old Mr. Wilkins and Roswell Sackett were boon companions. But father did not drink as much as usual, for it made him sick.

In the winter of 1850–1851 Alexander taught our school again and boarded at home. Our school was now quite large and this winter it went off as usual in good order and the teacher was liked by everyone.

This winter of 1850–1851 I again went to Mr. Paul's to make shingles. James Stevens worked there also. Jim and I were great cronies together. In stormy weather and evenings he made shingles also and how we used to race it shaving shingles. We had a fireplace in the shingle shanty and burnt our shavings.

In the spring of 1851 brother John went down towards Middleville to work and here he got acquainted with Mary Seymour and that summer they were married. John was thirty-two and Mary sixteen. They were an ill matched pair and my good old brother John had at last taken up with a very poor stick for a wife. Like the man looking for a cane and wandered for years in the wilderness to find a straight stick but at last cut the most crooked one he could find. She was kind hearted enough but no housekeeper for a poor man. She did not know how to cook and would throw out with a spoon faster than he could throw in with a shovel.

Mary's mother, Mrs. Seymour, was a widow woman and had two more daughters besides Mary. Their names were Marthy and Eliza. John's wife was quite good looking and good company but never could learn how to tidy up a house or be saving. It was always with them a feast or a famine and when she had plenty she would cook to waste and then scrimp and borrow and beg afterwards. I do not think she ever had a spark of genuine love for John. Good old brother John had loved us all so dearly through the long sad years of toil and now our hearts bled for him to think how he was situated. But soon after they were married they moved away off to Rutland, Vermont where they stayed a few years and how he fared there I know not. Another one was now gone out of the family but not out of poverty's vale or out of the wilderness of want.

Little Sammy this summer of 1851 worked for Uncle Joe Curtis and in the fall he married Jammy Curtis, Uncle Joe's youngest daughter. Soon after they were married they went to keeping house, living over on the Chauncy Furgason place. Now we had another place to visit and little Sammy had been more fortunate than brother John, for Jammy was a good saving woman and a splendid housekeeper and loved her husband and done all she could to help him along through Poverty's Vale. Our family were now like the birds of spring, choosing their mates and building nests and I think some of them had castles in the air. Jammy was the youngest of Uncle Joe's family and the idol of the household. Everybody loved and respected her for her good behavior. But when they were married they had but little to begin with and so they had to work hard like all the rest for a living. My brother Sammy ought to have had something ahead by this time, for he had brought not much home for years.

The spring and summer of 1851 I worked at home helping brother James clear land and get in the spring crop. We also peeled some hemlock bark. James built a new frame barn this summer and father and I hewed most of the timber and when we got it hewed James got old Mr. Simmons to come and frame for him. I also helped to frame it and here I got my first lessons at the carpenter's trade. Our old log barn had almost gone to ruin and was not fit any more for hay or cattle or horses. By haying time we had the new barn ready for use and we then tore the old one down and burned it up.

James was a regular home boy, kind and good to father and mother and all the rest of us and when any of us come home we were always welcome. He had raised him a young team and we had three or four cows and a plenty of hay and pasture and in fact we were getting along quite well. I think sister Julia worked in a lumber camp kept by Samuel Connell up on the Gulf Stream about a mile from the creek.

Us boys had our fun this summer as usual hunting and fishing. Early in the spring it was hunting pigeons and some springs the woods were full of them for they nested back in the swamp only a few miles. So our table was well supplied with pigeons, partridges and trout, and sometimes it was wild duck.

Along in the summer every season we had a duck hunt when the young wild ducks were nearly grown. There were lots of them along the creek. So this summer we started out for a duck hunt. We generally went up to Noblesboro, five or six of us, and then come down the creek, some on each side and when we scairt up a flock or litter we would fire into them. The young ducks could not fly, only skip along on the water with their feet while making their wings go. It was fun for us but not for the ducks.

So one day we started out. There were six of us. James and George Stevens, John Wilkins, John Flansburg, brother James, and myself. Off we went with a lunch in our pockets. We all had shotguns, the old fashion muzzle loader, and we could fire but once and then we would have to stop and load up. We were as jolly a lot of boys as ever hooted in the wilderness. We soon got up to Noblesboro. There was an old bachelor lived here and we always called him "Old Daddy Green." I think by his talk he was both Scotch and English. Anyway he talked broken. He was always kind in his way and accommodating and full of songs and jokes and odd speeches.

Well when we got on the hill and going down towards the house, we began to hoot and yell like a pack of Indians and out he come to see what was the rumpus and as we come up to the gate we all took off our hats with a good morning to the old man. When he says, "Where ye goin a rom banin and poonin and speelin aboot." "Oh," I says, "we are going a hunting." And then he says, "Oh the diedle hoont ye for ye're na good iny whas only to fright the life out of a body like me."

Here we separated. John Flansburg, James Stevens and me waded over the creek and come down on the south side and the three other boys on the north side. Well we did not see any ducks until we got just below the Chesly fishing place. Jim was just ahead of me a few feet when all at once a flock darted out from under the alders and went flapping down stream. Jim yells out, "There they go," and then the guns went too, bang, bang, bang, from both sides of the creek and two of the ducks keeled up. We could not tell who killed them but after they were secured we saw Jim a looking at his gun. I says, "Jim what ails your gun?" When he says, "Whish by g——d boys, I don't believe the charge went out." "Oh yes," John F. says, "I seen the smoke." But Jim was not satisfied until he tried it with the ramrod, then be believed it.

On we came and when we got most down to the mill we got another shot at them and killing two more where the creek was quite rocky, and in getting one of the ducks I slipped in feet first and went away under, gun and all, and then the boys had the laugh on me. From there we got two more and then we had one duck a piece and I had a ducking besides. Before we got down to our house it come up a heavy shower and we all got wet to the skin and such a drabby and bedraggled lot of boys you never saw. But we tormented Jim about the charge that did not go out of his gun and for years after we used to laugh over it when Jim came to see us.

In the fall of 1851 I worked for Hinkley and Ballou and boarded with Charlie Christman. He kept the boarding house in one part of G. Hinkley's house by the Four Mile Creek just below the sawmill. Mr. Hinkley lived in one part of the house also. Mr. James Abbott of Forestport was the foreman of part of the company works. That fall we went from there, taking our dinners to our work, away down below the Gulf Stream on what is now the old Potter place or depot. It is now owned by Gibb Johnson. Peter Hane also worked there with us. There were six in all I think.

It was all woods then and we went to clear a place to build the headquarters of the lumber camps directly back of the place. It was to be the depot of their supplies for several years.* As I said, it was all woods and Mr. Abbott picked out a spot for the buildings in the worst old smash of fallen timber, so I thought then, there was on the place and told us to go at it. Well I and Peter struck the first blows. The timber was all green and we made fires and burnt the great logs and brush and soon the carpenters come on and put up a house and barn and blacksmith shop. The house and the barns they built then are all gone but the shop remains and is rigged over in a dwelling house. After we got a building place cleared we went to cutting the main log road up the Gulf to the old Colnell shanty.

That fall old Mr. Simmons moved over to the saw mill over the creek on what is now or was then called Fly Brook. The old mill was later tore down and little James Cummings built another and that is not used anymore and in a few years it will be said of that too: "The mill has gone to decay and the rafters have fallen in." When I look back at those years it don't seem possible there could come about such a change.

---

* By "they" Henry means the firm of Hinkley and Ballou, which established a supply depot to service their lumber camps, which were located farther back in the forest. Because a team of horses could pull a third as much weight on the rough forest roads as they could on the graded town roads, lumber firms established supply depots near the terminus of town roads.

**13** IN the winter of 1851 and 1852 I worked for the lumber company repairing roads and helping unload sleighs on the bank at the Potter place until they got the logs in and when they went to skidding again I went in the woods to help. So did my brother Abiah. We worked at the Gilman shanty on Mad Tom Brook. Abiah and I sawed together most all summer and fall with the exceptions of about ten days in September. Abiah was a good sawyer and easy to work with. David Dunn also worked there.

About this time the California gold fever was raging and my brother Abiah and Mr. Dunn were smitten down with it quite badly and all summer long it was nothing but going to California as soon as they could save enough money to go with, and how they scrimped and saved, and my brother especially.

We used to come out every Saturday night and go back on Monday morning. This gave me a good chance Sundays to go and see Almira. Sometimes she would be up at our house visiting my sister Amy, for Amy was now my mother's standby, for Julia and Cassie were out to work and Mary was married. Well Almira and Amy were together quite frequently.

Almira was up one Sunday the last of summer and stayed until evening so I went home with her and on the way down we talked over our future prospects in a businesslike way not with any dilly dally foolishness as some lovers style it. But it was sincere, frank, open, plain hearted. Well I stayed quite late that night and before I came away we were engaged to be married sometime the next spring. Well I believed I loved Almira with all my heart and had all reason to think she returned my love. As we parted that night I gave and received a kiss of our betrothal. Oh those sweet kisses in love's youngest dreams. They were not, like the kisses exactly of my boyhood love, devoid of passion.

As I came along home that night or rather in the small hours of the next day I was happy and heeded not the darkness for it was most two miles of woods and darker than pitch. In the darkness I was laying my plans for the future and building castles in the air when Almira and I would have a home of our own when all at once I ran against a great bear who stood up in the road. *"Whugh!"* the old cuss growled as I hit him and kicked at the same time. I gave a yell and he dusted for the bushes as I dusted for home not stopping for mud or anything else. My future plans with Almira were for the moment forgotten and the castles were already tumbling down on my head. But I never told her how I got frightened that night and after that I made up my mind I would never stay courting till after twelve o'clock and I think I never did. I reasoned thus, if you could not talk enough in the evening until twelve why not go a little oftener and when you did go talk business. What would you think of a man staying all night and keeping another up to transact a bargain that you could consummate in five minutes?

The summer of 1852 old Mr. Wilkins lost his second wife and two little baby boys and they, strange to say, all died with the same disease, cholera morbus, the others died with two and a half years before and this was such a sad blow to him he determined to break up keeping

house. He offered his place, that is his claim, for sale so I bought him out for one hundred dollars, taking a quit claim deed.*

* In a quit claim deed, the seller of land gives up his own ownership of the property but does not guarantee the title. If there are legal or equitable flaws in the title, the purchaser assumes responsibility for them. In contrast, a warranty deed guarantees that no third party has a defendable claim on the property.

There was eighty-one acres in the lot. I had it in my possession until 1861. After I bought Mr. Wilkins out my brother James worked the place until I was married. I now had a cage and the promise of a bird to put in it. Mr. Wilkins now went to live with Mrs. Jane Dunn, his daughter.

Sister Julia worked for Mr. Colwell in the lumber camp this summer and next winter. She had got acquainted with a young fellow by the name of Andrew Krellis and they were courting each other and Sundays they would come out to our house for a visit.

Towards the last of September, 1852 I came out of the woods and brother James, my mother, sister Mary, Alex and I all went to the Black River visiting. James drove his own team going all the way by wagon. We were two days on the road and at the end of the second day we drove through Theresa village. On the way from Carthage my mother knew every place we passed and here was where they lived such a time and how long they stayed there and so on. The next place they stayed so long there and from there they moved to somewhere else and so it went. Mother was our guide now as none of us had ever been there and she knew every turn in the road and directed us to her old homestead where so many long years before she played when she was a little girl.

We found grandfather Curtis's family all well and surprised to see us and what a greeting to my dear old mother as she grasped her father's hand, now trembling with age, and her sister and brothers all gave her the hand of welcome while the tears trickled down their cheeks, for my mother had not been there since they moved from Watertown over twenty years before.

After my mother's greeting we all had to be introduced for they did not know us although my grandfather,

Uncle Henry, Uncle Philander and Aunt Sebra Ann had been once to visit us in the town of Ohio. Aunt Lydia us young folks had never seen before. She was an old maid and almost blind. She was still very good looking yet with the bloom of womanhood on her brow. She was kind and good and flew about trying to make us comfortable and wanted to help Aunt Sebra Ann all she could but she could not see to get around, and so she sat down beside mother and visited. Grandfather was old and lame and bent over and walked almost double and carried a cane. Still he could get about and do a good many chores. Uncle Philander was a tall spare man [and] an easy sort of a go ahead worker and was not able to do half the work the farm needed to keep it in former shape and he was too stingy or something else to hire help. His buildings were all out of repair, patched up with rough timber and no paint on any of them and the fences were in a sad condition. They kept over twenty cows, two teams and a lot of sheep. Uncle Henry had lately been married to a large fleshy, fat, squad of a woman. Her maiden name was Harriet Rider. She was just as good natured as she was fat and when she laughed she shook all over like a bowl full of jelly. Uncle Henry was a poor long scrawny looking man and they were an odd couple.

Well, I have told you something of all the family except Aunt Sebra Ann and cousin Ruth Elsey. Aunt Ann was slim and spry and was yet quite good looking and was the mainstay of all the housework, and I might say the calculator and foreman of the whole farm as well as the house. She had filled her dead mother's place as far as toil and work was concerned in looking after the whole family and she had nobly acted her part. Cousin Ruth was then a shy blushing young girl not yet in her teens and wore short dresses. She like her mother was all business. She had her hens and her geese, her lambs and her cow and an old mare and colt and she knew enough to look after the proceeds of them all, and young as she was then she had money in the bank. She was the pet of the whole household and as good as any of them to calculate. They let her have all these things to encourage her in looking after the interest of the stock and the farm.

Grandfather Curtis and most of his family were church members and belonged to the Methodist Church and were faithful Christian people. They had their family altar and family prayers and Grandfather said grace at the table. This suited mother to gather again around the old family altar with brothers and sisters and the dear old loving father and hear his voice once more in prayer and praise, reviving as it were the days of her childhood and memory of the bygone days of the long ago when there was a dear old mother also to gather with the family group.

We had a good visit and my dear old grandfather could not bear to have me out of his sight. I had to go with him around on the farm, to the garden and barn and to see all they had, and James and Alexander and I and Uncle Philander took a stroll down on the river flats and Pine Bluffs on the lot that my father lived on when first married and Uncle showed us some of the black ash rails that my father split nearly forty years before while clearing up the farm. The remains of the old stone chimney still lay there where the log house stood and while standing there he pointed out to us the bend in the river below where wolves had chased my father.

Uncle Henry was an awful hector and he was tormenting Aunt Lydia about her beau. It seems she had had a beau that fall a short time before we come and he had stayed with her till most morning. So she thought she would make her feller think she was alright for work and went to work getting breakfast. She put over the potato kettle and went out in the shed for the potatoes, but instead of getting the potatoes as she supposed she got a lot of walnuts with shucks on that cousin Ruth had gathered. These she washed and put them in the kettle and she was so blind she did not know the difference until they tried them to see if they were done and then they all had the laugh on poor blind auntie.

After we visited a day or two we went over to Uncle Cheesman's. He lived about three miles east of Redwood on a new farm in the woods near a nice little lake. Uncle Cheesman had married Mary Chatman and they had there children, Sophrona Ann, Eliza, and William, and they were about James' and my age. They were lively, full of fun and jokes and good natured. I think we stayed with uncle two days and two nights. Uncle's folks were Christian people and my mother, how she did enjoy the visit with her brother and Aunt Mary. They were not rich but in good circumstances, peaceful and happy.

After I got back home I went in the woods again to work with Abiah at the Gilman shanty until about the first of December when they quit skidding logs and then I went home. I had scarcely got home when James Stevens and John Flansburg wanted I should go to Jock's Lake [Hannedaga] with them still hunting. I had never been there so I went with them taking grub enough to last about five days. Off we started with great expectations of getting each a deer. We were young and spry and got over the ground quite lively and about middle afternood we come in sight of the lake at the Herkimer camp. We had no knapsacks but carried our dinner in a bag over our shoulders and by the time we got to the lake everything was all crumbled together.

There was no camp at the lake then, only a little one, big enough to hold four or five, made of logs covered with bark, and it had a fireplace. There was another

little camp up at Big Rock Bay, occupied by Robert Griffith and Joe Downer, trappers from Prospect.

Well, the first night we stayed at the lower camp and we had just got our supper when in came three more hunters from over the lake. They had been over to Jones Lake and had got a nice deer. I forgot who they were but we made them welcome even if we were crowded, and although we had been to supper we partook of a venison steak with them. In the morning they come out and we prepared to go out to the slaughter, so we took a lunch in our pockets and loaded our guns with buckshot. We all had single barrel muzzle loading guns. When all was ready we got in the old scow and started over across by Gull Rock. Here we left the boat and went sauntering up through the woods by the sand bar. The snow was about six inches deep and hung on the bushes. We soon come to deer tracks a plenty and this excited Jim so we could do nothing with him. When we come to where there had five or six gone, Jim says "Whush by g——d here they go," and on he went pell mell, crashing after them. We hushed him up, got him to go slow and as we come up over a little hill we saw them running and Jim hauled up and fired and at the same time yelled out "There they go, there they go with tails flying, shoot 'em boys, shoot 'em boys." Well John and I fired at them but they were too far away for buckshot so we did not hit them. We followed them for an hour or so and then came to camp, all wet with snow and slush, and after dinner we decided to go up the lake and take our dinner bags and stay that night with the trappers. We got in the old scow with our guns and dinner bags and up the lake we went, keeping all the way near the shore afraid we would upset. All the way up along the shore we could see where the fish had been spawning but they had left the beds now.

When we got most to Big Rock Bay we met the trappers going out to look to some traps. We were quite well acquainted with them and we talked a few minutes. They said they would be back before dark and we were welcome to stay with them, so we come on and left our dinner at the camp and then we went over to the flat rock (that is just where this camp stands now) and there we pulled the boat out and went up over the hills to look for deer. We saw lots of tracks but did not see any deer so we returned and went to the camp and found the trappers at home.

Their camp was made of logs under a great shelving rock. That point was then covered with forest growth timber. I was almost afraid to sleep under the great rock for fear it would tip over on us. The camp was nice and warm and we had a good night's rest. At breakfast next morning we decided to dig for home as our grub was

146

getting short and it was all mixed together in such a shape it was like succotash.

We bade the trappers good morning and launched the old scow and started for down the lake. The west wind was blowing a good gale and by the time we got to the narrows the whitecaps were rolling and we were drifting with the tide. John was rowing and he was full of fun and to see the boat rock and go with the waves he let it drift towards the middle. Jim began to get scairt, for he sat in the back end, and the water dashed over and got his seat wet. He got so scairt he began to pray and says, "For God's sake John row the boat to shore." He was white as a sheet and sat right down in the bottom of the boat and clutched the sides with his hands and begged to John to go to shore. We got to the landing all right but Jim was in such a hurry to get out he came very near up-setting us all and Jim declared he would never ride again with John on this lake.

This was the first time I ever saw Jock's Lake or Hannedaga as it is now called and although early in December it was still beautiful in its winter dress. The ruthless hand of the tourist, hunter, fisherman, guide and hotel and cottage builder had not left their devastating, cruel and haggling mark around its fair evergreen points and bays. With the exceptions of a few little notches at Herkimer camp and Big Rock Bay all was forest growth to the water's edge. A few years before there had been a fire over on Jock's Point and the forest growth along the shore there was down and rotting but the place was covered now with a growth of small things four or five feet high intermingled with evergreens. Rocky and Raymond Points were the most beautiful of any on the lake.

After we had got our dinner we started out. The road most part of the way went where it does now and was a better wagon road than it is today. It was not worn into deep channels and down among the rocks and mud as the road now is. We had some lively walking going out, racing it most of the way, and a little after dark we hauled up at Mr. Stevens's and stayed over night. Thus ended our still hunting trip and no venison of our own either, yet we had the fun out of it all the same.

That December, I think it was Christmas Day, anyway it was on Sunday, old Mr. Wilkins, Roswell R. Sackett and my father went over to the sawmill to visit old Mr. Truman Simmons. They all four of them liked their liquor and would have a gay time among themselves now and then. On this day Mr. Simmons had invited them over for a social, Mr. Simmons furnishing the old rye, as they called it. Well, they played cards, penny ante, using buttons for change, and when they got merry they went pitching pennies at the crack and then they tried to walk the crack and getting tired of this they danced the French Four and so it went. Mr. Simmons wanted his wife to get dinner but she wouldn't do it and says to her husband, "You're a damn purty Christian dancing and swearing and drinking on Christmas Day." "Well, all right boys," the old man says as he set the gallon jug on the table, "Here boys help yourselves. This is meat, bread and drink for it is made of corn and rye."

Well we knew where they were and towards night began to look for father home and while we were looking for him Mr. Wilkins came along and I went out to inquire for father. He said he and Sackett were coming and would be along soon so we kept watch, but no father, and while we were looking we heard someone over the bridge towards where C. Flansburg lives now and all we could hear was, "Help, help." As we listened again the sound came again borne on the gust of wind, "H-e-l-p," in a more fainter voice and our folks says, "That is father." The remark was made by someone, "He is drunk

148

and may as well die in the snow as live and be a disgrace to the whole family." I was the only one at home at the time of the menfolks and was considering what to do when I looked at mother as she sat trembling with the tears rolling down her cheeks but said nothing, yet this was enough for me. I grabbed my coat, hat and mittens and bounded out in the storm and snow drifts almost waist deep. I soon reached the bridge and as I got up the little rise beyond I saw my father trying to walk plunging in the snow from one side of the road to the other and every time he got his face out of the snow he tried to call for help but it was now getting more faint and the word help was scarcely above a whisper. I soon got to him and his bare hands and arms were wet with snow to his elbows and his face and hair was nearly frozen. I took off my warm mittens and put them on his hands, tied my scarf about his neck and ears and led him home, but it was no easy task for he could scarcely drag his feet in the snow. We got him by the fire and gave him something to eat and then he felt better. He had been without his dinner which made him worse. He was too far gone to be funny that day but afterwards told what they had been about.

This was a sad lesson to me as well as all the family and while the rest of the children were scolding and taking on I happened to go in the bedroom and saw my mother's Bible laying on the bed open where she had been reading and then and there I laid my hands down on the open pages and made a vow to myself that if I ever had a wife or children they should never see me come home drunk or under the influence of liquor and that I would never have it said their husband or father was a drunkard. Right here dear reader is the secret of my refusal to drink with my fellow townsmen and associates. My vow taken that day come fresh to my mind whenever any of the accursed stuff has been tried to be thrust upon me. The memory of my dear old mother and her open Bible and my solemn vow have kept me these long years from the habit that my father was addicted to from his early sailor life.

Well, after my father got warm and so he could talk I asked him where Mr. Sackett was. He said the last he saw of him he was sitting by a stump over on the sawmill road. So I started to go and see but met Mr. Samuel Colwell coming with a team, and he had picked him up out of the road and brought him along. We carried him into our house and laid him by the stove and by next morning he was able to walk home.

The next day father felt pretty blue and sick and could hardly get about. I watched my opportunity and when I got him out by himself I gave him one of the most straightforward and earnest temperance lectures a man had ever got, especially a father from a son. I talked to him until he cried and promised he never would get so again. It done him lots of good for he kept his word to me. Although he would sometimes take a drink, yet he never after got down so low as he did that time.

During the last few months I had not lost sight of my affianced girl Almira, but frequently went to see her, and in those pleasant autumn Sabbaths we took many a ramble in the grand old woods and enjoyed those happy days as lovers only can.

The lumber company was drawing logs this winter down the Gulf Stream and banking them on the Potter place, and so I hired out to them. My work was to fix road and help unload on the bank. I boarded at the depot and some evenings went to see Almira. Our old friend and neighbor Mr. James M. Gallt worked there and done the blacksmithing that winter. He shod horses and mended sleighs for the company.

**14** ALONG in the fore part of January 1853 there came a crust and John and Philo Flansburg teased me to go up to Jock's Lake fishing and hunting deer. So I got away from my work a few days and went. We took a gun, two dogs, snowshoes, fishlines and our packs and off we started. We had one little dog named Gunner and the other was Beaver and neither one of them had ever killed a deer but all the same we took them along. We got an early start and passed the Hubbard place early in the morning (old Mr. Francis Wilkinson and his son Ed lived there then). When we got to the Big Brook we came to an old deer yard and let the dogs go but they did not find the deer and come back to us in a little while and then we ate a lunch and went on, arriving at the lake at Herkimer Camp at middle afternoon.

Here we found a party of four who had come to fish and hunt and the little camp was now full and overflowing but they made standing room for us. Well, we rigged up some lines and went out on the lake fishing, cutting holes anywhere, haphazard, as we were green then and knew nothing about fishing on the lakes in winter. We had no luck so the other party told us to go over on the sand bar and fish in their holes and in doing so we got a fine mess of trout. They were the first I had ever tasted out of this lake. That night we slept heads and points and sitting against the logs in the corner by the fireplace.

The next morning we tried the fish and they would not bite so we thought we would go up to the head of the lake and see if we could get a deer. The lake was all a glare of ice and not a flake of snow on the whole surface and as the winter sun shone down on it, it was like a great mirror flashing in the sunlight. We took our fishlines wound up on the poles and on we went slipping, sliding and scatting along and the dogs sprawling after us. We halted at the trapper's camp at Big Rock but the trappers were not at home now and on we went up to the head. Here we cut a few holes in the ice which was about one foot thick but the fish did not bite. So we took the dogs and went hunting over the hill and started some deer up fresh but the confounded dogs did not know anything about crusting deer and in fact they knew nothing anyway.

We gave up the deer hunt in disgust and returned to the lake and started down and when we come to the fish holes Philo, who was a perfect devil in his way, was always up to mischief and the torment of the rest of the children and not only mischief but abuse and domineering and woe to any of his brothers or sisters if he got a grudge against them, yet he was good natured, full of fun and frolic with any except his own family. Well this day he had got a grudge against the poor dogs, Hunter [sic] and Beaver, and he let them eat the bait on the hooks and got them caught, saying if he could not catch fish he could catch dogs and he dragged the poor dogs along over the ice and they were yelping and whining for dear life until John and I put a stop to it. We got the hooks out of their mouths and put the lines in our pockets.

We got back to Herkimer Camp a little after noon and concluded to go over to the fly shanty and stay all night and next day go home. The fly camp was two miles from the lake and there were some people staying there with their cattle feeding out the fly hay. We were not long skipping over there. There were three of them and they said there was no room for any more and we thought so

152

too, for the camp was only four by six feet inside with a fireplace in one end. So we dusted for out and if ever snowshoes went clicking over the crust they did that afternoon.

We passed Wilkinson's at dusk and hauled up at the Ballou farm. Old Daddy Green lived there then, our old friend and fun maker. We asked for lodging and the privilege to cook some supper. Oh yes we were right welcome and he says, "Coom in, coom and lay your bags doon in yon cooner." We got our supper and stayed all night. It snowed that night about four inches and the boys said we ought to have a deer to take home and we would try the dogs once more. So we went up in the Mill Creek Lake Swamp but found no deer and started for home, Philo leading the way through the swamp, when we come to snowshoe tracks and Philo says, "Who is in here?" and he counted the tracks of three men and two dogs and then he hellowed as loud as he could yell but no answer and on we went, Philo ahead. John and I were laughing in our sleeves to see him circle around again to the same place. We told him he was lost but he would not believe it until he took his back track and come again to the same place and then he gave up. Now John took the lead and brought us out home just at night with no fish and no deer. But I did not care, for it was cruel sport to crust the innocent creatures, and yet I had helped do it lots of times for food.

On arriving at home I learned with sadness that my brother Abiah had started for California. As I said before, he had caught the gold fever in the fall before and now he was gone and I did not even have the privilege to take the parting hand or say the word goodbye. He had started for the land of gold, taking all his money with him. All the summer before we had worked together pulling cross cut saw in the Hinckley lumber woods, and many a time when he was talking of going, I asked him if he was not afraid to cross the ocean. "No," he said, "others are going and I can get through if they do."

At that time they went across the Atlantic and across the Isthmus and then the Pacific ocean and they were from a month to six weeks going. When he got across the Isthmus he wrote back to us that he was well and had not been seasick and everything was fair and prosperous with him, and as he said his goodbye in his letter he said he would write again when he reached the land of gold, but alas that was his last goodbye to us, and the hand that wrote it was soon still in death. We waited and waited but no more letters came from him and thinking something had happened we wrote to the captain of the "Winfield Scott," for that was the name of the steamer he took passage on from Aspinwall and after awhile we got our answer from the captain stating that he came on board ship February first and was taken with yellow fever and died on February 11, 1853 and was buried at sea. The captain further said that Mr. Conklin had all due attention shown him by the physicians and officers of the ship and especially by his friend David Albright, who made oath he was a relative and all of his effects and a wallet containing twenty dollars in silver was handed over to

154

him. We never had any relatives by that name so we put him down as an imposter and we wrote several letters to find out if we could find out more about it. But soon after that the "Winfield Scott" was burned at sea and most all the officers perished and we never heard any further news of him. After paying his passage he must have had over two hundred dollars left and no doubt that Albright put this in his own pocket unknown to the captain. But Abiah was gone and his grave was beneath the rolling waves of the Pacific Ocean, down, down in its dark and gloomy depths.

This was a sad blow to mother and all the rest of us and it seemed as though mother never could give him up. She often said in her silent mourning and grief for him that she could not hardly believe he was really dead and buried beneath the ocean waves. She often carried the idea that there was some mistake somewhere and he was still alive and someday would return to her, but alas for her false hopes of years waiting after he was gone and finally she gave up to the inevitable. We all loved Abiah and we all have mourned his sad fate. He went down in the bloom of youth.

Thus another one of our family was gone from poverty's vale. He who for so many years had aided us to live and distributed his generous gifts to mother and sisters, and his sweetheart looked in vain, for he never returned to her. He never reached California's land of gold, but we hope and trust his home is in that beautiful land whose golden street will never rust.

It was now getting towards spring and I was at the depot to work yet and frequently went down to see Almira and talk over matters for the future and the day was set for us to get married and that only one week ahead. The next Sunday was to be our wedding day and Wednesday I received a note from her requesting me to come down as she had something to tell me. After my day's work was done I went down and called at the house of her father and no Almira was there but her mother said she was over to Alvin's shaving shingles. Well this was nothing strange, for the girls and women in the north woods frequently made shingles. I went over to Alvin's. It was only a little ways west of where the old folks lived only on the other side of the road in a small log house with a log shingle camp built on one end of it.

I found her in the shingle camp sitting on the shaving horse shaving shingles. Our good evenings were said pleasantly and I asked her what she was doing there and she said she was shaving shingles for Alvin for twenty cents a bunch to get her some clothes. I saw she was not very good natured and I asked her what the trouble was. Well, she said she would be honest and tell me that she had made up her mind not to get married for the reason she had no clothes fit to wear and her folks were too poor to get what she wanted and then she said too that she had no furniture to keep house with, such as dishes, bedsteads, bedding and chairs and table, and she wanted all these first before she got married. Well I tried to reason with her but I could not and finally she said she would tell me another thing that was this. "That whoever she did marry she would never have any family and that she never would wear her life out taking care of a mess of squalling brats as her poor old mother had always done." Of course I could not promise her this, for we were both young and in nature's course a family might be expected.

I talked with her a long while but it did no good and finally Alvin's wife spoke through the crack of the logs where they had pulled the moss out for a peek hole and she says, "Almira shall I tell you what I would do if I were you?" "Well," Almira says, "If you have anything to say, say it and have it done." Well Ellen, that's Alvin's wife, says, "I would tell him he might go to hell." "No," Almira said to me, "I won't tell you so, for sometime we may get married." I said, "Maybe sometime." We talked low then so Ellen could not hear and agreed to part as the best of friends and if we never got married we would be as brother and sister always and always respecting each other as such and if either of us found someone else to marry it was our privilege to do so. So we parted not as affianced lovers with a kiss but a shake of the hand and a good night and a goodbye.

I went back to my place of work sadly disappointed and reflecting on the course events had taken, and all the consoling thing I could make out of it was I had lost a wife and gained a sister, an adopted sister by agreement. The next night I went home and told mother she need make no preparations for me for next Sunday, for Almira had gone back on me. I had made a confidant of my mother and had told her what had been going on. Well, mother said Almira was a good girl, and she was sorry but said I was young yet and I would see trouble enough if I waited ten years yet and maybe I would find someone I would like better than Almira. So I did not pine myself to death over it or grow to be a shadow. Mother said there were just as good fish in the sea as were ever taken out of it. Thus ended my courtship and no marriage and all my imaginary happiness was dashed to the ground, for all my air castles had crumbled at my feet.

That spring of 1853 Alexander and Mary moved to Forestport and so did Mr. Phelps' family and after I helped James to get in the spring crops I went also and worked all summer with Willard Phelps at the carpenter's trade. I was getting quite handy at it and liked the business first rate. Forestport was quite a small place then and was mostly surrounded by a dense forest growth of timber on the west, north and east.

**15** The summer of 1853 while working with Willard Phelps at Forestport I made it my home with sister Mary and her husband. They lived on the hill west of the canal bridge on the road that goes towards Boonville. I liked it there first rate and it was then a lively place. Almira was teaching school that summer at the old Webb schoolhouse near Northwood. She had a good education and after our match was broken up she went to studying and got a certificate and went to teaching. We corresponded by letter all summer as particular friends but never a word said of marriage, and along in the fall I came home and stopped and made her school a visit. It was Friday afternoon and after school was out I walked up home with her and had a pleasant chat with her and the old people and took supper with them. In our conversation along the road the subject of marriage was spoken of but I did not care now to enter into any more agreements, only that I told her I never should get married until she did and there it ended. The old lady wanted I should stay but I told her I must hasten on to see my mother for I had not seen her since spring. On parting with Almira I gave her a nice pocket Bible for a present.

In the fall of the same year my sister Julia Ann and Andrew Krellis got married. They went up to Noblesboro and old Mr. Francis Wilkinson married them. He was justice of the peace then and done lots of town business for the Town of Wilmurt. Shortly after they were married they went up to Morehouseville to live on his father's old place, the last house before going in the woods to Piseco Lake. So there was another of the family gone from the family circle but not from poverty's vale, to keep and care for a home of her own. Andrew was a good worker, good and kind to her but he was born under the roving planet, something like my father only he did not drink, but he was continually moving from place to place and today while I am writing this, March 20, 1892, he and his family are away off in Nebraska and my sister and him are an old couple now doting on their grandchildren.

I saved enough out of my summer's wages to finish paying for my place and to buy a nice cow. The cow I left at home for mother's use until I wanted her for myself. That winter I made some shingles at home and some for Ammon Stevens and towards spring I worked in the lumber woods repairing roads.

That winter Almira worked for old Mr. Dorval at the Basfield bridge and I went and got her and took her to a donation at Ohio. It was in R. H. Wood's old house. I had to go around by Grant to get there and it was a fearful cold night. I stayed to breakfast with her and that was the last time I ever took her anywhere. I got home next day at night.

My little old log cabin in the lane or my bird cage, as some of the girls and boys termed it, had stood empty now most two years and early in the spring of 1854 my brother Julius, who now lived at Attica in Wyoming County, had been writing to me for a place to stay in through the summer, for he and his family wanted to come and visit and pass the summer away. So I let him the use of the house free and a garden spot and all the hemlock bark he could peel as I had some land on mine the fire had run over and the trees would die and the bark be spoilt so he and his family come down early in the spring.* They had only two children then, Lydia and George, and they were lively and full of mischief and when they got a going everything rattled. They went to school some that summer and my brother Julius enjoyed himself when not to work in the bark woods, catching trout, wading in the creek up to his arms. This was something new to him as he had never before lived on the banks of the old West Canada Creek and never had had such trout in his life.

Since I and Almira had had our falling out I had met another girl, or had known her for several years. It was another one of my old schoolmates, Elizabeth Flansburg. We seemed to take to each other as we got more acquainted. My brothers and sisters visited back and forth with her brothers and sisters and so we were great cronies all around. Mr. Ammon Stevens was her uncle. Her Aunt Mary Stevens was sick the last of the winter and Elizabeth was over there to work and so I called there quite frequently. I went there before frequently, for James and George and Henry and Will and Sarah were to home most always. Aunt Mary Stevens, as we always called her, was the best of company and Uncle Ammon was full of fun and jokes.

Well Elizabeth wanted to go home for something so I got a horse and cutter and took her home. Our bridge was gone then and we had to go around by Wilmurt Corners and out most to Ohio to get to her house. We had a good long pleasant ride and talked over the future prospects and the difficulties we had passed through, and before we got home again we were engaged for life if we both kept well and that sometime in the future we would get married. But she requested that I should not come

---

* The bark was used in the tanning of hides and, as Henry indicates at various times, was hauled to tanneries in the area.

160

to her house to see her much for she said her father was such an old tyrant he would kick her outdoors if he knew it. So we kept it quiet and whenever I did go there to see her I kept an eye on the old cuss and never dared to stay till twelve o'clock. I could see he had got a grudge against me someway and I kept mighty shy of him but her mother, brothers and sisters were alright. But Philo, he too like his father, had got a grudge against me and took every occasion to abuse me in public or anywhere else. Philo was the very essence of meanness and many a blow he gave Elizabeth.

So Elizabeth was now my best girl and her brother John my best chum. He was our mail carrier and many was the letter he brought me and carried an answer back to his sister. John and I were the best of friends and had always been and I loved John because I loved his sister, and I never had any doubts but that she loved me in return and would always be true, let what would come, but we were courting under difficulties.

We had another trysting place and that was to old Mum's Tripp's. She lived alone and had her cows and chickens and the place to look after. I used to work some for the old lady and so did Elizabeth. The old woman done the most of her own work only what some of the young folks did for her. Well, Elizabeth and I met here many times to enjoy a lovers' chat before the blazing fireplace and it seemed like the old time boy love in the long ago. The difference was I was no longer the boy.

That spring the old man drove Elizabeth out to work. She worked to Mr. Barker's at Cold Brook. Mr. Barker had a large family and come near working the girl to death. At the same time the old man would come and demand her wages to get tobacco and groceries with. After awhile she left and come home the work was so hard and then she went out in Norway to work for Mr. Carpenter on a dairy farm. We corresponded by letter all summer.

That summer I worked in Hinckley's lumber woods after helping James on the farm to get in the spring crop. They were lumbering then in the vicinity of Little Black Creek stillwater or between that and West Canada Creek. The last camp I worked in the fall was called the Godin Shanty. It was built on Little Black Creek below the stillwater.

During the summer my brother Julius and his wife Harriet had been teasing me to go home with them to Attica and stay all winter with them. So I finally consented and the last of November we went. My brother had sold the bark on the ground he had peeled and ranked.

This was the first time I had ever rode on the cars, and it was a new thing to me. I thought of the home I had left and the dear old place and all its familiar surroundings that I had known for so many years. I thought too of my dear old mother, father and brothers and sisters and my new and loving sweetheart and almost repented of going but I had said goodbye to them and turned my back on all that was dear and they would laugh at me if I did not go. So on I went with my brother and his family. We had a pleasant trip and got through all safe although I trembled sometimes when the cars shook us up, for the central [New York Central] did not run so smooth and easy as it does now.

When we got to Attica, Jerry Gilson, Julius' father-in-law, met us at the train with horses and wagon to take us to Vernal Corners where he lived, and what a pleasure it was to shake hands with him once more. I had not seen him since we left Tompkins Hollow in the Town of Fulton, Schoharie County. He greeted me with the same old loving smile as when I was a little boy. Mr. Gilson had grown old some, and his hair began to turn gray, but he had the same old sparkle in his eye and the same rosy cheeks as when he used to sing in those old revival meetings in the log schoolhouse on the hill.

Attica and its surrounding farms and orchards was not like the grand old forest I had left behind but it was a new world to me. Mr. Gilson was not long in driving up to Vernal Corners. It was quite a little hamlet then and I think it had a post office.* Mr. Gilson lived on one corner, Mr. Gordon on one, Mr. Mott on one and my brother Julius on the other, and there were several other dwellings extending each way, all occupied.

I made it my home that winter with brother Julius and had got among lots of good behaved young people and enjoyed their visits and parties and neighborhood entertainments and was a welcome guest at all their doings. The winter passed away very quick. I got acquainted with a good many of the young people and young ladies whose parents were quite well-to-do invited me to their homes and threw out their modest inducements for my company, but I was fireproof to their contrived allurements although they were beautiful, modest and becoming. None of them could compare (in my estimation) to the one dear "girl I had left behind me."

Mr. Gordon had two children at home, Henry and Melissa. I fell in love with Henry at first sight. He was about my age, blue eyes, red cheeks and auburn hair and so good that everyone loved him. Well, he was my chum and he and I were together the most of the time when not to work. Melissa was beautiful too but some other eyes were loving her and her heart was given away before she saw me.

That winter I worked some here and there helping

* The hamlet is cited as "Vernal" in J. H. French, *Gazetteer of the State of New York* (1860), p. 712.

Julius in his jobs about the place, threshing grain with a
flail and cutting wood for the Attica market. Towards
spring I went over to Mount Morris where my cousin
Benjamin Curtis lived. I had not seen him for several
years, not since he moved from the Town of Russia,
Herkimer County, and I had a good visit with them. My
cousin John Curtis was there too, he who was the cripple
and done the shoemaking. Cousin Benjamin had two

164

children, Lorenzo and Leovisa. I stayed over Sunday with them and we went to the Shaker meeting. I heard a good sermon and after preaching they marched and danced about an hour, men and women all together, but Cousin Ben said the men and women never spoke to each other. The women had their work and the men theirs and they were not allowed to marry, and if a husband and wife joined them they were forever debarred from sleeping together. But they were a true and honest sect, nobly acting out the true Christian character. Everything about their garments was clean and neat as wax and their church and dancing floor was almost white as chalk. A sort of marching of low sweet singing accompanied their dancing and I thought that was the way I would like to serve the Lord.

After I got back to Julius's I got a letter from my uncle Henry Curtis in Rock County, Wisconsin, and he wanted I should come out there. Henry Gordon was going to Wisconsin so I made it up to go when he did. He was going out there to work on a farm for some relative. So I settled with Julius, and Henry and I started. It was now about the tenth of March. We bought our tickets at Attica for Buffalo, and at Buffalo we got a through ticket. I was to get off at Footville, Wisconsin and Henry at Union, the second station beyond, so us two chums would be together the most of the way. We had our satchels and our lunch basket that we brought from home and ate as we rode. This was all new to me, traveling through the country on cars, and I looked over the country until my eyes ached as we flew over the prairies and through villages. We did not sleep much the first night and the next day we got so used to the cars we could ride and sleep, and we both got to sleep and lopped down against each other and something aroused me. I was awake and lay still with my eyes shut and I heard an old lady say opposite us, "See those two sleeping beauties. They must be twins."

The second day about noon the conductor called out "Next station is Union." We roused up and Henry says, "You have passed your stopping place while asleep." Well then I thought I would go with him and in a few minutes the conductor called "Union," and we got off, and on the cars went. We began to inquire of the people we wanted to find, but no one knew of any such men and after awhile we found we had got off at the Union in Illinois instead of the Union in Wisconsin. We were about a hundred miles behind. We had to put up with it and could not go on the cars until the next day at the same hour. Although we had our tickets in our pockets for the end of our journey we looked about the place a little and got tired of that, so to stretch our legs we took our satchels and walked down to the next village and stopped over night and the next day took the train and went on.

What a beautiful country we passed through going that hundred miles. To me it looked like the garden of the world with its green rolling prairies stretching for miles away on each side and then the groves of natural oak openings that formed a shelter from the storms for the farm houses.

It was almost four in the afternoon when I got near Footville where I was to get off and the minutes were drawing nigh when I and Henry should separate and he wanted I should go with him and stay over night and offered to pay my fare, but I like a fool declined and as the train stopped I bade him goodbye with a hearty grasp of the hand and that was our final farewell for I never seen him since. I stepped off the cars and on they went.

I says to myself now for a seven mile walk in a strange country and it was late in the afternoon. I took out Uncle

Henry's letter, for he had given me directions. North I was to go. I looked about the country but could not tell north from south. So I asked a man which way was north and said I wanted to go to Big Ball Tavern. He smiled and wanted to know if I was lost. Then he told me and I picked up my satchel and started over the prairie, following the wagon trail.

Oh what long miles. I kept going and going and the country looked alike all over. But I kept on the right road by inquiring of anyone I saw, and a little after dark I reached the Big Ball Tavern. I went in and rested a few minutes. I made inquiry for Henry Curtis and the landlord said go east on the road to the corner by the schoolhouse then turn north and to the second house. It was only half a mile so on I went and found the place alright.

They were up yet and I rapped on the door and Aunt Harriet opened it. I said good evening and said I had lost my way and wanted to stay over night. She asked Uncle Henry and he come to the door with the light and said they could not keep me for they had only one bed in the house. I looked them in the face but they did not know me. And then I says, "Now Uncle, you must keep me tonight. I will sleep on the floor."

They knew me then and yanked me inside the door and I thought they would eat me up they were so tickled. Well, Aunt Harriet was the same old fat good natured body and Uncle Henry the same long lean, crooked man, and I was right welcome and they told a story about the bed. I found it so too, for I never slept in a better one.

Well, we visited and talked quite late. I had not seen them since the fall of 1852 when we were out in Jefferson County visiting. Uncle Henry had several jobs on hand, cutting wood out of oak tops where the farmers had took the bodies away for lumber. There were three kinds of oak here, the burr, the white and the red oak.

The burr grew quite scrubby and the white and the red grew long and quite tall and smooth. The shell bark hickory also grew here and the bark would burn like pitch pine and we used to get it for torches when we went to spear suckers in the outlet of the lake that spring.

**16**  I HAD again got into a neighborhood of nice young people and Uncle and Aunt gave me an introduction to them. Their winter school was not closed yet and they were preparing for an exhibition the last day. I was invited to take part in the drama. I went several evenings and practiced with them and acted a part in several pieces. I procured one of Uncle's old fashion suits, small leg pants, swallow tail coat and crumpled tall white hat and a false face and a cane. I spoke the piece of the old soldier which begins, "In manhood's morn I left my home to fight a country's foe," and when I come to the last verse which reads, "Then let a poor old soldier crave a morsel of your bread, a soldier hastening to the grave to join the slumbering dead," just then someway my hat and wig fell off and there was quite a roar of laughter. Well, little did I think then that I should ever realize I had been a soldier and in reality have the occasion to say, "Then let a poor old soldier crave a morsel of your bread."

I helped Uncle Henry about two weeks at his jobs and gave him the proceeds of the work. I had a little money left that I had taken from home. In about two weeks Uncle Henry moved about one mile west of Big Ball Tavern in one part of a house owned by a Mr. Webb whose son Julius and wife were going to California the overland route, and Uncle Henry was to look after the farm and the old couple.

After Uncle got settled I got a chance to work at the carpenter's trade to aid in building a barn for a farmer. I got one dollar a day and board. I worked two weeks at this, and then I helped a man do some breaking. They had three yoke of oxen on a great big plow and were breaking a piece down by the marsh. It was, near the marsh, all cradle knolls and oak bushes. The man wanted I should drive the oxen. I told him I did not know how but would try it. So I took the whip and started them up and they went alright to the corner and in coming around in some way got them tangled up, and it was, "Whoa, haw, buck, go where you are a mind to." I gave up in disgust and he took the whip and I took the plow handles and everything went off right. This marsh was called the Eleven Mile Marsh and was from one half to two miles wide and in the middle was water and mud, and around the edges it was all cradle knolls that the ants had thrown up advancing towards the middle as their work had dried up the water. Those farmers who owned any of this land found it to produce far better crops than the upland prairie.

The Big Ball Tavern was on the road leading from Jamesville to Evansville. It was twelve miles west of Jamesville and five miles east of Evansville. This was the main road for emigrants going west and all the while that spring hundreds of them passed going west to new homes. As I said, Mr. Webb was going to California. He wanted me to go along and offered to board me all the way through, but I would have to carry a gun across the plains and act as sentinel with the others as there were about fifteen different families going. But I told him I did not want to go for I thought of my poor old mother at home and brother Abiah who the year before found a grave in the ocean trying to seek the land of gold, and I was afraid my bones would lie bleaching on the plains and this would kill my poor old mother and blast the hopes of the girl I had left behind me. So I chose to go east instead of west.

The prairies were now covered with beautiful flowers and in answering letters I had got from Elizabeth I enclosed the most beautiful specimens. While there with my uncle that spring he and I and Julius Webb went to spear suckers at a lake about two miles northeast. As we went along through the woods we gathered a lot of shell bark, hickory bark, and made two long torches. The lake was about one mile long and half a mile wide and the suckers run down the outlet to spawn. The outlet was sandy and smooth bottom and for a long ways it was about twenty feet wide and along the sides were bogs of prairie grass. It was arranged that Webb was to do the spearing and Uncle and I hold the torches. We stood about twenty feet apart with Webb between us and when all was ready we lit the torches and took our positions. When the light flashed over water, what a sight, the bottom was covered and Webb went at them and it was pitch and throw, and as he threw them off the spear behind, their tails fairly snapped, and how this tickled Uncle Henry, and he says, "There they go, kitch 'em, there they go, kitch 'em." About this time he was so anxious to see the fun he leaned over too much and slipped off the bog and fell in the water, knee deep, putting out his light and before our laugh was over and his light in trim again the fish had all run back in the lake. But we had enough for a good mess and went home, but I never shall forget how Uncle Henry looked leaning over the water with the torch, his back bent down and his legs looking like a crane, and Aunt Harriet hectored him most to death about it, and afterwards nicknamed him *Pickerbum.*

Shortly after this another fellow and I started for the Wisconsin pineries, going north by stage up through the Fox River country and for sixty or seventy miles went through a beautiful rich farming country of rolling prairies and oak openings, but after we got further along we came to low ground along the Fox River Valley. On beyond, it was all sand, red sand and white sand and red earth banks with now and then a few stunted scrubby pines and white birch or something resembling birch. Along through this country were but few settlers then and they looked as though they had had the fever and ague all their lives.

The stage coach was full of men going back from the drive, for they were raftsmen and had went down the Wisconsin River to St. Louis with rafts of lumber and I heard them tell of their narrow escapes as they went down the river through the Wisconsin Dells.

Stevens Point on the Wisconsin River was the end of the stage route and we were three days getting there. In the forenoon of the third day we crossed a sandy desert of eleven miles and the sand in the wagon tracks was so loose and deep the axle-trees almost dragged on the ground. On each side of the road, as far as the eye could reach, it was drifts of sand, low stunted scrub oaks, ferns and brambles. Nearly in the center of this desert the driver pointed out to us away off to the right the love rock, as they called it, and said it was about fifty feet in diameter and sixty feet high, and from where we were it was a rough jagged looking object standing there alone and no other rocks or stones within miles of it.

Between this desert and Stevens Point was some fair looking farms but quite sandy. At the end of the third day we landed at Stevens Point having stayed at hotels two nights on the way, whose beds were filled to overflowing with raftsmen, bedbugs and fleas. At one tavern I slept up in the attic and after I had got to bed someone crawled in with me and got out again before daylight, so I did not know whether he was black or white.

Stevens Point was then a small place. One tavern, one store, one tinshop, one blacksmith shop, a schoolhouse but no church, as I remember, and a land office and about twenty-five dwelling houses.

I thought of going in the pineries when I left Uncle's but run across a carpenter by the name of John Mary who wanted to hire. I made a bargain with him for twenty dollars per month as long as we could agree. So I went to work the next day. Mary was a clever sort of chap but drinking some and knew how to shirk when at work by the day but it was hustle at the job.* He lived in the east part of the village and had a wife and two little children. They were building a new land office that summer and we worked at that quite awhile until finished or nearly so, and then we built a new tin shop for a man by the name of White next to the store.

There was a dam here twelve feet high across the river and it set water back thirty miles. A steamboat ran from here up to the rapids and carried freight, passengers and the mails. There was a chute in the dam for rafts to pass over and when there was high water the river was full of rafts of lumber in sections of ten or twelve cribs

* In other words, when Mary was paid a lump sum for a single task, he worked rapidly; but when he was paid a guaranteed daily wage, he was less concerned about production.

and the middle ones were loaded with pine shingles.

The raftsmen used to have fun with the Indians and get a lot of them on the rafts and when they went over the chutes they would whoop and yell and toss up their blankets, but their yell was soon stopped when the water and foam dashed over them at the lower end of the chute as they come to the rough water in the river below. But when the rafts tied up a little further down they would come back and try it over again. It was fun to see them.

There were a great many Indians then living in the vicinity of Stevens Point and the squaws brought their truck to market, such as venison, fish, partridges, pigeons, wild ducks, herbs, medicinal roots, and wild berries. The squaws had it all to do while the Indian would strut about in his gay attire, feathers, and paint, and do nothing, and when the squaws had sold the truck they would pocket the money and buy whiskey and ammunition with the most of it. They were a lazy, indolent, thieving set. The squaws brought their papooses on their back strapped on a board and when in the store or the dwellings they would set them up against a fence or the house outside. The young Indians and squaws were poorly clad and some were almost naked. One day I was taking my nooning in the store and a young Indian lad came in almost naked and one of the clerks measured off two yards of bright calico and cut a hole in the middle for his head and two more in the side for his arms and then tied a red ribbon about his waist. A prouder Indian you never saw as he strutted about the village in this comical dress making fun for everyone. There was not scarcely a day all summer but what they were around begging for something to eat or wear and when any ladies of the village gave the squaws any cast off dresses, they would put them on then and there over their other suit. The village witnessed many a comical scene.

I worked for Mary nearly two months and a half but could never get any money of him, only promises, and he put me off from time to time until such a job was done. Finally I got sick with the intermitting fever without the ague. It was caused by poor water and after I had been sick most two weeks and did not get much better I concluded I would leave Mary and as I could not get any money of him I asked him for an order to go to the store and get some clothes and boots and he said alright and went over to the store with me and told them to let me get what I wanted and have it charged to him.

This was what I wanted and I got me a good nice suit throughout and a pair of boots also. He owed me about fifty dollars and I traded nearly thirty and made up my mind this was all I would ever get of him. I took my bundle of new clothes and stepped over to Mr. White's, the tin man, and changed my clothes, putting on the whole new suit and doing up the suit I had taken off.

Mr. White wanted to know what was up and I told him I was going to leave Mary as I could not get any money of him. I was on good terms with Mr. White and wife and daughter Mary. Mr. White wanted I should stay with him and learn the tinner's trade and said he thought I could always agree with him and his whole family and was welcome to stay with them as long as I lived. But I courteously declined although his daughter Mary was all that any young man could ask for beauty, good behaviour, intelligence and virtue. She was lavishly endowed by nature and educated under the care of a Christian father and mother. But reader, how could I accept any such offer since I had given my promise to one I dearly loved down in York State?

I bade Mr. White and family goodbye and went over to Mary's, packed my things in my satchel, and started southward. Mrs. Mary and children were surprised to see me so dressed up and did not want me to leave but I told her Mary had not paid me a cent of money and I would not stay any longer. I further told her that her husband was welcome to what was back as I never should come after it. I had been good and kind to them while there but had not been used very well by them for I had to sleep in a little bedroom near the stove all summer and the bedbugs and fleas got so bad I had to take a quilt and go out in the shop and sleep on a work bench. I think of all the places where I ever was that Stevens Point beat all for bugs and fleas.

I bade them goodbye and as I started out I went by the Land Office where Mary was to work but he did not know me although he was looking at me when I passed. So on I went but was in no trim to do much tramping for I had been sick two weeks with the fever, and now dear reader you may call me a tramp on this journey for the most of my money I had left when I got to Stevens Point I had spent for writing material and stamps to send home letters.

I got along about half a mile, and a man with a horse and wagon overtook me and invited me to ride, so like a tramp that is beating his way I accepted. He proved to be a very nice gentleman and had been up to the land office to prove his claim. He lived south of there about twenty miles and as it was the way I was going I considered myself lucky and he proved the good Samaritan and kept me over night and treated me to supper, lodging, and breakfast, and would take nothing for it. He wished me good luck and prosperity as I bade him goodbye and trudged on with my satchel hung on a stick over my shoulder.

I traveled all that day and did not get a chance to ride. At noon I called at the house of a new settler and got a bowl of bread and milk for which I paid ten cents. On I went and nearly night I passed by a tavern but concluded not to stop, for I had only fifty cents left. I went on through a lonely woods looking for some farm house and at last I came to a clearing where lived a new settler. A man and his wife and the hired man. They had a very small house and when I asked for the privilege to stay over night with them they looked at me and my satchel so suspiciously that I was almost sorry I had made the request, but they finally said I could stay. The woman got me a dish of bread and milk—a tramp's supper.

When I went in the house I threw my old satchel down in the corner and thought if they robbed it they would find no money and nothing but an old suit of clothes. Before we retired for the night the man read a chapter in the Bible and he and his wife knelt down and prayed, but the hired man kept an eye on me and when we went to bed I slept with him in the hind side of the bed. But their suspicious looks kept me awake most all night. The next morning they questioned me quite sharply and I answered all their questions to their satisfaction. I asked them what the damage was and they said fifty cents and as I handed it out to them my heart almost sank within me for it was the last. My purse was empty.

I bade them goodbye and as I started the woman gave me a lunch of bread and butter. After I got thinking of it on the way I thought they had searched my satchel and clothes for money and when I got along in a piece of woods I looked in my satchel and it had all been over-hauled but there was nothing missing. Then I thought their reading the Bible was all a cloak.

The lunch came in very good as it helped me along the way but how was I to get the hundred and thirty miles yet to be traversed to get to Uncle Henry Curtis's. I had a good watch and this would have to go when I got to a place called Watertown only a few miles ahead. The cars run from there to Jaynesville but riding on the cars cost money. If I had been a tramp of 1890 I could have solved the problem some way.

There was no other way, the watch must go. When nearly dark and tired and hungry and nearly worn out I arrived in the village of Watertown and sought out the only watch tinker in the place. He was a fine looking man and as I stated my case to him I told him I had been to work for a man and he had cheated me out of my pay and I was sick and trying to get to friends down in Rock County who would help me. I was tired and hungry and had no money to stay over night and offered him my watch and he looked at it. I said it had cost me ten dollars. "Well," he says, "I don't dispute your story, for your looks show you have told the truth. But I cannot give you ten dollars, for I am selling watches just like it for six." He said he would give that for it and give me a cool glass of lemonade and a good supper and go over with me to the tavern and find me a place to stay over night.

I took up with his offer and handed over the watch and he paid me the six dollars and among the change was a gold dollar, and as I looked at the little yellow piece I thought to myself I will hang on to that at all events. This man also kept a lunch room and we went in there and I had an ice cool glass of lemonade and then a hearty supper. Then he went with me over to the tavern where I stayed over night. My lodging and breakfast I had to pay for out of the six dollars and in the morning after I had paid for my ticket to Jaynesville I had the gold dollar left and ten cents besides. That morning after I had got on the cars I felt much better although it was a rough railroad and jolted me up some. It was not like playing the tramp going through the country begging with an old carpet bag full of old clothes.

I landed in Jaynesville about four o'clock in the afternoon with a dollar and ten cents in my pocket. I was yet twelve miles from Uncle's. I sat down in the depot a few minutes thinking what to do. I made some inquiries if there were any teams in town going west to the Big Ball Tavern. They said there had been some there that day but had all gone. So I said I would go too and started going by a grocers where I got ten cents worth of crackers leaving my gold dollar alone in my purse.

I had heard my uncle say he lived almost directly west of Jaynesville. I had never been there before and the surroundings were new to me but I took my old carpet bag and started towards the setting sun which was sinking in the west. For quite a long ways out of the village it was thickly settled and after I got beyond this I slung my satchel on a stick over my shoulder and went to crunching at my crackers, for I was hungry. I walked along quite fast at first but soon got weary and took it slow and began to consider what to do. As the old tramp saying is, "I was so hungry I did not know where I should stay that night," for I was quite sure I could not reach my uncle's that night, but on I trudged passing many fine farms and nice dwellings whose occupants were busy doing the chores for the night.

I made some inquiries and found I was on the right road yet but they said there was no tavern for six miles yet. I thought I would find a farm house to put up at when it came dark, but then I thought my gold dollar would have to go and I was too proud to beg even if I was a tramp. So when it was getting dark I plucked up courage and thought I could walk through yet. So on I went. A little after dark I came to two roads running almost the same way but diverging as they went. Now I was in a quandry and looked for the north star and decided to take the left hand road which led the most directly west and on I went for a mile or two and I discovered I was going too much south and must inquire or stop somewhere for I was almost played out. So the next farm house I came to they had been threshing wheat and near by was some large stacks of straw. A splendid place for a tramp to rest and as I turned in to seek a place of rest a great big dog come after me and I decided to let the straw alone and went on and when I got further on I got over in the wheat field and concluded I would camp for the night. I laid one shock down on the ground for a bed and gathered up enough to make me quite a camp, setting them up around and covering some over the top. Then I crawled in one end and set a bundle up at the hole and laid my old dingy carpet bag down for a pillow and laid down to rest, thinking over, "Now I lay me down to sleep etc." It was a good refreshing sleep and what a consolation there was no bedbugs or fleas for me to crush in my fingers or fleas for me to clutch in vain for. I was soon lost in sweet slumber such as I had not had for weeks and when I awoke next morning refreshed the sun was shining in through the bundles of wheat. I heard the threshers up at the stacks giving their orders to their workmen and I hustled out of my nest and flung the bundles right and left. In doing so a great long snake ran out from under my nest and darted away. I was just then too much taken up with something else to pursue him and I grabbed my pillow, the old carpet bag, and hastened to the road.

I soon got to the road and come along by a little brook. I call it a brook but up in the Adirondacks it would be termed a slew hole. That water scarcely ran but it was quite cool in the autumn morning. Here I stopped and washed my face and hands and combed my hair and took out my pocket looking glass and found I was looking quite well. After eating the rest of my crackers and brushing

the wheat heads off my clothes I concluded I would pass
for quite a good looking tramp. On I went and soon met
a rosy looking lad driving some cows and I made inquiries
of him and found I had taken the wrong road and must go
to the next turn and then go northwest until I struck the
first road. I was yet most five miles from Uncle's but I

felt so refreshed I was not long in going the rest of the way and about ten o'clock I got to the end of my tramp.

I was at home again or the place I called home while in Wisconsin. Uncle and Aunt were glad to see me and had been expecting me for a long time. In a few days I was well enough to work and the first work I done I cut twenty cord of wood for old Mr. Webb out of oak tops and he gave me fifty cents per cord and boarded me.

I had now decided to go home to York State as soon as I got money enough, for I was tired of tramping and depending on strangers for work. So I wrote home I would start in two weeks, and during the two weeks I got some more work at threshing about the neighborhood and thought I had money enough to take me to Attica if I was saving. So at the appointed time I started bidding my Uncle and Aunt goodbye and farewell, for this was the last I ever saw them.

My Uncle and Aunt had been like a father and mother to me. Our parting shake was given in hopes of meeting again some time, but alas we never did. They moved about from place to place and finally got back to Theresa, Jefferson County, New York, and from there to Cattaraugus County where they both died long ago. My good old aunt had occupied all the spare room I had in my old carpet bag with a lunch big enough to take me back to New York State she said.

I had seven miles to walk that morning to get to Foot-ville but I now knew the way and there was no danger of getting lost, but I came near being left. When I got most to the depot the cars were starting and I run and grabbed on while they were going. I caught the railing in the steps all right and jumped, but my confounded old carpetbag swung around and threw my feet off and I hung with one hand and my feet dangling under the cars. Just then the conductor came to my rescue and grabbed my collar and pulled me in, carpetbag and all. I thought I was gone sure and my whole life seemed to come before me in a minute. "Well," the conductor says, "Young man you have run a narrow chance. Don't never try to get on the cars again while they are in motion." A lesson I have always heeded ever since.

I had no time to get my ticket at the depot so I had to get it off the conductor. I bought my ticket to Detroit and it cost more than I expected but the conductor said I could take the boat at Detroit and it would be cheaper and told me what it would cost. While on the way to Detroit I counted my money and after finding how much I had I would have to let my gold dollar go anyway for sure now.

When I got to Detroit I went where they sold tickets to go by the steamer and bought my ticket to Buffalo taking a steerage passage, the poorest and cheapest passage, but I had one consolation, if the rest got there I could, and I could stand it one night to lay on a bench.

We started from Detroit at eight o'clock in the morning and all that day until almost night the lake was terrible rough. They had a drove of cattle on the lower deck and the men who had care of them had to stay amongst them and keep prodding them with sharp sticks from side to side to keep the boat in trim. The hands who belonged on the boat also had to roll barrels of water from side to side. The wind blew so and the waves sometimes would dash over the deck where the cattle were. When it came night the lake was more smooth. I went down in the steerage and tried to sleep on the benches the same as the other steerage passengers did, but I could not sleep for fear of rolling off the benches. And then the bilge water from beneath was enough to make a horse vomit. I came on deck again and walked about the decks until near morning, when I lay down on a pile of baggage and boxes with my carpet bag for a pillow and went to sleep. When I waked up it was broad daylight and the passengers were all up and walking about the decks. We landed in Buffalo at nine a.m. and I was right glad to get off the old stinking boat.

When I got to the railroad depot I counted my money again but did not have enough to take me to Attica, but by walking to Lancaster I then could get a ticket to Attica. So I shouldered my old carpetbag once more and counted the ties to Lancaster and the first train east I jumped aboard for Attica. I come down into Attica flying just as though I had had a thousand dollars in my pocket, when in fact I did not have enough to buy a postage stamp. I had eaten the last of my lunch while walking from Buffalo to Lancaster and was not very hungry. So I shouldered the old carpetbag again and wended my way east out through the village and up towards Vernal Corners.

Mr. Gilson and brother Julius had moved the spring before, after I had went west, over southwest from Vernal but exactly where I did not know. So when I got up to the first schoolhouse from Attica I inquired for them and found I must go directly south over the hills about two miles and I would find them. Well, I sauntered along slowly, eating my fill of good mellow apples that were wasting by the hundreds of bushels along the road, and at supper time I arrived at my brother's and was welcomed once more to their humble hospitality, but I dared not tell them how poor I was for fear they would laugh at me.

I was once more with friends and relatives but was indeed down low in poverty's vale, not a penny in my pocket. I wanted to write home to brother James and mother and my sweetheart but I was too proud to beg a stamp or borrow for fear they would find out how poor I was, and so it was "Pride and Poverty" with me.

But here again I met my old and tried friends, Mr. Jerry Gilson and family, for they lived close by my brother Julius and here too I met two more of my old schoolmates. They were George Fulington and his wife Debby. One of Jerry Gilson's girls. They had been my classmates and playmates in the long ago in the old schoolhouse on the hill by the grove and to greet them here seemed like a dream of the long past.

Mr. Gilson said I was just in time as he had a lot of buckwheat to thresh and would give me seventy-five cents a day and all the cider I could drink and he would board me by filling me up with apples. The next day we went at it. George Fulington, Julius and I with flails and Jerry drawing it in for us as fast as we could thresh it and we had a pitcher of cider in the side of the hay mow and apples, all we could eat. But they did not stop our hunger, for we could eat at the table like ravenous wolves.

This of course was a help to me but it only lasted three days and I would not get my pay until I was ready to start home. I got some more work with Julius and George and in about ten days I had earned enough to take me to Utica and I told them I must go. So Mr. Gilson and the other men paid me and I bade my brother's, Mr. Gilson's and Fulington's folks goodbye and again shouldered the old carpet sack and started for home sweet home, the dear old home I had been dreaming of for the last month. . . .

I was not long in getting down to Attica where I bought my ticket to Utica and got aboard the eight o'clock train and was soon whirring towards the east as fast as the central could carry me, which I thought was a slow rate. When they stopped for only a few minutes it seemed hours to me. The central did not run as fast then as now and the trains had to stop a good many times before we got to Utica. When we arrived there it was eleven o'clock at night.

184

Then what to do I did not know and at first I thought I would go up in the city to a hotel and stay till morning. So I took a tramp up in the city a little ways but being a stranger did not know where the hotels were and then I thought too they must all be shut up by that time. I got as far as the canal bridge and didn't find any tavern. So I stopped and considered what to do. The moon was just rising and it was a clear night and I quickly decided I would hoof it home and not go to bed that night. So I clutched onto the old carpetbag and started down the street and over the Mohawk River bridge through Deerfield and over the hills north towards home. It was a bright moonlight night and just cool enough for a walk.

The roads too were good and everything was quiet along the way. I came through Graves Hollow and up through by Russia Corners and Pardeeville and when I got here it was getting daylight, but on I went and when I got within about three miles of home I met my brother James going to the post office with a letter to mail to Attica with inquiries concerning me. After our greetings I told him I had come to answer the letter. Our folks at home, not hearing from me, had written to Uncle Henry up in Wisconsin and he wrote back I had gone home and so they thought I was lost or dead.

James turned about and we went back home where I greeted the dear ones I had not seen for most a year and the old home, although an old log house, seemed dearer to me than it had ever been before. At times I had been as hard up as the prodigal son and had been hungry enough at times to eat corn husks if I could have got them. All the difference between me and the prodigal son was I had not spent my money in riotous living, but had spent it for railroad tickets and clothing.

I had two dollars left when I got home and had spent all my year's wages and forty dollars besides that I took with me when I left home. But after all I did not regret it for I considered it all in my lifetime and I was entirely my own boss. And if there was any value in experience, I had got my money's worth. The greetings and handshakes were a thrilling pleasure to receive from those who I had mingled with in the years before and if I had stayed at home I never would have known how valuable was the friendship of those I had not seen for only one short year, and what must the greetings be after a lifetime to meet with those who are over in the eternal home, where dear ones are watching and waiting for me beyond the portals of time, beyond the dark river, beyond the waves of death over by the Jasper sea.

17 HOME again, home again to enjoy the pleasure of mingling with those dear ones who had clung to me from my earliest existence to the present time. No bitter reproaches, no complaints, no bickerings, no turning the cold shoulder did I ever receive from mother, father, brothers or sisters. Oh the sweet contentment of home, and when I retired to rest in the chamber overhead, my bed was still in the same place where I could lay and reach the rafters and roof boards with my hands and hear the patter of the rain on the roof soothing me to a slumber and sweet repose. Oh blessed humble home sweet home.

There had been quite a good many changes while I was gone. Some neighbors had moved away and other people had moved into the neighborhood. I will go back to the fifteenth of April, 1855, and record another marriage in the family. This time it was Casandana, our little fairy as we called her in the story of long ago, and now she had grown to be a woman and a blushing bride. But not a very large one for strangers sometimes called her "sis."

Francis Flansburg had carried her off bodily and she was presiding over their humble home up in the Town of Wilmurt. Frank, as I shall now call him, had been courting her (that is the fairy) for several years and in the meantime working out among the farmers in Norway and also for the lumber company of Hinckley and Ballou, carefully saving his wages. Before he was married he had bought the west half of subdivision fifteen, Remsenburg patent and when I come home from the west I found them living on their place in an old log house that had been built several years. They were not rich but had their place paid for and so I considered they were out of poverty's vale. Our sister Cassie had got a good home, a good husband and was out of the wilderness of want, and they both were surrounded by loving relatives and friends on both sides. There they have lived until now, having built a new house and two barns and cleared up the farm. Here have been born and reared their children and here the grandchildren also now come to visit them as they are quietly and peacefully enjoying the good things of this life they have accumulated by a life of honest toil and sweet contentment.

And it was here at their home I again greeted my sweetheart Elizabeth on my return from the west, and now I had a double reason to spark her, for Frank had got my sister and I thought it only fair play to take Elizabeth. I did not venture very often over to her house to see her for her father was cruel and tyrannical to her, and to save her from his tyrannical meanness I kept away as much as possible, yet I did venture there sometimes under the pretext of visiting with the boys and Elizabeth's mother, Aunt Amy as we always called her. She was one of the best of mothers and had always been an old drudge to Old Bat as the whole family styled him. None of them ever had any love for their father.

Sometime in the spring of 1855 my brother Sammy moved over the creek in the Town of Wilmurt and located on subdivision sixteen next to the lot west of Frank Flansburg. (It is the lot I own now.) There was a little log house on the lot but after my brother come there he built a log barn and here he lived several years, clearing land and peeling hemlock bark. He was doing very well and making a good living and his wife Jammy was neat and saving and a good housekeeper. That is one of the most essential parts of the advancement to prosperity. Still they were in the vale of poverty.

My brother John and his family came back from Vermont that fall looking for a place to locate. They now had three children, Francis, Edwin and Hattie. Dear old brother John was in the meshes of poverty and so poor they were not decently clothed and the children in rags and so was John, but his wife Mary was togged out with gewgaws and ribbons. Well, he had nothing left to begin with, not even an axe, no furniture, for that they had sold to get money to move with. He looked around a little and finally decided to squat on subdivision fourteen. It is yet called the John lot.

The neighborhood got together one day and went to work cutting and hauling logs and put him up a log house. Some brought nails, some lumber, and some shingles and before night we had it nearly completed. Then it was corked up with moss and in a few days he moved into

188

it and his furniture was given him by the relatives and
neighbors as a donation. He lived from hand to mouth
and while the neighbors and relatives gave freely and
helped John to work to earn something his wife was
wasteful and negligent and had no knack of being neat
or saving.

One Sunday afternoon late that fall I went over to see
Elizabeth, and as I went past Mr. Farnicrook's, Alida
came out to the road to have a little chat with me and I

thought it nothing out of character as we had been old schoolmates the same as Elizabeth was. She says, "You better not go to Bat's to see Lib for you will be turned out of doors and you better stay here." But I said I would go on anyway and see about it, so I went on and was welcomed by all with a handshake except the old man and he looked awful grouty at me but I did not stay any longer than twelve o'clock. We made it up that night to not spark it any later than twelve thereafter in order to keep peace with the old *gentleman*. They lived in a log house with one big room and two bedrooms below, and the chamber was all in one room. Lib's sister Hattie peeked down through the cracks when we were sparking. That night we talked in whispers and as the clock was striking twelve I snatched a kiss and bade her goodbye and good night and dusted for over the creek. On my way I got a glimpse of some wolves chasing a deer acrost the road. I thought I was a goner for sure but they passed on towards the West Canada Creek one way and I ran on the other way.

In the winter of 1855 and 1856 I made shingles on shares for my brother James. I helped him get the timber and he boarded me and give me one half and I made a good winter's work. My brother James was drawing tan bark to the Pardeeville tannery and we had a splendid winter for teaming. Father did not go on the road teaming anymore and my brother James stood the brunt of the hard labor and done the planning and calculating. We were making a good living and did not lack for the necessities of life.

My youngest sister Rinda was now eleven years old and a good scholar and well behaved. She too was good looking, rosy cheeks, black hair and sparkling black eyes and her sister Amy sometimes would torment her to see her eyes snap. Many a time Rinda would chase her with the broom or poker and pelt her until she would beg. I think Rinda was more sensitive than any of the rest of the family and yet we all loved her. It was all school with her.

We had our meetings yet and that fall and winter there had been a revival at Ohio and frequently when it was good going a load of us would go over to meeting. I counted myself still on the Lord's side and loved the meetings as well as ever. I was then a member of the Methodist church and thought there was nothing like the Methodist, yet I respected all denominations. On New Year's Eve 1856 there was a watch meeting at Ohio. (They had now got a new church.) My brother James went with his team with bobs and bark rack.* The sleighing was good and he began to pick people up when he started, and all along the way they piled in, and before we got to Ohio there was over forty in the load. We had a speaking and singing meeting on the way and everyone who belonged to the meeting gave in their testimony on the Lord's side and to top it off with, Spencer Wilkins Jr. gave us a thrilling exhortation. The singing was glorious, for they all sung and as the notes of those glorious revival songs rang out on the clear midwinter evening it could have been heard for miles around. How it sent a soul stirring thrill through the believer's heart and at the same time it was music in the sinner's ears.

That night in the Ohio church we watched the old year out and the new year in and on the way home we had a singing meeting. How many times have I looked back over this one hallowed night. At peace with God, at peace with man and no cankering care—all was calm and sweet as the days and years flew by.

Sometime in the fore part of January, 1856 Philo Flans-

* That is, James had replaced the wagon wheels with two sets of bobs—double runners, as on a bob sled. The racks, which enabled him to increase the wagon's carrying capacity, were left in place.

burg got up an oyster supper and had it over the creek down at Hinckley's lumber depot. There was a family living there but the company did not use the building. They might have had it over in their own neighborhood but Philo done this to spite Elizabeth his sister and John his brother, and me also and my brother James and our sisters, for they had to come right by our door to get down there. As they came past they were all singing. Well, I suppose they had a good time but the next day there was a song out about it and it did not set very well on Philo's crop. Uncle Bat (that is, Philo's father) was up in end about it also and these two meddlesome creatures after that pursued Elizabeth and me with renewed vengeance, and Philo, to show out his evil nature, began to write letters of insinuating meanness. Almost every day he would send over some of his obscene literature. Philo and his father were teaming at something over the creek that winter. We (that is James and me) watered our cattle down by the bridge and I was there one morning as old Bat came along and handed me a letter and stopped to see me read it. I saw it was Philo's handwriting and I stuck it under the water without opening it right before the old man's face and that was the last letter I ever got from Philo.

John Flansburg and Elizabeth were over the creek that winter quite frequently at Frank's and our house and sometimes up to Uncle Ammon Stevens's. One time Elizabeth was over to her brother Frank's, and I and her started to go to a donation up to Ohio. It was good sleighing and we were with a horse and cutter, and when we got most to the Hane's hill all at once the horse ran out of the thills and left us sitting there in the cutter. The harness also was left behind, all but the collar, headstall and lines. The hame strap had broke and the horse slid out of the harness. Well, it was laughable and we were glad it was in the night. I soon stopped the horse and toggled up the harness and went on. We also went on with our sparking.

At the donation I and Elizabeth met my adopted sister Almira Conkling and what friendly greeting to us both, and that night after the tables were cleared away us three were walking about the room singing some of our old sentimental songs, arm in arm, for I had one on each arm, and when I looked at Elizabeth I thought she looked the best and then when I looked in Almira's face I thought she too looked the best. So I was in a quandry. I concluded I loved them both but could have only one of them. Elizabeth was now my affianced and Almira our sister and when the donation was over and we got ready to come home we bid Almira goodbye and that was the last time we saw her for years, for that spring she got married to Alfred Parks of Grant and went away up to Mankato, Minnesota, to live. Almira had made it her home to Dr. Wiggins of Grant since she and I had the falling out and she had been teaching school summers. She lived here when she got married to Parks.

When the creek broke up that spring the logs and ice took our bridge away so that ended our visiting back and forth so much, and there was a little less sparking also, yet we had a way over the difficulty. Our common byword then when we met was "What's the Program?" So we established a program line. John and Elizabeth would come to the abutment on the south side of the creek and I and my sister Amy on the north side, and with pencil we would write a message and tie it fast to a small stone. This I would throw over and they would read it and send an answer back the same way, and thus it went, the same string and the same stone carrying love and fun over the foaming and dashing waters of the West Canada Creek.

One day in April when the snow was most gone they come down again and the first message Elizabeth sent over was that she had hired out to Frank and Henry Stanton out to Russia Corners and was going the next day and that she had come down to bid us goodbye. As the stone went back whirring over the water it carried our goodbye and well wishes over to them, and a wave of the handkerchief as we turned to leave was our parting salute.

That spring, the ninth of April, 1856, Uncle Ammon Stevens and Aunt Mary Stevens and their sons Henry and Wilson bade their friends and the Town of Wilmurt goodbye and started for Illinois. Their daughter Sarah had married Dormer Phelps a few years before and they had moved to Illinois, so the folks had to go too.

James and George were young men then and lived here with the old folks working out summers and staying at home winters. But the boys did not want to go with their father and mother. This did not set very good on the old folks and they went off rather mad at the boys and to show their displeasure towards them they took everything but one old straw tick, one quilt, an old cast off stove and two knives and forks. I was there when they went and helped them pack up. My brother James took them to the depot in the night while the road was froze. They went with a sleigh.

I stayed till morning with the boys and we had to use shingles for plates and pass the knives around to one another. After the old folks were gone and the boys saw how their father and mother had stripped them of everything, they sat down and cried like babies. It was too bad, after the boys had done so much for them. But they soon rallied and in a few days had got things to keep house with of their own. I stayed with them a good many nights that spring. They lived here alone almost a year, and before the year was up the old folks sent to the boys for money.

But the boys never sent them any, to my knowledge. Uncle and Aunt were always kind and good neighbors, but always wanted everything that James and George earned.

18 ANOTHER new neighbor had moved in the neighborhood early in 1856 and that was Chauncey Potter's family that lived at Ohio when we lived in the old log schoolhouse. They moved on the depot lot on the north side of the creek. They had bought it of the lumber company of Hinckley and Ballou. They had a large family and at that time were all at home. I will name them, as some of them are connected with this story and act the part of heroes and heroines. Chauncey and Margaret, or "Old Mag" as some called her, were the parents and the children were Katharine, John, Hiram, Elizabeth, Mary-Jane, George, Esther and William.

Well, here on this place they all went to work clearing land, peeling tan bark, Mag and the girls working outdoors too, helping the men. I tell you they were the music of the neighborhood, always full of fun and good nature and ever ready to do a kindness. Old Mag especially was the staff of our little neighborhood in sickness and distress at all times far and near. People in sickness and trouble was always glad to see Mag come. John worked out most of the time at the carpenter's trade.

I worked on my place that spring putting up fences and got in some spring crops for I expected by fall I would need some potatoes anyway if I got Elizabeth. After the spring work was done, father and I hewed some timber and framed it and put up a barn for little Sammy, and he finished it off himself. When we got done for Sammy I went to work for Frank Flansburg building him a barn also and we raised it on the fourth of July. The whole neighborhood was there from far and near, the girls included, and we had lots of fun and a splendid time. Mr. Stanton's folks had brought Elizabeth home for a few days visit and she was over to Frank's too. This suited me for I could spark and work also.

The next day a whole load of us went up to Noblesboro for a picnic. We went strolling all over those old clearings gathering strawberries, and when we ate our lunch we had strawberry lemonade. My brother James, sister Amy and Rinda, Cassie and Frank Flansburg, Cornelius, John, Elizabeth and me. Cornelius was then sparking my sister Amy and had been for some time. After lunch we lounged about under the shade trees up on the side hill and here I and Elizabeth talked business once more and we named the month for us to get married. We decided it should be sometime in October but did not fix the day and left that for some other time to talk about. We wandered about over those old clearings until four o'clock and then started for home having had a pleasant time and lots of fun. And now as far as I was concerned I was thinking of October and counting the weeks and wondering what day it would be.

In a day or two they come after Elizabeth and she went back to Stanton's and I did not see her again till September but we wrote letters back and forth. September came and I went out and had a visit with her and before I came away the wedding day was set to be the twelfth of

October on Sunday. I was to come after her that day with a horse and carriage and she said she would be ready.

I had no fears of her giving me the slip as Almira did, for I believed whatever came she would be true to me for I knew she loved me. We had kept our business to ourselves and no one knew of our engagement for certain, and I had not even told my mother this time.

Well, mother had been talking for over a year of going to Jefferson County to see her dear old father once more. So the second week in October father, mother and brother James rigged up and went off to Jefferson County leaving me and sister Rinda to keep house and look after the place. Sister Amy had been away to work since the fifth of July, and Rinda now done the housework with my assistance.

Well, I had now engaged a horse and carriage of Mr. Alanson Bunce for the twelfth of October to go after Elizabeth. On the eleventh I went up to Frank's and got my sister Cassie to come and stay with Rinda the next day and have a wedding supper ready for us when we got home. On the morning of the twelfth I was up and dressed early. I had to wade the creek that morning and did not dress my feet until I was over at the end of the *programme line* on the south abutment. The town had not built a new bridge yet and we had to ford the creek. Well, on I went and found the horse and carriage all ready for me.

I was not long driving to Russia Corners for the horse was young and spry. I arrived safe and put my horse out at the tavern. I think Varney kept the tavern then. I went over to Mr. Stanton's and not seeing Elizabeth I inquired for her of Miss Jane Stanton, and she said Elizabeth had just gone out in the orchard with a lady friend. So I went out and found her, and had a good long talk with her under the apple trees, and then we went to the house, and Elizabeth told Mr. Stanton's folks she was going away with me to get married. At first they declared they would not let her go, but seeing she had promised me they let her go after we had had a lunch, and Miss Stanton cried when we came away.

We started on our way back and when we got to Grant I inquired for a justice and I was directed to Squire Jones. He lived in the little old wood-colored house just opposite where the new tavern is now. I see the dingy old house everytime I go to Grant, and I think of the time I and Elizabeth stood up before the squire to be spliced. The squire was at home and when we went in I told him what I wanted and he said alright and sent his little girl out after witnesses. Who should pop in but our *old mother school teacher,* Elizabeth Wiggins, for she and the doctor now lived at Grant and so we greeted our dear old teacher once more. She had to come in to see two of her children married, and happy was the greeting. We were hardly done shaking hands with her when in came Phillip A. Conradt and his wife, two more of our old friends to greet, and two more to see the knot tied. Mr. Conradt was the merchant there then, and I had dealt with him a long time.

When everything was ready we stood up and were soon spliced, the ceremony was short but to the point and we said yes to all the questions. It was over so quick I did not hardly realize there had been much done. When it was all over and the squire got his chink, a twenty shilling gold piece, we bid the company good night as they wished us much joy.* Oh I almost forgot to tell you I gave my bride a rousing good kiss, and so did our dear old school teacher.

* The shilling was not a coin but a unit of account worth 12½¢. Henry is referring, therefore, to a $2.50 gold coin.

198

It was now almost night and getting dark but when we got up to Pardeeville the moon was rising in its autumn beauty. It had been a clear cool sunshiny day for our wedding and now it was a beautiful evening also and so we had the bright sunny day for our wedding and was now having the bright moonlight to go home in. I thought according to the old proverb we always ought to live happy together ever after. We had come past where the Flansburgs lived, and I asked Elizabeth if she wanted to stop a few minutes, and she said no, her father would not make her welcome if she did, so I drove on. When we came to the creek we had to drive through it, and as the rays of the full moon shone on the rippling waters we could see the gravelly bottom all the way across. When we drove up to the house Cassie, Frank and Rinda came out to greet us. We were welcome there and Elizabeth did not hesitate to stop here. We were soon seated at the table and done ample justice to the chicken and berry pie and all the goodies our sister fairy had fixed up.

Well, I had got now a wife and a house to put her in, although it was a log cabin it was a home. I had also kept my cow, and the spring before I had bought a good bed of our old friend Mum Tripp. I had raised hay and grain, garden sauce and potatoes that summer and thought now we could live like two mice.

In a few days our folks came home from Jefferson. They stopped over night to Forestport with sister Mary and her husband, and while there had heard we were married. In a few nights after we were married the young boys and some of the old ones too came to horn us.* We took it all in good part and mingled in the fun and helped the cause along. This shamed them out and they

* Horning is an ancient custom, often called a chivaree, whereby the newly married are teased by nocturnal noisemakers.

soon went off home declaring they would never go to another horning. We invited them in but no, they all had some excuse and sneaked off home and they said afterwards we were the funniest couple they had ever met and they had got fooled for the last time. We made more racket than they did, blowing the horn in their ears.

After our folks had got home from Jefferson County and found I was married for sure, my brother James wanted I and Elizabeth to stay with him that winter, for mother was not able to go on with the housework and sister Amy had got a place to work for the winter. Rinda wanted to go to school so he would be rather short for help. So the woman and I (you see I now had a wife to council with) talked it over and consented to stay. James was to furnish me in all the shingle timber I could work up and board me and give me one half, and Elizabeth was to help Rinda about the housework for her board and clothes. In doing thus we came out very well in the spring and had something to go to keeping house with, and as to the garden sauce and potatoes good old brother John got his share, for none of us would see him and his children go hungry, if he did have a poor stick for a wife.

The first of sleighing that fall a whole load of us went out to Forestport to visit sister Mary and her husband Alex Gallt. They were keeping a boarding house east of the village in the old red house for the hands who worked in the old steam mill. We had a right down good visit with them.

My brother James hauled tan bark that winter to the Pardeeville tannery. The old tannery has long since been burned down.

In January 1857, my brother James, Elizabeth and myself went to Schoharie County to visit our oldest sister Ruth. She had not been to see us for three or four years, so we rigged up and went to see her. We found her and her husband, Nathan Peaslee, and their daughter Fanny all well, but how changed was my sister Ruth now. She was fading and the wrinkles were gathering on her brow. Hard toil and care and age were doing their work and she had lost her sprightly step and the bright sparkle of her brown eyes were now languid. But in her disposition and goodness and loving kindness she was the same loving sister of the long ago. We had to make our visit short for fear the snow would go and the roads be bare before we could get home. So we visited a few of the old neighbors and cousin Mehala and her husband Sheldon Peaslee and the rest of the family and then stayed the last night with sister Ruth. In the morning we started bidding them goodbye with a handshake and the parting kiss from my dear old sister Ruth with the tears running down her cheeks as she said farewell. This was my last farewell to her, for I never saw her again although she lived for years after.

We did not have time to go around and see the old familiar places where we used to live when we were struggling through the vale of poverty in Schoharie County. How I longed to go over in Tompkins Hollow in the Town of Fulton and get a glimpse once more of the dear old home we occupied in my early youth, but time was short and we must get home. We reached home alright but found the road bare in many places coming through the Mohawk Valley and up through Norway.

In the spring of 1857 we went to keeping house in "the little old log cabin in the lane," after repairing it up a considerable. This was a new experience to us to get all alone by ourselves. Only two of us, only two to cook for, only two chairs to slide up to the table, only two plates, two cups and two saucers to place on the table, and only two to eat unless we had visitors. And how very odd it seemed to us after we had been living in such

large families. I went to work with a good will on the farm while Elizabeth helped all she could in the garden and her flower beds. After the spring crop was in I went to work with my father's help and built a nice new frame barn, twenty-four by thirty feet, and finished it all by haying time. We did not have very costly furniture but we had a good cow and a horse and lots of chickens and with our crops now growing we bid fair to make a life of it.

My father-in-law, after he found I and Elizabeth were married, began to tone down a little towards us and thought I was not such a bad son-in-law after all. He frequently called in to see us as he went by. He was always made welcome to our humble shelter and our goodies on the table. If anything ever pleased him it was a good meal of victuals. Yet he had his spells of being contrary and meddlesome, especially with his own relations.

He had a claim on the schoolhouse lot by a quit claim from someone and he used to come over and work it during the summer and haul the crops over to his place in Ohio. He was always very good to me when he wanted help to get his work done in a hurrying time, but never cared whether my crops were in or not in season, and about all the consolation I got after helping him through, he would come along and say, "Henry it is too late to put in your crops now."

202

That was a happy summer to us and our table was well supplied with berries, trout, and garden sauce. It was a home in the wilderness, a bright spot in Poverty's Vale. I had nothing but a quit claim deed for my place, all the same I worked it with courage and hope. Fall soon come and the crops were secured.

On the ninth day of September our first born came to town. A nice rosy cheeked boy, and our good old Dr. Wiggins, our mother-in-law, Mrs. Jane Dunn, and Mrs. Spencer Wilkins Jr., and my own mother also was called in to share in the rejoicing over the brand new baby, and how proud we felt over the kid. What a beauty he was, how fat and chubby and how we did love him, our first born. Now there soon would be another plate to put on the table and lots of little shoes and dresses to be added to the bill of goods through Poverty's Vale. All the same he was welcome.

Our old friend and neighbor Mrs. Potter as soon as she heard we had a little boy had to come up to see it, and what a fuss she made over it with her baby talk, and said it looked just like its father and all that. She had to kiss it and I thought she would eat him up but she didn't. We had another angel of mercy in our little place now.

Spencer Wilkins Jr. had married his second wife, Miss Ann E. Bowman of Little Falls, and they lived among us. Mrs. Wilkins was one of our old standbys. Always pleasant, friendly and sociable and ever ready to help the needy, and care for the sick, and lift up the fallen with words of encouragement for all both old and young with a friendly smile and love greeting for all whom she met. It is a pity there are not more just such in the world today than there is now.

James H. Sackett also lived in our place now in the old log house east of the schoolhouse on lot seventeen. He had married Sarah Flansburg, Elizabeth's sister, a few years before and had moved about from place to place, and now he had settled down for a time here. Sarah was a splendid looking woman, rosy cheeks and blue eyes, good and kind to all. Everybody loved her but she had married against her father's wishes and the old gentleman did not respect Harve (as we called him) anymore than he did me. They had two lovely children, Phenie and Jay (both dead now).

That spring of 1858 they had another daughter born while they were living in the old log house, and they named her Ada. But the mother took cold and in a few days died with a fever, leaving little Ada to be cared for by others. This was sudden and sad to part with one so young and blooming in health. Sarah was only twenty-six years old and as she lay silent in death she looked like a marble statue. This was the first one of the family of ten children they had lost and it was a severe blow to them, and as she lay in her coffin, to the surprise of all, her father bent over and kissed her, she being the first one of the ten that he was ever known to kiss in his life. She who now lay silent in the cold embrace of death had at last received a father's kiss but the closed eyes and silent compressed lips gave back no sign of his last touching farewell.

Little Ada was taken home with us for Elizabeth to care for for a few days. But as we had a bouncing boy to feed and look after it was too much for Elizabeth to care for both. So she went to live with her grandparents who brought her up and she is now a middle aged woman and married to Mr. William Topp of Johnstown, New York. She has a kind husband and a splendid home. We had named our first born Milo Dewitt and by spring he was quite a load to carry.

**19** In the summer of 1858 sister Rinda went to Blenheim, Schoharie County, to live with sister Ruth and go to school. She was now in her fourteenth year, a good scholar and good looking young girl. She too had bid the old home goodbye for a time to finish up her education and fit herself for teaching. She had lived here most all her life through childhood and early youth. She had grown up with the place and she had seen the wilderness bud and blossom like the rose. Sister Amy was now the helper at home after Rinda went away, for mother had to have someone with her all the time.

That year of 1858 Mr. David Dunn and Cornelius Flansburg went to California. Mr. Dunn left his place and his family in the care of old Mr. Spencer Wilkins, Mrs. Dunn's father. The match between sister Amy and Cornelius in some way or other was broken off and they were never to marry each other after all, although they had been courting for years. But the gold fever had taken Cornelius away and he was wholly oblivious to everything but gold, gold. Even his letters to us was dedicated to gold.

The summer of 1858 I worked out some in Hinckley's lumber woods up on the Morehouseville road. Philo Flansburg was boss over the shanty or camp and Alexander Gallt and my sister Mary kept one camp. They had come back from Forestport that same spring.

This summer and year our little neighborhood had lost quite a good many of its inmates by death and removal. I came home in the fall to harvest my crop and as usual to go trapping in the fall and fore part of winter. My money for the fur helped me along quite a considerable through poverty's vale. My brother little Sammy and his family had also picked up and gone. They moved to Allegany County, New York, up south of Attica.

While I was away to work this summer I had got an old lady to come and stay with Elizabeth whom I shall call "Grandma Dunn" as everybody else did who knew her. She was David Dunn's mother, a queer old body, good and kind but not over bright. But her religious faith was firm as a rock and nothing could swerve her from the even tenor of her way. She was good company and loved children and everyone that was good. For several years she made it her home with us and old Mum Tripp. Oh yes Elizabeth and I had a place to visit now and we used to go over and see the old lady and take our little kid with us and set and spark by the old lady's fireplace.

Time went on with us as usual during the winter of 1858 and 1859 and not much of interest took place until the fifteenth of April 1859 when we had another son born to us. This event was looked for with interest to both of us as I wished it to be a daughter, but my wife was well pleased because it was a boy. We named him Aurey Cornelius after his uncle in California. But as for me I had already nicknamed him Melissa. At his birth we had quite a gathering. There were present both his grandmothers, Mrs. Jane Dunn, Mrs. Ann Wilkins, Grandma Dunn and Mrs. Potter. Midwives enough for a town.

I was making sugar this spring in my father-in-law's sap bush on shares up on lot seventeen, north of the schoolhouse. Jerry Flansburg stopped with me and brought his own provision and Elizabeth cooked it for him.

That year, 1859, Philo went to California. He too had been saving up money to secure a passage to the land of gold. Philo never used to call in to see us and most always

206

went by as a stranger, but we did not care for that, for neither one of us did think much of him. Just before he went away he and his father came over to Frank's and Philo borrowed sixty dollars of Frank to take with him to California and never told Frank he was going away. Philo never said goodbye or farewell to any of us over the creek and a short time before, he went and bought a nice black horse of R. H. Wood at Ohio and gave his note with his father for a backer. Philo sold the horse and pocketed the money and the old man put his property out of his hands, and so Mr. Wood was cheated out of the horse. Philo never was the *man* to pay his brother Frank the sixty dollars or Mr. Wood for the horse. Although it was said that Philo was doing well and handled thousands of dollars in California, all his own money, he never wrote to me or Elizabeth or any of the family except his father.

That summer after Aurey was born we had our door yard all fixed up nice with flower beds and nice flowers of all kinds and a great row of hollyhocks of all colors next to the road. How beautiful it was with everything neat and clean about the house and its surroundings, and how happy we were though we were poor with two little kids to look after. When we went to pick berries we took them along or left them with Grandma Dunn for she seemed now to be one of the family.

Her son David had gone to California the year before and he had promised to send her some gold, and with what great faith she looked forward to her son's promise. How happy she was, and when the birds were singing in the trees outside she would go out and sing with them, and I can see now just how she looked with her arms across her breast and her cycs looking up at the birds, her form weaving to and fro while she sang most everything with a gushing heart. She had many songs of her own make for the birds. I recall one to mind now and it ran like this. "Pretty little birds how sweet do you sing, flying from branch to branch amongst the trees, amongst the trees. How I love you little birdies so happy singing in the branches amongst the trees, amongst the trees."

Thus the time went by pleasantly with about the same routine of business and happiness with all the families in our little settlement. We were all alive to the interest of the favorable reports from the gold fields of California and the Dunn family especially for they were expecting to go there when David sent them money.

Sister Rinda had got home from Schoharie County and during her absence she had taught down there her first term of school and had given good satisfaction. This spring of 1860 she had got a certificate and a school to teach here in the Town of Wilmurt.

Along about the first of May it was all excitement in our little settlement, for Mr. Dunn had sent for his family. So they made an auction and sold all their things except what they could carry in two trunks. There were five of them to go, Mrs. Dunn, Jane Ann, James and two younger children. Jane Ann was about Rinda's age and they had always been playmates and schoolmates and had grown up from childhood together. Sisters could never have thought more of each other than they did and sad was their parting. The Dunn family had always been loved and respected for their kindness and quiet good behavior. But now they were to go, and what an undertaking for the sad distracted woman to start off from the dear old home and place with her little family to cross the two oceans and the isthmus through dangers and storms to meet her husband in California. But such it was to be. When they got ready at last to go they bade their old friends and home farewell for the last time. The tears ran down their cheeks like rain, and Mrs. Dunn said she never should see the old place again.

The home was left for her father, old Mr. Wilkins, who now was living with his third wife. He had married Mary Simons, an old maid, a daughter of Truman Simons. But the saddest part of all was that Mr. Dunn had made no provision for his poor old dependent mother whose heart was broken to see all the rest go and her to be left to strangers or to the charity of her old friends, and sad was the picture to see her weep and wring her hands and cry. She was a poor old frail body, and odd it was true, but then she was his mother and it did seem to me then that he did not do his duty to her. He never fulfilled his promise to her or ever sent her anything that I ever knew of. She lived with us and old Mum Tripp until after the Civil War and then she drifted back to Oppenheim near Fort Plain where she was born and raised, and here she lived the rest of her days among and on the charity of those who were her true and early friends.

We missed the Dunn family more than others that came and went, for they came in the place with us when it was a howling wilderness. Mrs. Dunn and her family reached the land of gold all safe but almost worn out and tired the letter said. But she did not enjoy the happiness of a long life in California. In a year or two she sickened and died, and her grave was made under a live oak tree where she is now sleeping her long last sleep. But the memory of lovely character and Christian influence still lingers like the scent of the faded rose leaf. She was sadly missed in the prayer meetings and in the homes of those who needed care in sickness and trouble. The remainder and increase of the Dunn family are somewhere in California, for they never returned.

I will mention here too that Herman Sackett and his family had gone to California. Old Mr. Marvin Sackett and wife were living at this time up in Ava northwest of

Boonville and they never returned to Wilmurt to live again and have long since been dead.

In the fall of 1860 we began to hear of war and rumors of war but not many thought then we were on the eve of a great bloody war and that its great dark cloud of bloodshed and disaster were already hovering over us.

I worked at home that season and in the fall as usual set up my traps and went to catching fur. Often times Elizabeth would go with me to the traps (leaving the kids with Grandma Dunn) taking as much an interest in the catching and care of fur as I did. In the winter after I had got my pay for the fur we went down to Newport to trade, she of course to get a lot of mysterious things to make up into little garments. Fur was then bringing a good price and mink pelts were bringing from two and a half to three dollars. I made more out of fur while I was at it than I did get elsewhere.

On January 22, 1861, our third boy was born, a trapper. He was a little bit of a nugget but all the same he was welcome. The most of our neighboring women was present and we sadly missed the kind genial face of Mrs. Dunn, but "Old Mag" Potter made up for all deficiencies. We called him Burton James.* Now we had three little kids and all boys. I was dissatisfied but in after years I was glad he was a boy.

Well, now I had five in the family and it kept me working and planning to supply all their wants. I began to realize what it was to take care of a family. I managed to get enough to eat and supply the children's wants but Elizabeth and me began to be pinched for a second suit of clothes, and rags were not uncommon to dangle about our garments. Since I had been married I had by accident

---

* Burton James Conklin, whose son Roy is the present owner of Henry Conklin's manuscript, became a famous Adirondack trapper.

lost one valuable horse and I had only now partially recovered from the loss. I was indeed down in poverty's vale groping my way along, and as people sometimes say, charity begins at home. My brother John, dear old brother John, was still on the place and my brother James and the rest of us had contributed to his comfort which would leave us a little short every time.

The year before, sister Julia and her husband Andrew Krellis lived away up in the woods within three miles of Piseco Lake in a little old clearing and an old dingy house and my sister Julia was taken sick, and they came after mother. Well, my mother was now a rickety old body with her nerves unstrung and scarcely able to walk and she tottered as she went. She could not say no to the summons. So brother James took her up there and also medicine and the necessaries of life for her comfort. We made up a donation among ourselves for their relief, for Andrew could not get out to get anything and it come very good, for they were now down so they dealt out the rations with one slice of bread to a meal.

Well, mother stayed there for six weeks before sister could be moved out. She came very near dying and would have gone if she had lacked a mother's care. I went up there once during the six weeks to take them some things, and such a place to live in. Andrew had a little log barn and the door was so low a horse would not put his head down to go in and so we turned the horse around and backed him in. After my sister got well enough to move we went up and got her and the family out. There was a doctor woman at Morehouseville gave my sister the wrong medicine, and her hair all fell out and it was several years before it grew out again.

In the spring of 1861 war, cruel war, was upon us and men from all over were enlisting and leaving their homes to go and fight for the old flag. All that summer the pa-

pers were full of the war news. Victories and defeats and
the terrible disasters of war. I had not thought much of
going, for I thought how could I leave my wife and little
boys to go out with my life in my hands and perhaps
never return. So the spring and summer went and then
there came a time when more troops were called for and
recruiting officers were around enlisting men and holding
meetings to arouse up those who had not already gone.

On the twenty-third day of October, 1861, there was to
be a patriotic gathering at Ohio, Herkimer County, and
I with many others went. At this meeting the wants of the
government were so vividly portrayed that I forgot all
about my family, listening to the patriotic speeches, and
when the opportunity came, I with others walked up
and enlisted. Let me see, there was James Hane, William H. Hane, Edgar Hane, James Ostrom and myself.

Well, on our way home we talked it all up about going
off to the war and as they dropped out one by one going
home that night, it was "Good night comrade." I went
alone the last half mile and began to consider what I had
done and almost repented of signing the paper. But it
was too late now, so I made the best of it and began to
harden myself to what must come sooner or later, and
that was a soldier's adieu. When I told my wife what I
had done she did not scold me, but the silent tears trickled
down her face as she looked at the little boys who stood
gazing at us in wonderment.

On the thirteenth day of November a lot of us went to Prospect Depot to be mustered into the service and I was so hard up for clothing decent to wear I had to borrow a coat of my father until I got my uniform. I remember it was nearly white or very light colored and afterwards while drilling at Rome the boys in fun called me the white Mohawk. When we were mustered in we were such an awkward squad the mustering officer could not get us in line so he made us toe the railroad track in front of the depot.

Rome was to be our headquarters as old Colonel Pearce of that place was getting up a regiment of *Mohawks* as he called us.* So in a few days we all went to Rome with a promise we should have a furlough to come home once before we went to Virginia. A promise he kept in most every case. So it was not so very hard to part with my wife and boys this time and I went to Rome with the boys and stayed until the last of December when a lot of us got a furlough for two weeks to come home. We hoofed it all the way from Rome, not having money enough to buy our ticket on the cars.

The snow was half knee deep part of the way and towards the last we dragged our weary legs along by inches and it was now night and James Hane was the first of the seven to get home. When the light of their window was in view he knew they were up yet and he would soon greet its inmates. Next to drop out was James Ostrom at the Farnicrook place, for he had married Alida, and she now was stopping with her father and mother. Next was Edgar Hane at the corner on the Ash place. Next was

---

* Colonel O. B. Peirce of Rome formed a regiment called the Mohawk Rangers, which, as Henry later notes, was combined with Colonel Edwin Rose's Oswego Regiment in February 1862 to form the 81st Regiment of Infantry. See Frederick Phisterer, *New York in the War of Rebellion*, 3d ed., 5 vols. (Albany, 1912), III, 2877.

Jasper Hollenbeck who lived where Madison Bunce does now. Next was Isaac Davenport where he lives now, and next was William Hane where Mr. Bussy now lives, and from there over to just across the bridge about a half mile was my place.* I was so tired I could have lain down in the snow and went to sleep but I thought of the dear ones just over the bridge and kept going and at last I was home, almost tired out.

I found my wife up yet talking with Grandma Dunn, but the kids were abed and as soon as they heard me they were up and climbing onto me and such kisses and hugs I got from them I did not forget very soon. The next morning was New Year's Day 1862 and I had only two weeks, only two short weeks to stay at home with those I dearly loved and then must come the sad parting. So I began to school myself to reflection and hardness of heart.

Well, I tried to improve those two weeks to good advantage, fixing up the cabin a little so Elizabeth would be comfortable, and getting up some winter's wood, and finally visiting evenings about the settlement with relatives and neighbors. But two weeks was a short time and it soon rolled away and the day before I was to start back was mostly spent in visiting and bidding farewells with a shake of the hand of my old neighbors and relatives. The evening before I started I called in and bid my dear old father and mother farewell, not knowing as I should ever see them again. That evening brother James, sister Amy and Rinda came down to our house and stayed awhile and there was also a farewell to them. When they went away we were all alone, as Grandma Dunn was over to "Old Mum's." I tried to be as cheerful as I could but I know my feeling betrayed me.

We stayed up late that night although I had to get away

* The location of these several homes is given in Nichols, *Atlas of Herkimer County*, p. 26.

early to go with the other boys who were going in the morning. Not much sleep that night and I kept [the] fire all night. Milo and Aurey would not undress for fear I would go before they got up and so they lay down on a quilt by the stove. At three o'clock we were up and the mother got our breakfast, but little did we eat and not much words of comfort could we say on either side, for the parting must soon come. The moments were drawing nigh when we should sever, and when I began to get ready and put on my things the tears stood in their eyes. When I got ready to go I says, "Now I must bid you goodbye." Elizabeth got her arms about my neck, weeping on my shoulder. Milo was on one side with his arms about my waist and Aurey on the other side clinging to me, and little Burt with only his nightdress on had crept to me and was clinging to my knees in front. There I was and they were all crying. I thought I was in a vice with all their loving arms about me and the time was come I must get away someway, and it was done so quick I hardly knew how I done it, but it seemed so cruel and cold. I snatched Milo's arms loose and pushed him away and as I stooped to loosen Aurey's arms he looked up in my face with tears in his eyes and says, "Oh papa don't go to war," and all I could say, "Oh I must go now" and pushed him away. Then I stooped still lower with my wife yet clinging to my neck and with a kiss to little Burt tore him away, and then raising myself gave my wife a kiss and goodbye and thrust her away with the others. As I grabbed the latch and darted out the door one glance saw they were all in a heap clinging together and crying.

I darted out in the cold winter morning, the snow up to my knees, and I scarcely knew how I got over the ground but it seems now as I look back upon it I almost flew until I got to the middle of the bridge which is only about twenty-five rods from the house. Here I halted a moment to take one more glance at the dear old place and my "log cabin in the lane" where so many loved ones had clustered around me. As I glanced at the creek as its gurgling waters were running under the ice, whose music had often lulled me to sleep, I looked back at the cabin and the light was still burning, and I fancied I heard their cries of anguish. And then I almost repented of going to the war and the temptation came up now as I looked over to the north star and whispered, "Why don't you go to Canada?" But no, I would be no coward or deserter. Better die a thousand deaths on the battlefield than leave to your wife and children the everlasting stigma of coward or deserter. I turned my face to the foe and dashed off southward on a run to join my comrades who were already waiting for me and I found them all ready and saw some of their farewells, but oh how different from mine. Little did they know what an ordeal I had passed through that morning. I never want to see another such parting and would rather go into fiery battle than pass through another such scene.

And let me say here dear reader that those fathers, mothers, wives, children, brothers, sisters, and sweethearts who were deprived of dear ones during the war were entitled to the highest praise for the part they acted and sufferings they bore, and no words from the pen of mine can estimate the sacrifice and how nobly and well they give up the best of the ones that the land could furnish. It was not the old and feeble that went out from their embrace, but those in the bloom of youth, manhood, and middle age, and if I had my say about it a higher and better monument should be erected to them than to any one particular general who led the brave boys through the fiercest fight. Suffered, yes they suffered all the bitter anguish and privations and care and hardships as well as the soldiers in the field. And such torture of mind when

216

listening and watching the dread of an impending battle.

We went to Rome that day in a sleigh and got there alright. My eyes that day seemed burning in their sockets but when I lay down that night to sleep I wept till my pillow was wet with tears for the cruelty I had practiced on my family at home.

20 WELL, we all went back to Rome and were being drilled for further use in the field. We first occupied a large room in a brick building that stood down near the canal and we were up in the third story. When we all got in there stomping and drilling we made the old building shake and the people living in the lower stories got scared and raised a fuss and we had to get out.

Then we went up to the old armory in the west part of the village but this did not suit old Colonel Pearce for it was an old empty shell. He finally got the court house for us to stay in to drill in the exercise of manual of arms, and here the old colonel give us a lecture every day as he occupied the judge's chair. Before this we had boarded at the Seymour house but now we were scattered all over the village to board and sleep and such a mess of tramps Rome never housed before or since.

There were nearly four hundred of us. I and James Ostrom boarded to Baman's next door to Colonel Pearce. He was quite an old rickety played out man with one lame arm and in my estimation poorer financially than a church mouse. They called him Colonel. Whether he had really been one I do not know, and lots of the boys got down on him, but as far as I am prepared to say he done just as he agreed to by me and will further say I believed him to be patriotic and done all he could in the nation's

peril to recruit a regiment. But failing in this he had to turn his men over to the government and when we were consolidated in the Oswego seven companies more younger and more competent officers were selected.* Colonel Pearce had to step out and succumb to the inevitable. He might have got something for his trouble and that was right and just. It was no money out of our pockets if those who took the best positions in the regiment handed him over a present out of their own pockets. My motto is, "Honor where honor is due."

Well, we were not long to stay at Rome and were soon off to Albany and here we were consolidated with the Seven Oswego Companies, and when mustered we were eleven hundred strong. They were from all over the state. They came from the east end of Long Island to the eastern shores of Lake Erie and from the St. Lawrence to the southern line of New York State. We had men of every trade and occupation represented to America, from the preacher of the gospel and professors of academies down to the boot black and wharf rats of the slums of New York City. And from the statesmen in the southern part of the state to the guide and trappers of the great Adirondack of the wild woods. A heterogeneous mingling mass of men standing together in line swearing allegiance to the dear old flag and all at one command presenting arms to the command of our dear old Colonel Rose. No matter where we came from or what we were, we were now a band of brothers and as such were to go on to hardships, privations and peril and some to death. Some to promotion and fame and some to be mangled and maimed. We had all left behind us our friends and our homes mid the perils of war and its dangers to roam and taste, yes taste a soldier's woe. But little did we realize then how bitter would be

*See note on page 213.

219

the taste before we should return again to our homes and friends.

Well now dear reader, as I have got along down to the army scenes, it will not be out of place to mention some of the boys in the rear guard, in addition to those already named, from Wilmurt and Ohio who had enlisted. There was John Flansburg, Jerry Flansburg, James Stevens, George Stevens, Edward Fallen, James Pruyn, John E. Potter, Hiram Potter, and afterwards George W. Potter, Smith Conkling, William Conkling, Morris Conkling, and George Conkling, Jaspar Halenbeck, Isaac Davenport, and John McIntosh.

And my good old brother John, although in his forty-third year, could not resist the temptation and the sound of the recruiting martial music, and had enlisted in the ninety-seventh New York stationed in Boonville. He too had left his home and family to the mercies of the civil authorities and the charities of friends, just like myself. And on the eighth of October 1861 my brother-in-law Alexander Gallt also enlisted in the ninety-seventh at Boonville. Our regiment was at Albany and the ninety-seventh at Boonville.

At Albany, Camp Rathbone, we got our uniforms and from there I sent my father's old white coat home with my other cast off clothes. After I had donned the new suit of blue I was no more afraid of being call the "White Mohawk."

After leaving home the last time I began to number the letters I sent home and named them "soldiers sketches." I kept them and wrote them as a sort of diary but am sorry to say there is only a few left out of what would fill a volume. But from what is left I shall give in these pages for the interest of the reader a few extracts. Here is one: "Soldiers sketches" no. 5 Camp Rathbone, Albany, February 8, 1862.

Dear Wife and children:

I am well and will pen you a few lines hoping you are all well at home. We have just got our new uniforms today and you can't imagine how well we look. We also got our knives, forks, spoons, cups, plates, and canteens. Our fare is a little better but all the difference is we are getting used to it. I have been in the cook room for three days and I have got the run of the whole concern. We are detailed for three days and my time is out to-night. We have to be here at five in the morning and stay until ten at night. It is my work to wash and rinse dishes and I never had such a long tour of washing dishes in my life. They cook ten barrels of potatoes a day, five barrels of beef and they have four men cleaning potatoes, carrots and beans. I saw them make a pudding one day. They put in four bags of meal. It was the largest pudding I ever saw. Our bread is good and baked in the city and drawn here by the load as you would cord wood. I fared good in the cook room. (Sunday 9th) About four hundred of us went to the Baptist church in the forenoon. I enjoyed the meeting and the walk as I had not been out of line before. This afternoon had soldiers service at the brick barracks in the open air. It lasted for half an hour.

Sketches no. 6, Feb. 16. Sunday evening we went down to Methodist church to hear Stratton preach. He was formerly of Little Falls. On our way we went cross lots and down a flight of one hundred forty three steps and concluded Albany was a hilly place. I sent father's coat and you will find it at Grant with the other boys' things there. Tell James Ostrom to hurry up and get well for I am lonesome without him.

Write soon and my love to all and remember your absent soldier.

Henry

While we were at Albany we thought our fare was poor. Well it was, beside what we had been having at home. But there was so much to cook and so many to cook for, no wonder it was a mixed up mess, and then every day a new detail of men were sent in the cook rooms and some of them didn't know enough to cook for a goose let alone a human being. The beans were a swishy, swashy mess and poor miserable coffee and generally once a day we had meal pudding and black strap molasses. Lots of times this would get tipped over on the floor and we had to track through the sticky stuff and this would sicken a good many and make them almost vomit, and they would turn and go out to their barracks, taking their slice of bread and cup of coffee. The only good thing we had here was bread and that was splendid.

Well, we stayed here over two weeks and then we went to New York City and stopped at the park barracks two nights and three days and while here we had good fare and quite a lot of luxuries, but that could be accounted for as it was more directly under the eyes of the authorities. The government was not to blame for our poor fare in a place where everything was so plenty but it was the contractors that were coining fortunes out of the government and scrimping the poor soldier. Our next move was over on Staten Island and here we had quite good barracks and bunks but our grub was about the same as at Albany only a cleaner place to eat in.

For the past year before I enlisted it had been a hard struggle for me to keep my family in provisions and clothing and in fact we were down quite low in the vale of poverty and letters from home were sad and discouraging for they had to depend on charity or go hungry and this grieved me more than the poor fare and hardships. My wife had to sell my carpenter tools and a colt and farming utensils to keep hunger away from the door. And at last the cow was sold. Then about this time the county of Herkimer granted some relief to the soldiers' wives and so my wife and little ones at home became for the time being county paupers. When we enlisted we had the promise of pay every month and now here it was in March and I had been a soldier since October and my

222

family were reduced almost to beggary, and I could not grant them any relief. It was a sad thing to leave them as I did and all I could do was to write words of encouragement, but what is words, they will not keep away hunger or repay the dear ones who had given their husband and father a sacrifice to the country.

I began to learn the fortunes of war were terrible. We had left some of the boys at Rome who were sick and then quite a good many more at Albany with the small pox and the measles. The roll called numbered less every move we made.

While at Staten Island when not on duty us boys were strolling along the ocean beach, which was all new to us Ohio [township] boys, gathering up shells and wading in the salt water. It was quite cold yet but how refreshing to our feet and legs.

Some of the boys had caught the small pox at Albany and got sick with it on Staten Island. Among the number was Eli Boyce and I sat up with him part of the night to give him medicine and then I slept cuddled up to him the rest of the night on the narrow bunk cot. In the morning his face was a solid blotch of small pox, but strange to say I never took it and after that I was never afraid of the small pox. We left Eli here when the regiment moved.

We were on Staten Island two weeks and then shipped by steamboat to Amboy and by railroad to Philadelphia. We were on the train all night and were quite badly shook up. The eighty-first were all on one train and it was a big load with our guns and all our traps and tents and accoutrements of war. When we got to Philadelphia we were tired and hungry and wasn't we glad when word come to us on the cars that we were to have a breakfast on the generosity of the ladies of Philadelphia and how the boys did hurrah and swing their hats.

At eight o'clock we were marched into those great

rooms and around to the tables set for the whole regiment. The tables were loaded with all the good substantial food and luxuries of every kind that could be piled on them. As we filed around and took our seats if there was ever thankful hearts it was here, and if ever grace was said in the spirit of thankfulness it was here and it was this: "God bless the ladies of Philadelphia for this bounteous repast, Amen." And as I glanced down the long line of faces I saw many of the boys with the tears trickling down their cheeks. And well they might weep, for scores of them never returned and never after sat down by another feast like that. After we had done ample justice to all these good things and to ourselves we boarded the train and started on, and the boys were cheering for the ladies of Philadelphia.

All that day as we passed through the country it was cheer on cheer. Farmers swung their hat in the air or anything they happened to have and women were out with flags, handkerchiefs, mops and brooms and aprons waving us on towards Washington. So it went until we got to Baltimore and here we began to discover the secesh scowl and teeth grinding, but all the same we got through Baltimore safe and went on to Washington.

Here we unloaded and went into the soldier's retreat near the depot. It was a great building covering nearly an acre and was built of rough lumber at the time of the first Bull Run fight and was named the Soldiers' Retreat for here was where thousands of our soldiers halted from the first hard battle and defeat. There were no bunks in it and all who stopped there had to lay on the hard floor if they had no blankets of their own. Here we stayed two days and two nights and were marched in by companies to the cook room with our plates and cups and got our rations and came back and set down on the hard floor to eat them. We thought it hard fare then to be so near the capital of this great and rich nation, going out to defend it, and live thus. No beds, no chairs, or benches, no luxuries of any kind, simply a cup of poor chicory coffee, salt beef or pork, poor beans and magotty hardtack with B.C. marked on some of them. Some of the boys said it meant Before Christ.

21 FROM the soldiers' retreat we were marched up on Kalorama Heights. Here we were furnished the little square tents large enough to hold five or six and each company had a street by themselves and the letter of the company was the letter of the street. Here too our cooking squad was established and no detail made from the regiment for that purpose. Edward Fallen and William Wilcox were the cooks for Company C. Our food was got up in good shape and how we did enjoy it. We were marched in line to the cook house with our cups and plates and got our rations and took them back to the tent to eat them. While here we were paid off and it was a joyful day with us. I know it was with me, for now I could send home some money to Elizabeth and the children. But I am sorry to say that some of the boys who had none behind dependent on them spent their money drinking and gambling.

After we had been here a few days the ninety-seventh New York came and encamped about two miles north of us and one day my good old brother John came over to see me, and how noble and manly he looked in his bright new uniform. I thought I never saw him look so well. He was shaved up and had his hair cut and that with his rosy cheeks and sparkling blue eyes made him look far younger than he was, for he was now in his forty-third year. His step was sprightly as any of us. We had a good visit that afternoon and talked of the dear ones we had left behind and the old home up in the wilderness and wondered if we ever should get back there again. When he got ready to go back to his regiment I walked along out with him about a half mile and we lingered by the way dreading the farewell parting, when at last I said I must go back, and we stopped and looked at each other and took the parting hand that was reached out. The tears were in his eyes and he could hardly say goodbye. This was our last farewell and last adieu, for I never saw him more. He went on to his regiment and I went back to mine.*

One day while here Edgar Hane and I got a pass to go down to the city and we went through the capitol and away up on the dome where we had a splendid view. It was a clear and beautiful day and we could see for many

* John, serving with the Ninety-seventh Regiment, was wounded at the second battle of Bull Run, August 29, 1862, and was discharged for disability in February 1863. In January 1864, at the age of forty-four, he enlisted in the Second Regiment of New York Heavy Artillery. Sometime between May 19 and June 21, 1864, in the campaign leading to the final assault on Richmond, he was again wounded. He died of his wounds, July 15, 1864, at the military hospital in Portsmouth Grove, Rhode Island. *Annual Report of the Adjutant-General of the State of New York for the Year 1902*, (Albany, 1903), p. 786; *Annual Report of the Adjutant-General of the State of New York for the Year 1896* (Albany, 1897), p. 576.

miles around. We tramped all over the city and the day seemed too short for us, but at night we hastened back to our quarters well paid for our tramp and visit.

We were now being put through a more thorough course of drill in company, regiment, brigade, and division drill and we were busy every pleasant day. On the twenty-seventh day of March we had orders to break camp the next day. So in the afternoon of the twenty-eighth we fell in line and we were pretty well loaded. We had our guns, forty rounds of ammunition, knapsacks, three days' rations, canteens and rubber blankets from our dog tents. We were the last regiment in the brigade and we had to go so slow, there were so many ahead of us. About seven o'clock in the evening we got across the chain bridge. We got within about one half mile of Alexandria and camped for the night and it was then ten o'clock at night. When we stopped, our regiment was scattered from Washington to Alexandria. An officer rode past the colors and wanted to know what regiment that was and they told him it was the eighty-first New York. Then he asked if the colors were in the center and the captain said yes. "Well," he says, "This is the damnedest, longest regiment there is in the United States."

Thus we camped for the night and every old barn and house was chuck full of soldiers and all who could not find shelter camped along the highway and under the bushes and burnt rails to keep warm. I and some of the boys lay under the thorn bushes and all we had over us was our rubber blankets. We laid by the road side until noon the twenty-ninth and by this time our regiment had got together once more and all the stragglers were in.

In the afternoon we marched up among the hills about two miles and pitched our tents which were made of our rubber blankets by looping two together and two sleeping under them. We got nicely to work at our tents and it began to snow, and it snowed, hailed, and drizzled and rained all night. We had a bitter time of it, camping under the dog tents the first time. But the boys put up with it with as good grace as possible. That night's song was "O Why did I come for a military man." In the morning we dried ourselves by the fire and cooked our breakfast and prepared for another march.

We started about noon for the steamboat landing at Alexandria where we arrived about three o'clock of the thirtieth. We had some fun marching in the mud all the way down, which was about four inches deep and just like pancake batter. We called it the "sacred soil of old Virginia." On arriving at the landing we were marched down in the cabin where we unloaded our traps, and oh what sweet relief to our aching backs. Here we had good bunks and a good rest. We were on board the "C. Vander-bilt." The ninety-third New York were also on board. She lay at the dock all night loading on army supplies and the next morning, March thirty-first, at nine a.m. we started down the Potomac. The "C. Vanderbilt" also towed three other sloops loaded with horses, hay and provisions.

From the boat we had a distant view of the house where Ellsworth was shot.* It was a pleasant day and we remained on deck most all day enjoying the scenery on both sides of the Potomac, and to make it more pleasant the band was playing as we passed down. About noon we passed Fort Washington on the Maryland side where we were greeted with three hearty cheers and music from the band in the fort and in response our band struck up "Hail Columbia." A little further down on the Virginia

* In May 1861, Elmer Ellsworth, of the 11th New York Volunteers, removed a Confederate flag from the roof of a tavern in Alexandria, Virginia, and was then killed by the tavern owner. The incident was widely publicized.

side we passed Mount Vernon, a very pleasant spot, and in the distance we could see the tomb of Washington. The setting sun found us entering Cheasapeake Bay where the water was so salty we could not drink it. We run all night and in the morning the first day of April we were in sight of Fortress Monroe. At eight o'clock we anchored and at noon marched off the boat and passed the fort and on towards Hampton where we had a view of the desolation of war which the tall burned brick chimneys and broken down walls plainly told us. We went about two miles further and camped for the night in the pines. Here we built fires and laid down in our blankets to rest and were soon in the land of dreams.

The next day, April second, we moved a little further and at night encamped seven miles from Fortress Monroe, and on our way from the fort we had passed a good many new made graves. We were camping on a deserted rebel plantation and were burning oak rails for wood and tearing things to pieces in general as we were now in the land of Dixie.

We were doing picket duty along the James River watching for the Merrimac who a short time before had come out and destroyed the Cumberland. One night I with others were detailed for picket duty on the river bank and our orders were to not let anyone pass and watch for small boats and see they did not land. Each one had his post or beat to walk and about eleven o'clock at night I thought I saw a boat in the distance and gloom. So I called the attention of the boys on each side of me and they came and looked at it and thought it was a boat and then we called to the corporal of the guard and he come and pronounced it a boat. About this time the grand rounds got along and after they were properly challenged and returned the answer, we called their attention to it. They too pronounced it a boat and decided to hail it and if we did not get an answer to fire at it. There were six of us now got together and stood in line ready to fire. The captain calls out, "Who comes there," and no answer. "Who comes there" rang out again but no answer and then the officer said in a loud voice if you don't answer we shall fire. He called again and no answer. Then he gave the word to fire and the roar of six muskets broke the stillness of the night air. Before we could load, a signal gun at the fort sent its booming sound over the waters and the whole army in their midnight slumber. Well, we fired three times at it and by this time the long roll and bugle of every regiment were sounded and thousands scrambled into arms and the cry, "The Merrimac is coming, the Merrimac is coming," rang through the post. Every man was up and in arms and every steam-boat and monitor were getting up steam to go out and fight the Merrimac. The order "fall in, fall in" was heard far and near. The object was still there and apparently getting larger and the captain called for volunteers to go out and see what it was. The moon had risen and we could see quite plain out on the dusky waters. So two of the boys stripped off their clothes and started out in the water, and they could wade it now, and when they got out to the object they ha ha'ed and laughed and said it was a great long rock. So it was, but as the tide went out it began to show itself and in the night it looked just like a boat. After that it was called "Merrimac" Rock. We did not hear the last of it for many days.

In a few days we passed on up the river going by Newport News where we saw the Cumberland with her masts sticking out of the water and her flag still floating. It is not my purpose in this little story to write war history, for other more competent men have written long ago the peninsular campaign, but I will hasten on with my narrative giving you a sketch now and then that may prove interesting. We were now, April 1862, tramping up towards Richmond over the deserted plantations and over the lawns and garden flowers, through pine groves from the James to the York River. Beautiful indeed was the scenery if it had not been for the devastations of war. The air was laden with sweet perfumes from the gardens, the flowering almonds and the peach orchards, which were in full bloom. And that is thirty years ago.

Thirty long years, and it don't seem possible. I was then in the bloom of manhood and my cheeks were red and rosy, auburn hair and bright blue sparkling eyes and elastic frame. Alas, this April 1892 finds me with my cheeks wrinkled and thin and streaked with furrows of care and my hair almost white as the winter's snow and my eyes growing dim and my frame shattered with age and pain, away up here in the Adirondacks writing out this narrative in a rustic mansion all by myself. But dear reader I am digressing from my story and must hasten on with my pen, for I have 30 long years more to write about and resurrect.*

The cry now of the whole army when we moved was "On to Richmond." So on we went up past Young Mills and past the Warwick Courthouse, and on April twenty-third were within a few miles of Yorktown, and here we encamped and stayed quite awhile. We had now got the "A" or wedge tents as they were called and were quite well sheltered from the rain and damp of the swamps. Our little dog tents were a thing of the past, yet we clung to our rubber blankets. The night of the twenty-second the supply train did not reach us and the next morning the boys were yelling *crackers* at the quartermaster. That night for the first time we slept with all our traps

---

* It is not certain whether Henry fulfilled this intention or not. See Epilogue.

on and our guns by our side. I wrote home I had as soon get in bed with a baby as to sleep thus.

While camping here some of the officers went up in a balloon and discovered the rebs were leaving Yorktown and then there was hustling and our forces moved quite lively. The next day or two when we moved on we went past their breast works on the road south of Yorktown where they had a lot of great wooden guns, and in crossing a ravine some of the boys stepped on a torpedo and three were killed and several wounded. In the woods just beyond, their campfires were still burning and they had left raw dough ready to bake. Here I gobbled on to a frying pan and carried it along but did not get much use of it I had to lend it so much.

Some of our boys were getting back to the regiment and some were dropping out. Eli Boyce had got back (we had left him at Staten Island) but he was so pitted up we hardly knew him. Then a letter came from home stating that James Ostrom had answered to the last roll call and they had laid him away in the Ohio cemetery. James went from Rome sick with the inflamatory rheumatism caused by sleeping in damp sheets while there. When we left home, of all the boys I thought the most of Ostrom but now I and Edgar Hane were the twin brothers.

Another of our Ohio boys had gone and that was Jasper Hollenbeck. For quite awhile as we came along on our route he was sick and could hardly keep up with us. Still with a will and good courage he would not give up and go to the hospital, but he got so bad he had to linger behind at Warwick Courthouse and here we left him with some of the boys to care for him. But he soon passed away and they buried him here under the pines amid the spring flowers. [Henry later went back and wrote a poem in the margin of the manuscript. See

232

Appendix 2, poem 2. It may be of his own composition, but "bonny blue flag" usually refers to the Confederate flag.]

After we left Yorktown we began to come to where the rebs had more recently deserted their homes but we found some that did not go, especially the old and infirm and some of their slaves. Some of their young men had been conscripted in the rebel army. On we went and the day of the battle of Williamsburg we stood in line all day expecting to be called into action, and we could hear the cannon and roar of battle. But we were spared, and towards night we were permitted to lay off our things and stack arms and make fires, for it had rained most all day and we were wet to the skin.

We got a little rest that night and the next morning early we were on the march and soon came to the battle ground. Here the eighty-first stacked arms for the day and a detail was made to bury the dead and help pick up the wounded. I escaped the draft for that day thanks to our orderly sergeant, Edgar Abeel. Our friend Edgar was a noble manly fellow and sometimes showed his favors to those who never refused when called on and pitched on some who continually had some excuse. So Edgar Hane and I were excused for the day and we went over the battlefield and what a shudder ran over me at first. But we soon got used to it and the sight of the dead did not move us. We also went to the great log barracks the rebs had used for winter quarters. These were now dissecting rooms and here the surgeons were busy with scalpel and knife amputating arms and legs. This seemed to me a too horrible butchery but then it had to be done, yet I always thought and always shall that many and many arms and legs were taken off that might have been saved if the soldier could have been in some quiet hospital at home.

These were the first dead I had seen killed in battle and the blue and gray lay scattered side by side. But I never wanted to see another sight like that. By night they were all buried and all the wounded were picked up. We lay on the battle ground that night. The next day as we marched along the road we saw where the rebs had scattered their things by the way as they were fleeing towards Richmond. Feather beds had been ripped open and the feathers scattered to the winds and furniture of all kinds had been abandoned and stove in pieces. Along in the afternoon we passed a plantation and rebel storehouse and the beans, flour and meal was strewed all over the ground. Some of the boys gathered up beans enough to last a week but we did not stop to get the feathers. We came to a ravine where they had got stuck in the mud and had smashed their stoves, furniture and wagons and killed the mules and cut the harness in pieces. So on we went up to Bottoms Bridge and into the fatal Chickahominy Swamp where the boys began to dwindle out by sickness. Our band had left us long before this and either went into the ranks or went home, and when we marched at night it was by the tap of the drum and the tune of the fife.

Towards the last of May we were getting well along towards Richmond. So near that we could hear the church bells and the tooting of the car whistle and everyone with strong hopes expected to enter its gates in a few days. But how foolish the thought to imagine the rebs were tamely going to submit to us and give up their stronghold without a struggle. And that struggle soon came, to our sorrow. As we moved along we kept driving in their pickets. Casey's division was now in the front on the left and we had gradually moved up and encamped in an open field on quite a rise of ground. To the right of us was a forest growth and in front towards the rebs was a long clearing and towards the left in front was a second growth of about ten acres and over beyond this another long open field. Along the highway directly south was an open field and a high rail fence and here is where the eighty-first were assigned their place in case of an attack. To the left of this beyond the clearing was a forest growth of woods running almost square angles to the fence and highway. There was also a rail fence along these woods. The thirtieth of May we thought they would attack us and had been called to our positions but the battle did not come. In the morning of the thirty-first a detail was made to chop down this ten acres, and volunteers called for who could chop. Edgar Hane and I went and lots of others to the chopping bee, as we termed it, and there were little ponds of water in the swails and we got wet to our knees. Well, if there was not music with axes now there never was before and by eleven a.m. the whole place lay in windrows.*

When we got to camp I and Edgar made a fire and took off our stockings and washed them and hung them on a pole to dry and set our shoes by the fire and then we got our dinner, running about in the dirt and ashes in our bare feet. After dinner we were out cutting up our capers in our bare feet when all at once we heard the rebel cannons booming and the shells came shrieking over our heads, and the word "Fall in boys" was the next and we did fall in in a hurry. Our stockings were not dry so we put on our shoes without them and Edgars says if they get me they will have to furnish me stockings. We slipped on our shoes, darted in the tent and threw on our traps and got to our places in time to answer to our names.

* The action described here and in the following paragraphs was the Battle of Seven Pines, or Fair Oaks, May 31–June 1, 1862.

In a few minutes the whole regiment was marching to their position, but before we got that short distance the battle was fiercely raging on the right. As we halted by the fence we could look over the slashing we had made and see the rebs coming up in columns over in the long clearing to the right of us. Our artillery and men in the rifle pits and those supporting the batteries were mowing down the rebs by scores. Their flag went down several times but in an instant it would be up and floating again, and the gaps in their ranks closed up again. While we were looking at this an orderly came galloping down the road with an order to throw down the fence and march out in the open field by left flank. In a moment the fence lay flat and we were swinging around at left flank. The left of our regiment stayed where they were and the right swung around about twenty-five rods so we were directly facing the forest growth of woods on the south side of the clearing.

As we halted we could see the rebs along these woods and from their shelter they began firing at us and we at them. They had all the advantage of us. They could see us plainly out in the field but their smoke and the green leaves hid them from us. But we done the best we could and had just got over our tremor and were loading and firing without a nerve shaking when the orderly came again riding pell mell out in the field and gave the order to the colonel to fall back slow to the road. It will be well enough to say here that Colonel Rose was home on sick leave and Lieutenant Colonel DeForest was commanding the regiment in the battle. As the orderly gave him the order to fall back he repeated it to the captain. I was loading my gun and glanced around at the colonel just then and saw him falling, but the adjutant caught him in his arms and kept him from falling. When he was falling he was white as a sheet and as he partly turned about I saw the white cotton in the hole of his coat on his back and the next instance the blood spurted out. The boys says, "He is gone and is killed." * In a twinkling they were after him with the stretcher and carried him off. The adjutant's name was Cook.

As we were falling back to the road a ball struck me in the right hip and run over the joint and stopped. I could feel it grind its way over the joint and then it began to slow up and stopped. I thought my hip was gone it was so numb. I said to Captain Hannah, "I am wounded in my hip." He told me to go to the rear and I started hobbling on one leg for awhile with my gun for a crutch. After I had gone quite a ways the feeling came back in my leg and I felt of my hip and knew then the ball was in there. I got along as fast as I could and soon had lots of company, for the boys that were wounded and could walk got to the rear as quick as possible, out of the reach of the minie balls and bursting shells.

When we got back to the reserve line we were halted and all that were wounded passed on and the stragglers were detained. At this line of soldiers I sat down and rested a few minutes and while I was there two soldiers were carrying off a wounded comrade who was shot through the body near his heart and he begged them to set him down and let him rest. As they did so I saw a trail of blood on the grass and flowers. Then he began to tell the boys what word to take home to his wife and children and father and mother, brothers and sisters. He said he had only a few minutes to live and asked of the color bearers to lay the flag down over him. What a smile there was on his now pale face. He looked up at the boys who brought him and said, "When I am gone bury me

* His full name was Jacob J. DeForest. He survived and was discharged for disability in September 1864.

238

under the pines." Then the word goodbye almost in a whisper and he was gone. (In after years I wrote a poem of this subject for a school exhibition which will be copied in this narrative.) [He did not copy the poem into the manuscript but did insert a copy on a separate sheet. See Appendix 2, poem 3.] After this touching scene I got up and went on and just at sundown I got to savage station and the hospital on the railroad, and when one of the surgeons was at liberty he came and cut the ball out of my hip.

That night I lay in a stable on corn stalks for a bed and could look out on the barn floor where the surgeons were busy all night cutting off arms and legs. There was only one besides me who I knew of Company C and that was Edward Cornstalk of Greig, New York. He had a ball shot through his foot and we lay side by side all night.

I traded my gun and belt for two blankets and an overcoat. One of the ninety-third New York boys had helped bring up a wounded officer and had no gun to go back with so I traded and took the blankets which came in good for us.

All night long they were bringing the wounded but I did not hear any names of the eighty-first. The next morning we were put on the cars and taken to White House Landing where we were put on board the steamboats. The boat I was on went to Annapolis but I did not see any of the places along the route for I was down below in a bunk and had to lay still. I got on the boat about noon and the next day in the afternoon we arrived at Annapolis where I had good care, enough to eat, a corn husk bed and a quiet place, and all the papers to read and peruse.

**22** IN the hospital at Annapolis, Maryland I had the best of care with a plenty to eat and everything quiet. My bed was a spring cot with a tick filled with corn husks, a feather pillow, sheets and blankets. This was the best bed I had slept in since I left home. My wound was not a dangerous one but very painful for a long time and I had to lay on my left side or back. I did not try to walk for several weeks until my wound was healed up, and my meals were brought to me.

I had all the papers to read. Besides, there was a reading room close by and the ward master brought us books until I was able to go and get them myself. As soon as I could hobble out I was out every pleasant day and would go down to the dock to see the convalescents swim in the salt water.

While I was here there were two boat loads of sick and wounded and those who had been in rebel prisons, some of them since the first battle of Bull Run, and such a sight to see these poor emaciated forms get up and walk and nothing but skin and bone, trembling, walking skeletons. Those who could not walk were carried on stretchers. Many of them were delerious and were talking everything. Oh my god I said to myself, can it be possible that these skeleton forms only a little while before went out from their homes and loved ones in the bloom of youth and manhood with health and vigor beaming in their countenance? Their own mothers would not have known them now.

240

I was here ten weeks and could now walk quite well without a cane if I went slow. They were now sending men back to their regiments and so the doctor sent in my name for examination. So I went over and was examined for my regiment which was now at Harrison's Landing on the James River in Virginia. The doctor decided I was well enough to take the field and do duty again and must go in the morning with a lot of others who were going to the same place.

So I went back to my ward and picked up my letters and little trinkets I had been saving and made them into a small package. The ward master gave me an old haversack to carry them in. Then I went over to the post office for mail if there was any and to tell the postmaster where to forward any letters to. The next morning I bid goodbye to my ward master, Orin A. Green, and my other chums in the ward and at nine a.m. I went on board the cars for Washington with about fifty more of the convalescents who were labeled for Harrison's Landing.

It was a good consolation to me for I was not alone. Some of them I was already acquainted with, and as we went along we discussed the situation quite freely. We were not long in getting to Washington and here we were put in the old soldier's retreat which I have described before. It was the same old place only there had been a great bath tub constructed in one corner where we took a good bath on our arrival. But there was such a sickly stench to the water we soon got out of it. But the same old hard bare plank floor was there and no bunks, no chairs or benches.

That morning when we left Annapolis none of us were furnished with knapsacks, coats or blankets, so when it came time to sleep we had to lay down side by side on the cold hard floor with nothing over us. I had no pillow that night to wet with tears, so they fell on the hard floor. The next day we made complaint to the officer in charge and the guard who stood over us, and the next night we had a blanket apiece but had orders to leave them there when we left the retreat. Our grub was hard-tack, bread, coffee and salt beef or pork, and the coffee was miserable. We had beef steak and eggs and tea or coffee while at Annapolis and lots of other delicacies. Some of the convalescents began to sicken of this poor fare we were now getting and wished themselves to Annapolis or home or anywhere but in this old castle almost in the shadow of the dome of the capital.

They kept us here three days and three nights and then they marched us out and through the city down to the steamboat landing. Some of the squad (which was now increased to nearly one hundred) were in no shape for duty, for our usage since we left Annapolis was enough to sicken a well man. Some of the boys fairly reeled as we marched through the streets of Washington and down to the dock.

As far as I was concerned I was well at heart but my hip was paining me so I could hardly walk and I did not care where I went. I had bid adieu that morning to the miserable old soldiers' retreat and never wanted to see it again. As it turned out it had received my last farewell.

As we were going from the city down to the landing an officer came along past us and asked the corporal where he was taking us. He said we were going to Harrison's Landing to our regiments. "My god," he says, "There is men more fit for duty just come from there and are now here in the hospitals." Well, the corporal said we would have to go there now unless the order was countermanded and it never was.

Well, on we went to the boat and got aboard. It was a poor old stinking steamboat and they had a drove of beef cattle on board to take to the landing. Some would have to endure the stench of the cattle all the way. The captain seemed to be a nice fellow and put us in the rooms farthest from the cattle and gave us bunks and blankets. We had good coffee, bread, hardtack and good corned beef on board the boat.

We left Washington about eight a.m. and started down the Potomac. Instead of a band playing the national airs while passing down the river it was the mournful looing of the poor cattle. We stayed on deck all we could to see all that was to be seen and get the fresh air until night drove us to our bunks where we were soon in the land of dreams, for we had not slept much since we left Annapolis.

That afternoon we met a good many boat loads of soldiers coming up the Potomac to land at Aqua Creek to head the rebs off at Fredricksburg and to defend Washington. These very soldiers, and there were thousands of them, had just come from Harrison's Landing and we poor half crippled fellows were going back there. We heard the captain of the boat talking to the other boatmen and we knew what was up. The next morning about eight o'clock we got to Fortress Monroe and the captain of the boat wanted to leave us and the drove of cattle there and not take us to Harrison's Landing. But no, the commander of the fort told the captain he had got his orders from Washington and he could not land the cattle there, he must go to Harrison's Landing. Oh how the captain of the boat did swear and tear and gave order to open the valve to its utmost and sent the boat up the James.

The man at the engine obeyed the captain's order and the man at the wheel headed the old steamboat towards Newport News. Away we went but had to run against the tide and the current of the James and our progress was slow. On we went up past Newport News and along close to the masts of the Cumberland which still lay there with her flag still floating, a solemn reminder of the sad havoc of war. It was now getting late in the afternoon and we went very slow and slower still when it got dark. Then we poor, tired and lame soldiers sought our bunks for the night.

In the morning when we awoke we were still going up the James and after we had our coffee, beef and hardtack we clambered on deck to view the country along the river and get a glimpse of the deserted rebel plantations and the old historic places we used to read about in Hale's *History of North America,* and especially James-town. All we could see of that now was an old crumbled down church, three or four old brick buildings, a few immense shade trees, and old neglected orchards. When we got above Jamestown we passed quite a number of gun boats guarding the river and occasionally they sent a shell over south of the river a mile or two at the rebs for they were prowling about along the river on the south side. Along in the afternoon several balls came whistling over our boat which made the captain look a little scary.

It is a beautiful country along the James River and if it had not been devastated so by the war I thought I would like to come down there and locate for life. About three o'clock we arrived at Harrison's Landing and when the boat had been fastened to the dock an officer came on board and the captain delivered up his orders. But the officer in charge said they did not want the cattle there as all who were able to march were going across the peninsula to Yorktown, and the rest who could not march were going down the river in the morning and he would have to take the cattle back to Fortress Monroe. The captain flew into a rage and swore by all that was great and good he never would take them back and he opened a gate or slide door on the side of the boat and made his men jump the poor cattle off into the river and such a ducking they got, some of them going way under and then coming up snorting. Then they all swam to shore. The captain felt a little better then and told the officer he would take anything else down the river but them damned stinking cattle.

Well, while all this was going on the soldiers were going ashore and the first one I ran into was Morris Conkling of the eighty-first New York, Company C. Then I found William A. Wood also of our company and they wanted to know where I was going. "Why," I says, "to my regiment." I was so lame I could scarcely walk. They looked at me and said I could not stand it to march to Yorktown. Morris had come over from the regiment which was about two miles from the landing to bring some mail and he said he must hurry back to get ready to go with the boys. So there I was, but the officer in charge of the convalescents and the sick said I would have to stay there with them that night and go back to

Fortress Monroe in the morning. So he took my name, regiment and company and I went and stayed with William A. Wood. Not one of the boys found their regiments that went from Washington with me but all had to come down the river in the morning. We got on to another larger and better boat but it was loaded down to its utmost capacity. All who were able had to lay on deck, for the rooms below were full of the sick ones who needed hourly care and nursing.

I and Wood lay on deck [except] when we went and drew our rations of hardtack and coffee. My wounded hip was now a running sore again and not much sleep did I get the night I stayed at Harrison's Landing. We had a pleasant ride down the James that day although I was lame and in pain and had a hard plank deck to lay on. Wood had a blanket which he put over us when it came night and here we lay on the hard deck and not a thing for a pillow. But after all we got some sleep.

In the evening I and Wood went down in the cabin to see the doctors take off an arm for a young soldier who had been wounded sometime and it did not heal so they had to take his arm off. He was a young pale looking lad but he stood the terrible ordeal with courage and bravery and came out of it alright.

We got to Fortress Monroe sometime in the night and anchored at the dock till morning and after we got our rations we were taken off the boat and taken in ambulance wagons over to Hampton Hospital about three miles from Fort Monroe. Here we had good comfortable quarters with cot bedsteads with straw or husked mattresses and feather pillows, and what a luxury.

It was a quiet healthy place with the sea breeze wafting over us. Our fare was good and nearly equal to that of Annapolis and sometimes we got oysters and clams and chicken and fruit. There was over fifteen hundred soldiers here most all the time. We had good care with the best of ward masters who kept everything neat and clean. William A. Wood was here also and two boys of Company H. I kept to my bunk pretty close for over a month and suffered more with my hip than I did when first wounded. Then too I was worried about the folks at home.

I had not been paid since we left Washington in March and my wife and little children had been dependent on charity and were groveling along through the vale of poverty on *cold shoulder* and the charity of neighbors. This did not set very good on my crop but I could not help it. I had been drifting about on the breakers of war. I tried to get my pay but could not.

After I got able to walk again I frequently went down on the sea shore near Hampton with the convalescents and went in the salt water bathing, getting clams and oysters and roasting them on the shore. Sometimes I passed away many an hour writing letters for some sick one who could not write.

Our regiment was now at Yorktown and I tried to get a furlough to go up and see the boys but the surgeon in charge would not let me go.

Along in October I asked the surgeon if he would send me to my regiment and he said no and thought I would get my discharge first. I went to Hampton about the sixteenth of August and stayed there until the sixteenth day of December when they gave me my discharge and transportation home.

I came over to Fortress Monroe in the ambulance and from there to Baltimore by steamboat. Here I went to the paymaster's and drew my pay from March in the spring before until the sixteenth of December. From Baltimore I came by steamboat to New York. But it was in the night and I did not see much of the sights along the coast from

Fortress Monroe to New York City. From New York City I came to Prospect by cars and by stage to Grant. Here I met many of my old friends and neighbors and acquaintances who seemed to be glad to see me. It being just at night and no one down from Wilmurt I stayed all night with our old friend Dr. R. H. Wiggins and the next morning my father-in-law came down after me with a wagon. It had been an open winter and they ran with wagons yet.* The old gentleman did not seem to be very glad to see me and met me with a scowl or a haughty frown and a hand shake of a cold shiver.

* By "open winter" he means little snow; therefore, sleighs could not be used.

# Epilogue

And so, with that cold shiver of a handshake, Henry Conklin's story comes to an anticlimactic conclusion. Not that his return from the war was an illogical stopping place, but a reunion with his wife and children would have provided a warmer final scene than the cool greeting of his irritable father-in-law. The fact is, however, that Henry did not intend to end his reminiscence at that point. Sometime after he began writing he went back and pinned a note to his original introduction: "In connection with this story will be given my religious experience, Grand Army experience, and as guide to different parties going to the Adirondacks. Also my experience as chainman with surveying parties for private individuals, the county, town, and Adirondack League Club. The names will be given, and pen pictures will be drawn in each event."

Whether he fulfilled this intention will never be known. Sometime after his death most of his possessions were lost when a house belonging to one of his children was destroyed by fire. A continuation of his narrative could have been lost in that fire.

It is known, however, that after his return from the war Henry Conklin moved his family to Attica, New York, where his daughter Lillian was born. The family later moved to Indiana, where Henry worked in a factory for a time, and then returned to the Town of Wilmurt in Herkimer County. Here he purchased subdivisions sixteen and seventeen, comprising several hundred acres of the Remsenburg Patent.

In time he cleared a major part of this acreage and built a barn and an eight-room frame house, which stands near the point where New York route 8 crosses the West Canada Creek, and which is owned today by the Harvey Bussey family. Here, five more children—Roscoe, Harriet, John, Ruth, and Lyman—were born to Henry and Elizabeth. It was impossible to support the family by farming alone—though he grew corn, buckwheat, and garden crops, and had several cows—and Henry supplemented his income by shingle-making, trapping, and carpentry. In addition, as his note indicates, he worked as a guide and a chainman for surveying parties. And in 1890 he served one term as supervisor of the Town of Wilmurt.

It was Conklin's skill at shingle-making that led to his winter job at Snyder's camp where he wrote his narrative. He had, according to his note, assisted in the survey of a 105,000-acre tract purchased by the Adirondack League Club, a society formed by a number of men from several northeastern states, and incorporated in 1890.* He then was employed by the club to make shingles for its lodge on Hannedaga Lake. Evidently, Mr. Ole L. Snyder of Buffalo, a member of the club who had a camp on the lake, then hired him to make shingles for that camp. Henry did this in the winter of 1891–92, while living at Snyder's camp. In his introduction he says that he was "in charge of" the camp; thus, he was also acting as caretaker. Henry's home was about ten miles from the camp—too far in that day for daily commuting, but his grandson Roy thinks that he did return home from time to time that winter, perhaps on weekends. Since there was no place at the camp to keep a horse, he traveled to and from the camp on foot.

Of Henry's nine children, only Lyman—now in a Johnstown, New York, nursing home—survives. In time, the three daughters married and one of them, Lillian, moved to Herkimer. Of the six boys, five married in the Wilmurt area while Lyman moved to Johnstown where he worked in a glove factory. The others did some farming or lumbering, and all five did a bit of guiding and trapping. Burton James Conklin became one of the best, if not best known, of the great Adirondack trappers, with a trap line extending over a broad portion of Herkimer and Hamilton counties.† In the early 1900s Aurey moved to Montana where he spent the remainder of his life.

* See *Adirondack League Club* (New York, 1896). This report includes maps of the tract and Hannedaga Lake, with the precise location of Snyder's camp.

† See Lloyd Blankman, "Burt Conklin, The Greatest Trapper," *New York Folklore Quarterly* XXII (December 1966), 274–97.

Henry Conklin's mother and father spent their declining years in Attica, New York, undoubtedly in the home of one of their children. Mary died there in 1879 and Samuel in 1882. The former, despite her weakened constitution, was seventy-eight when she died; and the latter, despite his attraction to grog, was ninety. Henry's brother Julius died in 1895. But no information about his other brothers and sisters is available in family records.

Henry recorded, however, that his grandfather, Abiah Curtis, died in Theresa in 1861; Aunt Lydia died in 1870, Aunt Sebra Ann in 1890, and Uncle Cheeseman in 1884. Cousin Ruth Baker, whose forlorn letter appears in Appendix 1, lived to be over ninety and died in Theresa, February 1, 1931.

Henry Conklin spent his final years at his home in Wilmurt. He died there in July 1915, in his eighty-fourth year. Before he died, he purchased one of the largest plots in the cemetery in the village of Ohio, as a last resting place for himself and his descendants. He rests there today at the side of his wife Elizabeth, who died in 1925, and four of his children. His descendants, in the pattern of American migrations, are dispersed throughout New York State and in several states of the Union.

# Appendixes

# 1

Mᴙ grandfather on my mother's side was Abiah Curtis, born September 5, 1777, whose ancestors at some time came from the old country, of what nationality I know not. But I think they were from Connecticut and were always spoken of as American born and were styled by some as Yankees.

My grandmother Curtis was a Holland lady and had emigrated to this country from Holland. Her maiden name was Ruth Cheesman, born in Holland February 20, 1777. She with her father's family was one of the first settlers of that name who came and began what is now called the Cheesman settlement near Theresa in Jefferson County. They came to this country from Holland near the close of the seventeenth century. That part of the country was then a howling wilderness infested with wolves and all the wild animals natural to an unbroken primeval forest and where the red man of the forest made it his happy hunting ground. And so these early pioneers had the treacherous Indian to guard against and the wild beasts of the forest to molest them.

My grandfather and grandmother Curtis were married at Theresa in Jefferson County, December 2, 1799. Soon after their marriage grandfather Curtis bought a farm about one mile below Theresa Falls on the west side of the Indian River. Their farm was partly on the river flats and part upland with ledges of stone and pine bluffs. Here they went in the wilderness alike with those early hardy pioneers to clear up their land and build homes for their wives and children.

To them were born seven children, four boys and three girls as follows: Polly or Mary B., born August 20, 1801. (This is my mother, of whom I will speak more fully hereafter.) Next was Betsy, born July 5, 1804. Aunt Betsy never married, but lived at home assisting her parents in clearing up the farm and caring for the younger children. She died in the bloom of youth and early womanhood August 2, 1825. Next was Lydia, who was born November 2, 1806. Aunt Lydia never married, for in her early youth her eye sight failed her, and for many years she was almost totally blind. She died January 9, 1870, in the ripe old age of a maiden aunt of nearly sixty-four years. Sebra Ann was the next, born February 18, 1808, of whom I will write more fully further on. Next was Cheesman, born November 26, 1810. Uncle Cheesman married Mary Chatman of Theresa. They lived on a farm a few miles east of Redwood for many years. Here I have visited them twice in my life. Once when I was in early manhood and once since the war. I found them to be Christian people trusting in the God of our fathers and a great inheritance of the beautiful time and life to come to the good and the Blest. In a letter from cousin Ruth Baker, dated December 24, 1891, I learn they are still alive and living at Plessis, Jefferson Co., but both are almost helpless. As I remember Uncle Cheesman and Aunt Mary how lovely and happy and trusting they appeared to me in their Christian character while gathered about the family altar. Philander was the next one, born November 2, 1818. Of him I will speak further on. Henry, the last, was born February 14, 1820. Uncle Henry grew to manhood living at the homestead and assisting in clearing up the farm. He married Harriet Rider of Antwerp. He was more of a roving disposition than the other two boys and wanted to move about from place to place and at one time went to Wisconsin, where I visited him in the year 1855 of which I will speak further on in my own recollections. Uncle Henry also lived for a good many years in the western part of the state in Chatauqua County. He died after wandering about from place to place April 13, 1884, leaving one son by the name of Augustus.

Grandfather Curtis died in a ripe old age November 9, 1861, having lived a widower since grandmother's death August 15, 1826. Grandfather was a member of the Methodist church. Always at his post on duty, faithful to the last, living in lovely peace with his family on the old homestead from the time he bought it when it was howling wilderness until the day of his death. Oh, sweet contentment, what a continual feast, and as the christian dies he has stepped over the line to his reward, as the poet sings. He has plowed his last furrow. He has reaped his last grain. No morn can awaken him to labor again.

Aunt Sebra Ann was married May 1, 1837, to a man by the name of Elcy [*sic*] who proved to be a wanderer and unworthy of the wife he had chosen. He lived with my aunt a year or two until a daughter was born to them when he disappeared as strange as he had come and no one knew where he had gone. They named their daughter Ruth after her grandmother Curtis. Thus my aunt, having been deserted by her husband, continued to live with her daughter Ruth on the old homestead taking charge of the old home and its occupants, as grandfather was a widower and never married again. Aunt Lydia was almost blind for many years and consequently needed the care of someone all the while. Uncle Philander never married and so was always at home. He had of his own the forty acres he bought of my father, joining my grandfather's place, and after grandfather was too old and feeble to work, [his place] also fell to the lot of Uncle Philander and Aunt Sebra Ann to look after. As soon as cousin Ruth was old enough to work she was their helper in all things, growing up on the old farm, caring for all and looking after the interests of all concerned. In fact she was the sole director of the whole affair for many years after grandfather and Aunt Lydia had gone to rest, and then Uncle Philander's health was poor for many years before he died and the whole business of carrying on the farm devolved upon Ruth. Uncle Philander died March 24, 1884. The all that was left to her was her own mother, decrepit and lame and almost helpless when also she died February 27, 1890, thus leaving Cousin Ruth alone, all alone, on the old homestead. The dear old home where so many of the now departed ones had been born, nourished and cared for from infancy to old age.

At my grandfather's death he willed the farm to Uncle Philander and Aunt Sebra Ann as long as they lived and at their death it was said the grandchildren were to have equal shares. Be this as it may, it at last turned out that Uncle Philander willed it all to Cousin Ruth, the old homestead and also the forty acres which belonged exclusively to Uncle Philander. Grandfather also gave at his death $50 each to the other children then living. My own dear mother got the $50, but did this compensate her or amount to what would seem to be her just due for the fifteen years toil of her early life spent in clearing up the farm and enduring the hardships and privations and discomforts alike with the others of the family? Yet without a murmur my dear old mother in her poverty accepted the gift as a God-send.

As I have said before, my cousin Ruth now inherits by will the old homestead of my grandfather and his numerous family, and also a forty acre farm adjoining the old homestead on the north which once belonged to my own father many years ago.

Cousin Ruth was married to Harvey A. Baker January 19, 1871. Mr. Baker was a soldier in the Union Army and belonged to Co. H. 14th N.Y. Heavy Artillery. But alas their married life was not of a very long duration, for Mr. Baker died (from the effect of wounds received in battle while in the service) on June 8th 1873 at Theresa. Thus, having been left a soldier's widow, cousin Ruth applied for and received a Soldier's Widow's pension of twelve dollars per month and yet with all these earthly goods, chattels and benefits she is not happy. I will quote from a letter from her, dated Theresa, December 18, 1891. "Dear cousin, I will try and answer your letter which duly came to hand. I am quite well. I now live in Theresa. I have a house and lot here but I do not like it as well here as I do down on the old farm where I was born and brought up. I go down to the old home once in a while but I soon get homesick and sad while there, for there is no one living on the farm at present, but I left a stove and some furniture there and when ever I go there I build a fire and call it my dear old home for the time being. I moved here at Theresa on the 23d of October 1891, and it seems to me I am only visiting and ought to go home. I am all alone now and so very lonesome and lonely. Yet I have plenty of company but they are not my own folks or kindred by no means. I never can forget my own dear mother and Uncle Philander. It seems as though I can never give them up. One of my neighbors carries on the farm and has done very well for several years. If I could see you I could tell you many incidents of our early life in grandfather's family. I will write out one. A great many years ago when it was all a wilderness here and Uncle Henry was a little boy he got lost one time in the winter and liked to perish in the snow. It got dark and the neighbors all turned out to find him, and they blew a great horn which he heard and came to them, and in this way he found his way home almost froze to death. I have the same old horn yet in my possession, it being a present from grandfather down. I send you our family record. My grandfather's folks were all Methodists. All of them lived and died in the Christian Faith. Wish I could see you. I could tell you more to write.

I remain your affectionate cousin,

RUTH E. BAKER

2

1.

Under the wild thorn they are sleeping
Side by side where the violets bloom
And their sweet silent voices in keeping
With the silence of their lonely tomb

Many years ago they bid us goodbye
With tears and with smiles and with love
From poverty's vale to mansions on high
To dwell in the beautiful Heaven above

Where the flowers never fade or decade
In the eternal bloom of youth they stand
Waiting and waiting for us dear ones to come
To join them in that beautiful land.

Beautiful and loved ones on earth
To lead us home to us were given
Departed in love from our family hearth
Our treasure on earth our treasure in Heaven

HENRY CONKLIN
March 1, 1892

## 2.

Where sleeping in his lonely grave
One of our boys so noble and true
Where the wild flower and grasses wave
Over his form there dressed in blue
Sleep on, sleep on while ages flee
The bonny blue flag still waves o'er thee.

[HENRY CONKLIN?]


## 3. *The Seven Pines*

Come freemen listen to my story.
Of battle fierce and fallen braves,
Where many a loyal boy in blue
Found 'neath the pines a soldier's grave;
When the traitor foe with maddening might
Were swinging round the Union lines,
While Union men the battle stayed
The battle of the Seven Pines.

Fierce raged the fight and battle din
And hearts of courage faced the steel
And wavering lines of boys in blue
Were striving hard to gain the field,
When soon they beat the traitors back.
A shout of victory! Along the lines
And the good old flag in triumph waved
O'er the battle of the Seven Pines.

When from the front two comrades bore
A soldier wounded to the death.
They knew that life would soon be o'er
By his glaring eye and shortening breath,
A crimson trail on flower and vines.
They halted at his kind request
There under the shade of the Seven Pines.

O sit me down and rest awhile
A message home to friends you'll hear.
For my blood is flowing and I am going.
I have no moments now to spare.
Oh boys, I'm dying, wrap the flag round me.
Its starry folds my form entwine
And when my heart's blood is done gushing
Then bury me under the Seven Pines.

Go tell my mother her prayers and tears
Were not in vain for one she loves:
That fairer sights and nobler scenes
Are dawning from bright lands above.
No more I'll hear her farewell words;
No more her arms my neck entwine
For the fallen form of her darling boy
Will soon be sleeping under the Pines.

Go tell my father his council good
Has been my guide for many a year,
With brothers kind have labored hard.
The toils and joys of home to share
And sisters with remembrance binds
A prayer for them for one and all
Before I sleep beneath the Pines.

Go tell my boys how their father died
And daughters fair will weep for me.
Oh how I miss their loving smiles
Their parting kiss how sweet to me,
Their eyes in tears like stars they shine,
But their father's form no more they'll see
For soon I'll sleep beneath the Pines.

Go tell them that in after years
They'll visit here a father's grave
A hallowed spot 'twill be to them,
Where rests the weary and the brave.
They'll pluck the early flowers of spring

And offerings here of love they'll bring
For him who sleeps beneath the Pines.

Go tell my wife to nobly bear
This honored sorrow of her lot
That she with love our children guide,
In our mountain home our humble cot,
In happier days and years that's past
A home of peace that love combines
But my country called me from that home
To find a grave beneath the Pines.

Go tell her that my love grows warm
In thinking of my home she blest.
Oh tell her not to mourn for me,
For in Heaven there is forever rest.
Farewell my friends, my home, my wife.
At duties call love not refine
And my bleeding heart will breath your name
While dying under the Seven Pines.

So farewell boys to the flag be true.
Those emblems bright my bosom warms
And when the battle's o'er then come
And bury me in my uniform.
He pressed the flag to his heart once more,
One lingering look along the lines,
And smiling sank in death to sleep
There under the shade of the Seven Pines.

Beneath the Pines they dug his grave
By the side of many a comrade true
And the moaning pines their requiem sings
To hearts of oak enrobed in blue.
They heaped the turf above his head,
A monument for freedom's shrine
And memory bless our honored dead;
Those loved ones sleeping beneath the Pines.

Those loved ones from each fireside home,
From hill and dale and northern land,
While every true Columbian heart
Hold memories in that fallen land
And history pens and poets sing;
While sun and moon and stars do shine
For a nation's pride, their nobler deeds:
Those soldiers sleeping beneath the Pines.

HENRY CONKLIN

3

Carroll, Wayne Co., Nebraska
Jan. 11, 1892

Dear Brother Henry,

I will try and write you a few lines of my early recollections for your narrative. I remember of living in Jefferson Co. in quite a number of places but distinctly remember when we moved from Watertown to Duanesburg. Brother James was a little baby then. It was in the winter and stormy and cold. The morning we got ready to start one of the neighboring women gave us a churn full of fried cake to eat on the road. The first night we stayed to grandfather Curtis's at Theresa, and next morning when we started there were two loads of us in the big sleighs. Father got a man and team to go through with us and paid him for it in things we could not carry. Mother took her loom and all that belonged to it. I wore on my feet cloth moccasins that mother made for me, and I never had any shoes until I was twelve years old. I lost one of my mittens on the road and father went back and got it. We were on the road a good many days and sometimes I thought we would freeze but there were taverns all along and we would soon get warm by the great fireplaces.

When we got to Duanesburg we stopped a day or two at a house. Father called them uncle Jacob and aunt Anna Wiggins but how they were related to us I never knew.

Then my father rented places here and there about Duanesburg for over three years. You and sister Mary were born here. Our great grandfather and great grandmother Curtis were alive yet and lived here. Great grandfather had the numb palsy, and I used to go and help my great grandmother take care of him, for he was helpless. A man lived next to us at one place by the name of Slauson, and they had two little girls Mary and Hannah. Hannah lisped when she talked, and would climb on the fence and call out "Maythe, Maythe mothy wanth ooth." Mr. Slauson had a big buck sheep, and he bunted me over, and father carried me in then tied up the sheep, and then I went and pounded him with a club.

While living here I first learned to spin on the big wheel. My first lessons were spinning rope yarn out of tow and we used a corn cob on the end of the spindle. I was so small I could not very well reach up to turn the wheel, and my brother John fixed a wide plank about a foot from the floor for me to walk on. I walked this plank many a day until my bare feet would ache.

One day mother was washing and I was spinning and brother James fell in the pounding barrel of water, head first, and came near drounding but mother grabbed him out and shook him until he got his breath and then took off his wet clothes and put him to bed until we dried his clothes, for he had only one suit.

We moved to Blenheim late in the fall when Mary was a baby. The roads were stony and rough. After moving to Blenheim we lived the first year on one of Uncle Joe Curtis's places in an old, dingy, smoked up log house with fireplaces in it. It was near a great hill and here we rode down hill in the snow, and running in by the fire to warm our bare feet. From here we moved over on the north road as they called it, near by a man named Delong who had a brother hung while we lived there. The winter we lived there my father went to New York to see his sister Aunt Polly as we always called her, and while father was away the boys had a high old time having fun riding down hill. This winter I and the boys went to school. I wore rags and cloth moccasins on my feet.

From here we moved to Darling Hollow and then up to John

Perry's house on the hill, and here we lived until father bought that place over in Tompkins Hollow. In regard to Julius and I getting lost will say: The summer that sister Ruth was married, 1842, I worked over in North Blenheim for a man by the name of Capman, and in the fall when I got done work I started for home on foot. I stopped and made sister Ruth a short visit and then went to Patchen Hollow and then to Hagers where brother Julius lived. Here I stayed overnight and next day after dinner Julius and I started to go home. It was October 16, 1842. We had ten miles to go and when we got to the great Wolf Swamp it began to rain and soon got dark. We ran against a tree that had fell in the road, and we thought we were out of the road, and then we began to wander about and got lost. We yelled until we were hoarse but no one answered, and then brother Julius gathered a lot of hemlock brush and we made a temporary covering by a big log and we sat there all night with a bundle of factory cloth wrapped around us. We had no fire for we were not prepared with punk, steel and tinder (matches were unknown then). And so we sat there in the cold till daylight, and hearing the roosters crow we knew in what direction to go to get home. Before morning it had snowed two inches and was bitter cold. We got home before our folks got up. Well dear brother, I have been a long time writing this letter but hope it will be acceptable. We had a severe winter here in Nebraska. Andrew and I are not very well and we are getting old, and how we would like to come and see you all once more but don't think we ever can. Write soon. Love to all. And I remain,

Your loving sister
JULIA KRELLIS

Through "Poverty's Vale"

*A Hardscrabble Boyhood in Upstate New York, 1832–1862*

was photocomposed in twelve-point Baskerville, leaded two
points; printed by photo-offset lithography on sixty-pound
Warren's Sebago Antique; and case bound in Canfield Denimweave.
It was composed, printed, and bound by Vail-Ballou Press,
Binghamton, New York, and published by

SYRACUSE UNIVERSITY PRESS
Syracuse, New York

| Date Due | | | |
|---|---|---|---|
| | | | |
| | | | |
| | | | |
| | | | |
| | | | |

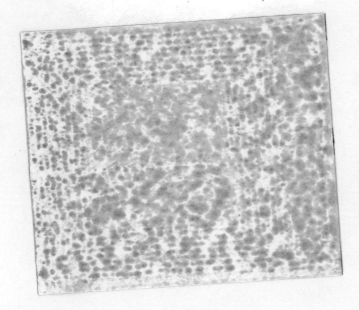